As I look back over my life, I observe many tough times. In retrospect, many of these times are humorous; some are even hilarious if you're not going through them yourself. Weighing the events of my life on the scale of time, I can see that the trials, temptations, tragedies, testings, triumphs and tough times did count.

There's not one of you reading this book who couldn't write a fascinating, unique story of your own life. As I share my life with you, I want you to ask yourself...

Was my life like hers?

Was it better?

Was it worse?

Have I learned to make the tough times count?

Also available from Here's Life Publishers —

Freeing Your Mind From Memories That Bind
by Fred and Florence Littauer
(Also available on LifeSounds Audio)

The Promise of Restoration
by Fred Littauer

The Best of Florence Littauer
Compiled by Marilyn Willett Heavilin
(Also available on LifeSounds Audio)

MAKE THE
TOUGH
TIMES COUNT

FLORENCE
LITTAUER

Co-author of *Freeing Your Mind From Memories That Bind*

Here's Life Publishers

First Printing, November 1990

Published by
HERE'S LIFE PUBLISHERS, INC.
P. O. Box 1576
San Bernardino, CA 92402

Library of Congress Cataloging-in-Publication Data
Littauer, Florence, 1928- .
    Make the tough times count : how to rise above adversity /
Florence Littauer.
        p.   cm.
    ISBN 0-89840-301-4
    1. Littauer, Florence, 1928- . 2. Christian biography —
United States. 3. Consolation. 4. Encouragement — Religious
aspects — Christianity. 5. Christian life — 1960- . I. Title.
BR1725.L487A3   1990
209'.2 — dc20   90-46855
[B]   CIP

Portions of this book were orginally published as *The Pursuit of Happiness* by Florence Littauer (Harvest House Publishers, 1981).

Scripture quotations designated KJV are from the *King James Version.*

Scripture quotations designated NIV are from *The Holy Bible: New International Version,* © 1973, 1978, 1984 by the International Bible Society. Used by permission of Zondervan Bible Publishers.

Scripture quotations designated TLB are from *The Living Bible,* © 1971 by Tyndale House Publishers, Wheaton, Illinois.

Scripture quotations designated NASB are from *The New American Standard Bible,* © The Lockman Foundation 1960, 1962, 1963, 1968, 1971, 1972, 1975, 1977.

Cover photography by Larry Lee/Westlight
Cover design by David Marty Design

For More Information, Write:
L.I.F.E. — P.O. Box A399, Sydney South 2000, Australia
Campus Crusade for Christ of Canada — Box 300, Vancouver, B.C., V6C 2X3, Canada
Campus Crusade for Christ — Pearl Assurance House, 4 Temple Row, Birmingham, B2 5HG, England
Lay Institute for Evangelism — P.O. Box 8786, Auckland 3, New Zealand
Campus Crusade for Christ — P.O. Box 240, Raffles City Post Office, Singapore 9117
Great Commission Movement of Nigeria — P.O. Box 500, Jos, Plateau State Nigeria, West Africa
Campus Crusade for Christ International — Arrowhead Springs, San Bernardino, CA 92414, U.S.A.

One Mother to Remember

I lovingly dedicate this book to the memory of my mother and acknowledge she deserves far more credit than this account gives her.

While I looked for flashy faces and worldly wonders, my mother stood on the sidelines, patiently waiting for me to abandon my fitful grabs for glory. It was she who gathered the family together on Sunday evenings and encouraged me to play hymns on the piano while she harmonized on the violin. Her sincere, Christian principles, her quiet and gentle spirit, and her devotion to motherhood prove the biblical admonition, "Bring up a child in the way he should go and when he is old, he will not depart from it."

Even though we grew up during the Depression and had none of the furnishings and appliances that we take for granted today, Mother made the best of bad situations and helped us all to make the tough times count.

Take the tough times
The whole amount
Turn them around
Make them count

Contents

Personal Preface

Before my brother Jim, a career chaplain in the Air Force, left for a year's duty in Taiwan without his family, his wife Katie said, "It will be tough here trying to raise the five children alone, but be sure you don't waste your time. Make it count."

As Katie cared for the children, Jim spent his year in creative and charitable work. He organized the Council of Concern which matched Air Force groups with charitable organizations in Taiwan to aid those in need. Through this council the base civil engineers built a two-bedroom home for a Chinese grandmother who was formerly raising her grandchildren in a mud hut. Along with the normal responsibilities of the chaplaincy and the additional charitable work, Jim managed to write his thesis for a master's degree in political science and organize the building of a new chapel on the base. Though their year apart was a difficult one, neither Jim nor Katie wasted the time.

They made the tough times count.

As I've looked back over my life, I've observed many

tough times. In retrospect many of these times are humorous; some are even hilarious if you're not going through them yourself. Weighing the events of my life on the scale of time, I can see that the trials, temptations, tragedies, testings, triumphs and tough times did count.

There's not one of you reading this book who couldn't write a fascinating, unique story of your own life. Even children growing up in the same house don't see the circumstances from the same point of view. As I share my life with you, I want you to ask yourself, "Was my life like hers? Was it better? Was it worse? Have I learned to make the tough times count?"

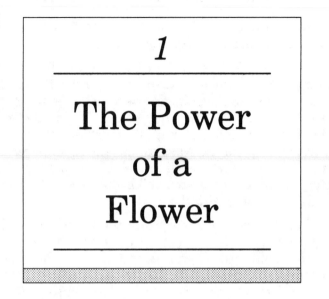

1

The Power
of a
Flower

*Miss Badashaw handed me the little clay pot with
one lonely geranium at the top of a long stalk. I
had a flower of my own.*

"Could we have wallpaper in the kitchen?" I asked
Fred as we discussed our new home. "Could we have
flowers?" I added. "That's what my name means—
Florence: 'blooming flower.' "

We were moving from a large house we no longer
needed to what we had already labeled our love nest: the
first place in thirty-five years where we would live alone.
Our last home was built during the energy crunch when
the aim of architects had been to make houses energy
efficient by extending the rooflines into massive overhangs
and setting the windows where even an aggressive sun-
beam couldn't seek them out. And although we saved on
air conditioning, for ten years we had lived in semi-dark-
ness. Now, in what was to be our final home—that last one
before "In my father's house are many mansions"—I
wanted light. We chose a town house on top of a hill with

tall windows and skylights grabbing each passing ray. We'd never be in the dark again.

Our last house had no wallpaper. It had been monotonously washed in Navajo white. Even though I had hung pictures and posters on every wall, the white stuck out behind them as if to say, "You can't get rid of me." I did paint one room brick red in a rebellious effort to take control away from the Navajos, but the room never fit in. It never got comfortable with itself or compatible with its sisters. It remained a step-child, the prettiest room but always out of step with the rest.

I could have done more with the house, but with my busy schedule it never seemed quite worth the effort. I could have put up some wallpaper, but I never had the time to go through those huge books and make a choice. But now it was different. This was to be my last house. "Whatever you want," Fred answered, "whatever will make you happy. Get it now, because this will be your last chance. We're not going to move ever again."

I'd never moved into a last house before. It was almost like decorating a tomb. There was an eternal tone to it. We'd bought a one-story house so we wouldn't have to worry about stairs when we were too old to climb. We had chosen a tiny yard in anticipation of being too old to weed. We had the eternal white walls, but I could paper those quickly before my eyes got too feeble to see the flowers.

"Could I have flowers?"

"Anything that will make you happy."

Instantly, a roll of wallpaper dropped from heaven. I looked up as eager as a child in a garden and began to pick pink posies off the paper and hold them in bunches in my arms. Suddenly all the flowers were gone from the paper and all that remained was a geranium—one lonely red geranium in a little clay pot. As I reached out for it, Fred asked, "Why are you crying? I said you could have whatever wallpaper you wanted."

"I want geraniums, lots of geraniums."

"Just geraniums? How come?"

For once in my life I didn't have a ready answer. Why did I want geraniums?

I suddenly saw myself as a little child standing on the steps outside our store. In front of the three cement steps was a blacktop sidewalk leading to the gas pump — an orange Gulf monster that spewed gas into the cars that honked for service. Behind the pump was a patch of weeds that belonged to the drugstore next door and next to our building was a strip of dirt.

I'd tried to plant some flowers there, but like the seeds in the Bible, they fell on hard soil and never took root. Some up close to the store forced their way up but died for lack of water. A few hardy seedlings popped up through the cracks in the blacktop sidewalk, but they were quickly trampled down by the feet of those who didn't know I cared. I'd sit on those steps in the evening and wonder, *Will I ever have any flowers?*

Say It With Flowers

Across the street from our store was the local church. It was the only social center we had and we were there every time it opened. Once a year we had Children's Sunday, a special day in June when we got our awards for perfect attendance and were given recognition for any honor we might have received throughout the year. It was a dress-up day when we happily put on the best we had because we knew we would be called up front by name. I remember the excitement as we met in our Sunday school rooms and were given our instructions on how to behave in "big church."

We marched in a quiet, awe-struck army and dutifully took our assigned seats. Helen Badashaw, our perpetual Sunday school superintendent, stood at the appointed time and walked to the platform. I always wondered why her legs puffed out over her shoes. Did it hurt to walk with legs like that? She would read off the winners' names and we'd walk forward with dignity. No one ran or giggled. This was church.

The most exciting part came at the end of the service: the giving out of the geraniums. The platform was ringed with little pots of bright red geraniums and we knew from the start we would each get one. The toddlers went first and I can still see my brother Ron's big eyes as he brought his first geranium up the aisle to his seat. My other brother Jim gave me a proud grin as he passed by and then it was my turn. I always wished I had a prettier dress or curly hair, but at least I was going to get a geranium. Miss Badashaw handed me the little clay pot with one lonely geranium at the top of a long stalk. I had a flower of my own.

I'd take my little pot home and each year I'd vow to make my geranium last forever. One year it fell off the porch railing where I'd put it for decoration. Once it shriveled up and died in the dark kitchen. Another time I planted it outside in the hard dirt and a hurried customer stepped on it. "Sorry," he called back to me as he hastened on, unaware that he had trampled the only flower I'd have for another year. I sat on the steps and wondered, *Will I ever have a geranium that will last?*

I realize now why my favorite hymn was always "In the Garden." The words expressed my childhood dream, that I might trade the blacktop and the gas pump for a garden. I wanted to find an Eden full of geraniums. I wanted to "come to the garden alone while the dew is still on the roses." I wanted to walk with Him and talk with Him and have Him tell me "I am His own."

When I chose this hymn for my baptism back in 1966, I didn't realize that my choice sprouted from that inner childhood longing for a garden full of fresh flowers—or at least one little lonely geranium.

As I thought about my childhood with no flowers and my desire for some touch of beauty, I asked Fred again, "Could I have a little pot of geraniums?"

"You can have all the geraniums you want," he answered. "You can have geraniums on the wall and on the curtains. You can have pots at the front door and window boxes full of them. You don't need to cry for a geranium ever again."

Reflections

How about you? Have you lived a bleak life without beauty? Did you long for flowers you couldn't find?

Whenever I share this story of my longing for a flower to call my own, women come to me in tears, crying out for some token geraniums. One lady told me how she grew up in West Texas where nothing was alive but the wind and the tumbleweeds. As she told me how she'd tried to plant some flowers and nothing grew, she got emotional and I put my arms around her. I looked toward her husband. He was obviously embarrassed that his wife would burst into tears over a lack of flowers in her childhood. As I gently moved her over to him I suggested, "Why don't you stop on the way home and buy her a geranium."

"She doesn't need any geraniums," he retorted as he pushed her toward the door. "She just needs to grow up."

How sorry I felt for that lady whose husband had missed the point and who was no doubt going to reprimand her for making a scene in front of the speaker. Here was a man more interested in himself than in filling some gaps in his wife's childhood.

Oh, let us be like little children. Let us reach out for the flowers we never had. Let's fill pots and vases and surround ourselves with beauty.

A pastor came to me that same day and told me a story about his first pastorate. He had decided to give every lady in the church a carnation for Mother's Day. After the service he had a box of carnations left, so he and the elders decided to take them to the mothers of the church who had been unable to attend. One suggested a certain old lady who had not been to church in years. "Oh, she won't even let us in," another elder said. "We've tried to visit her and she slams the door in our face. There's no point in going to see her."

The pastor's interest was aroused and his nature challenged. He determined to give it a try. Just as had been predicted the lady snorted out a nasty, "What do you want?" as they stood outside her screen door.

"We're from the church," one replied.

"I haven't been to church and I don't intend to go. Just leave me alone."

She was about to slam the inside door, when the pastor quickly said, "I've brought you a flower."

The lady looked out through the screen and saw the pink carnation. Her harsh voice softened and she replied, "Well, I guess you could come in for a few minutes."

The astounded men entered. The pastor pinned the carnation on her dress, and she burst into tears.

"This is the first flower I've ever had in my whole life."

The next Sunday she was in church.

Let's not ever underestimate the power of a flower.

One Sunday morning I was called to the platform in a church where I had told about the geraniums on the previous day. When I stood by the pastor, he reached under the pulpit and pulled out a little clay pot with a geranium. He had searched through every geranium at the nursery until he had found this spindly specimen: a few green leaves at the bottom with one long stem and a lonely little red flower at the top. It was so ungainly that it was laughable for the audience but I became nostalgic. I remembered that one day I waited for each year when I received my very own geranium.

Is it possible you had a childhood without flowers? Did you long to touch a tulip or reach out for a rose? You don't need to live another day without the smell of a gardenia, the smiling face of a pansy or the bright color of a geranium. Find some fresh flowers at your florist or purchase a potted plant in your supermarket. Hang silk flowers in a basket from your ceiling. Paper the walls with bouquets of lilacs and nosegays of violets.

Make up for what you missed out on as a child. You don't have to be without flowers ever again.

2

Shirley Temple Paper Dolls

Although I was too young to recognize this gathering as a charity affair, I was bright enough to observe that I was on the wrong side of the stage.

If ever a fairy godmother wandered through the state of Massachusetts in search of a child in need of a change, she would have chosen me. I was a perfect candidate for Cinderella—poor, plain and plump. Born during the Depression to a struggling shopkeeper and fragile violinist, I needed all the help I could get.

My parents, Walter and Katie Chapman, married late in life and when I was born in Newton Hospital on April 27, 1928, my mother was thirty and my father fifty. Because I was an eight-pound, first child of a ninety-pound mother, my birth was a trauma for both of us. She was hospitalized for weeks and I emerged with a twisted foot that had to be put in a plaster cast.

When I was born, my father managed an S. K. Ames Butter and Egg store, but as the Depression grew deeper, the stores were sold. After twenty-eight years with the company, he lost his job. By the time I was seven, my father, now close to sixty, was reduced to serving as a timekeeper for the Works Progress Administration. My mother, who was used to a comfortable life, taught violin lessons in her living room for fifty cents an hour.

Our lack of money did not dampen my ambition or drive for success. I was always attracted to wealthy people, large homes and big cars. I remember the day in the second grade when I looked up from my little desk to see a lovely lady enter our classroom. She asked the teacher for a list of names of the poor children who might not be getting any presents for Christmas and I heard my name mentioned. I tuned in closely to find out what was going to happen to me and heard the lady tell the teacher about a Christmas party she and some friends were sponsoring for poor little boys and girls.

When the day came, we were picked up after school by a chauffeur in a big black Packard. I didn't even know what a chauffeur was, and I had never been in such a large car. We arrived at the local Grange hall along with many other children and after some cookies and Kool-Aid we were asked to take our seats. I was on the end chair in the third row and I watched wide-eyed as the "lovely lady" came out on the stage and called us up one by one.

When my name was called, I went up front to receive my gift—three books of Shirley Temple paper dolls. Although I was too young to recognize this gathering as a charity affair and the terms "disadvantaged" and "deprived" had not yet been invented, I was bright enough to observe that I was on the wrong side of the stage. I wished then that I could be that lovely lady in the elegant gown giving out the books and toys. I wanted to be on the stage giving out and not receiving.

That night I began to look at myself in a more critical light. I decided I didn't like the dresses the Works Progress Administration turned out in three pastel colors: pink, blue and yellow. Once they were washed they all turned beige.

These little dresses had puffed sleeves, a peter pan collar and a sash tied in the back. They came in three sizes — small, medium and large — none of which seemed to fit.

I was tired of looking like all the poor little girls in class. I wanted a fairy godmother to give me a whole new wardrobe. My mother explained I should be grateful for the clothes I had. "There are some children who have nothing," she said. But because she understood my hurt, she embroidered a big black lion on the pocket of my plain yellow dress. I was hopeful no one would recognize this as a charity contribution.

From that time on I determined that when I grew up I was going to have plenty of clothes and they weren't going to be plain pastel colors — even with a lion on the pocket.

Reflections

Did you grow up in the lap of luxury or were you, like many of my generation, on the list of "poor children"? Did you long for the big car and the fancy home? Did you receive charity? Did you know you were on the wrong side of the stage?

Gratefully, I was able to get on the right side of the stage and today I spend my time giving out to others. But some of us stay on the wrong side of the stage for a lifetime because we were made to feel there was no hope for us. We believed the lie. For those of you who may have been forced into retaining a poverty mentality, you don't need to stay there any longer. Read my book *It Takes So Little To Be Above Average.* Get self-help books from the library. Have your hair styled. Give yourself a lift.

Think about the simple possessions you had as a child. See if you can find some replacements or perhaps the originals in your mother's attic or garage. My friend Patsy Clairmont loves to search through antique shops and for my birthday she gave me two pages of original Shirley Temple paper dolls from 1935. She also located a Shirley

Temple doll and a blue milk pitcher with Shirley's picture on it. When I saw the pitcher I remembered how we had sent in box tops from Wheaties to get the Shirley Temple dishes free. We had a cereal bowl with Shirley's picture on the bottom and we would race to eat all our Wheaties so we could find Shirley's smiling face beaming back at us. When I look at those objects some very happy memories come to mind.

What special objects did you treasure as a child? Bring them out where you can look at them. Have the fun searching for replacements. Don't blot out the simple and uplifting souvenirs of childhood.

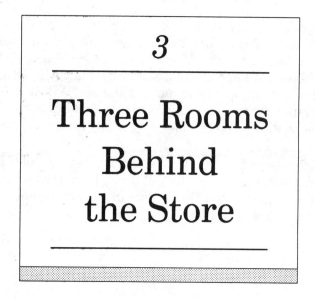

3

Three Rooms Behind the Store

With an air of optimism, Father showed us the rest of our new home. Mother continued to sob and clutched Baby Ron as if he were her security blanket.

When I was nine, my father borrowed $2,000 from his best friend, bought the Riverside Variety Store in Haverhill, Massachusetts, and went ahead to prepare for us. When everything was ready, Aunt Sadie picked us up from our tenement in her Model-T Ford. We drove from Newton Upper Falls to Haverhill with Mother sitting up front holding baby brother Ron and my five-year-old brother James sitting in the back with me.

As we approached our new town, Mother said, "So here we are, starting all over from scratch, and at our ages."

"I don't have much hope for this whole venture," said Aunt Sadie, shaking her head.

I left them to their thoughts as I eagerly looked out the window. I could hardly wait to see our new home.

As we drove up to the Riverside Variety Store, my heart sank. Our new house was a shabby brown building with peeling paint and faded orange trim. The yard was high with weeds and a few sparse hollyhocks struggled up the side of the store. Three cement steps led to the warped front door. Excitedly my father ran out, picked us up and hugged us.

I took James by the hand and walked into our newly acquired combination variety store and living room. I noticed a nickel on top of the *Haverhill Gazette* on the news rack at the front door and wondered if I should pick it up.

Behind the stand of newspapers was a long table piled high with brightly dotted loaves of Wonder Bread, packaged cakes and jelly rolls. I was fascinated with the prospect of a house crammed with cakes, free cakes at my finger tips. James tugged my attention to a big glass case full of candy — trays and trays of all kinds and colors of candies! Gum drops, Fleer's bubble gum and licorice twists.

A perfect heaven for children, I thought.

Soon James and I found the sliding doors behind the case holding the Tootsie Rolls. As we stuffed our pockets with goodies, I heard my mother crying.

"Chappie," she sobbed, "how will we ever fit our furniture into these three rooms behind the store?"

"Katie," said my father optimistically, "it's going to be all right."

I followed their voices past the cash register, the Coca Cola case and the ice cream freezer, through to the kitchen. There I saw my mother staring into a black slate sink edged with warped green linoleum. There was one brass cold water faucet and beyond the sink was an ugly black stove. Gurgling behind it was an upside-down bottle of kerosene. Faded flowered chintz curtains that had long since lost their glaze hung in shreds over the windows. Sagging squares of painted tin served as the ceiling.

With an air of optimism, Father showed us the rest of

our new home. Mother continued to sob and clutched Baby Ron as if he were her security blanket. The back hall was so narrow that Father had to go sideways past the wooden icebox that leaked its way to the back door where we peeked out into the backyard full of garages, mechanics, gas pumps and broken cars.

"Is that where my little boys are going to play?" asked Mother. It was.

Father quickly brought us back in and showed us the tiny den. The wallpaper looked like a jungle, and my father, trying to relieve the tension, said, "When you look at that paper, you almost expect a monkey to jump out at you." We children laughed although Mother didn't think it was funny. The final stop was the bedroom where we all had to sleep on unpainted bunk beds my father had ordered from the Sears catalog.

Mother was near collapse as the full force of her new life hit her. "How can anyone bring up decent children in three rooms behind a store?" she asked.

Yet Mother did. From that day on I remember Mama, serious and sad, trying to bring up decent children, and Father, enthusiastic and joyful, trying to make fun for us and force the frown off Mother's brow.

Visions of Grandeur

As I look back now, I realize how difficult it must have been for Mother to keep going at all. She was so frail the doctor made her drink heavy cream to put "some meat on her bones," and yet she worked night and day. Since there was no hot water, Mother constantly kept a boiling pot on the back of the stove.

She did our laundry in the black slate sink, where her tiny hands, made for the violin, wrung big sheets and heavy corduroy pants. It always embarrassed her to hang our clothes on the clothesline that ran from the back door to one of the garages. The mechanics would laugh, hold up their greasy hands and say, "Do you need any help, honey?"

My brothers loved playing with real cars in the backyard, but Mother constantly worried about the vulgar language they heard. One day little Ron asked one of the mechanics, "How come Jesus could walk on water?" My mother was aghast at the reply: "I guess it was because He had such g--d--- big feet." How could she bring up decent children in surroundings like this?

While my brothers enjoyed the cars, candy, cake and chewing gum, I picked up my mother's pessimism. I wondered why I had to live in three rooms behind a store where to go from the bedroom to the bathroom I had to pass the cash register. I wondered why the bathroom had no tub and why we all had to take baths in the kitchen sink while Mother held up a big towel to shield us from the customers. I was embarrassed and fearful that some day Mother would drop the towel and the customers would see me sitting naked in a sink.

To escape my unpleasant surroundings, I sat on our one couch and read romantic novels where the heroines all live in magnificent mansions with huge white columns. I imagined myself in a beautiful ball gown, sweeping down the circular staircase into the arms of an awaiting prince. I even wept a little when the hero marched off to the Civil War and the heroine had to spend long lonesome evenings in her wing chair by the bedroom fireplace reading love poetry.

I knew that *if only* I could live in one of those plantation houses with the columns, stairs and fireplace, I could be happy. But, as I closed the book and looked around the three rooms behind my father's store, I realized the only column we had was the rotating barber pole for the shop next door; the only staircase was a ladder that dropped from a trap door to the oil tank room where we pumped kerosene by the gallon for the customers; the only fireplace was a gas grate in the bedroom where all five of us slept in layers.

In order to improve our circumstances, I was constantly creating and cleaning. I made new curtains for the kitchen out of white dish towels scattered with strawberries. I repainted the drop-leaf table and chairs, and I tried desperately to keep the top of our old sideboard cleaned off.

One day after seeing a magazine picture of a mahogany buffet set in an elegant fashion, I swept away all the junk that had collected on top of ours and put tall candles at each end with a large bowl of polished apples in the center. When I came home from school later, I found that my brothers had used the candles for hat stands and had eaten all the apples and left the cores turning brown in the bowl. Where was that pleasant plantation living that I longed for?

I desired to be a heroine, but instead I was a discouraged damsel in distress; I wanted to go to important places and be with beautiful people, but instead I was stuck in three rooms behind a store in Haverhill, Massachusetts.

Family Fun in Spite of It All

Although I felt sorry for myself, we did have family fun sitting around our one table in the store. My father kept us laughing and our dinner table conversation, frequently attended by an audience of customers, was often sharper than today's situation comedies. While Mother jumped up to wait on customers, Father kept us sitting at the table by giving a running commentary on politics and current events. He stimulated our imaginations with provocative questions.

One day during World War II he asked, "Do you think it would be possible to make buildings that would go up and down to save on elevators?"

Immediately we started on the plans and verbally designed a skyscraper on pulleys. We began with the economy and ease of eliminating elevators and having the building move so businessmen could walk out from their own floors. We put light switches on the outside so that when the building sank, each floor would automatically light up. Our design was also a great boon to window washers as they could do a whole skyscraper without ever leaving the ground.

One of the outstanding advantages of our brilliant creation was its versatility during air raids — the building could sink rapidly into the ground! We planned the roof as a pasture with peacefully grazing cows so that when the bombers flew over they would have no idea that under the cows was a business building.

Sometimes customers would join in with additional ideas. One night a man phoned from his home to tell us he had just figured out how to put toggle switches on nearby trees to increase the leverage of the pulleys. With his timely suggestion, we were able to add five more floors to our building!

As we spent night after night on our inventions, Mother would just shake her head and say, "This is ridiculous. How can I bring up decent children when their father keeps their minds on foolish things?"

Not only did Father keep us laughing and thinking, he kept us playing. One of our favorite pastimes was Monopoly. We always had a game in progress on our one table in the store. Some of our steady customers even owned property and we rolled their dice by proxy if they were not around. Father taught us how to buy and sell wisely, how to build hotels on the right side of town, and how to expand our fortunes while avoiding bankruptcy. Our longest game lasted thirty-seven days!

While Father and the three of us focused on the fun of life, Mother's steady hand kept a quiet, even keel on our tipsy boat. She washed and ironed our clothes, cooked on the oil stove and had good meals on the table on time. She helped us each night with our homework and faithfully went to PTA. She kept us in church and made us sing in the junior choir, listened to me recite my elocution pieces and played the violin to keep me practicing the piano. She encouraged James with his piano and singing lessons, and scrimped to buy Ron a trumpet. On Sunday evenings she gathered us around the piano and led us with her violin as I played hymns on the piano, Ron strained at the trumpet, and James and I sang. In every way Mother tried her best to bring culture and dignity to a family forced to live in a variety store surrounded by garages.

Reflections

Where did you grow up? What kind of a house did you live in? Were you ever ashamed of your circumstances and afraid to bring your friends home?

When I share my story of the three rooms behind the store, people laugh and cry as they think of their childhood homes. One lady told me she'd lived in three rooms over a saloon. My friend Emilie Barnes grew up in three rooms behind her mother's dress shop in Los Angeles. And one girl had come from a one-room depot at a railroad crossing in the desert of Needles, California. No matter where you lived, it has had some influence on your adult life and choices. For me the lack of a normal home gave me the driving desire for a large house with a real front door and furniture that matched.

On Christmas Day, 1989, our whole family gathered at our Redlands home to open presents. Marita was unusually excited about the gift she was giving me. When it was time to open it, she went out into the garage and made me shut my eyes while she brought it in. Even without peaking, I could tell the object was large. She and her husband Chuck struggled to get it through the door! The item was placed in front of me, covered with a sheet. I was told to feel it and see if I could guess what it was. I ran my hands down the side and I guessed it was a table. I felt the drop leaf on the side and I cried out, "It's the table from the store!" And it was.

My mother had kept that old table which she had purchased new as a bride. When she moved to California, she had left the table in Aunt Jean's basement where

Marita had found it. Chuck had taken it apart, put it in a box and brought it back to California on the plane. They had stripped off the different layers of paint we had put on through the years and had it stained and polished.

When I opened my eyes and looked at the table, I was transported back to those many years in the store. Sitting around that table we would play games, piece puzzles and do homework. Often customers would watch us eat. I could see mother mopping off the oilcloth after supper and picture Daddy and me sitting there reviewing the newspaper and listening to politicians on the radio. That table was our gathering place, the center of our lives in the store.

Though that table doesn't match my other furnishings, I display it proudly as a memorial to a life long ago and far away.

Perhaps there's a piece of furniture, a family picture or a doll that has been ignored in your family. Revive it and revere it. Let it serve as a remembrance of what once was.

4

The Barber in the Attic

We couldn't understand how a person who was our friend, who was intelligent and had a sense of humor, could turn into an incoherent, babbling old man within a matter of hours.

It wasn't enough that we had to live behind the store and that a heavy-footed family rented the apartment overhead, but we also had an alcoholic barber who made his simple home in the attic. His name was Bill, and when he was sober he was Ron's best friend. He called Ron "Snookie," and when there were no customers in his store, he would pump Ron up and down in the barber chair. Barber Bill dropped by our store each day and sometimes ate with us as a family.

The stairs leading up to Bill's room went right by our bedroom. On those nights when Bill had been out drinking, he would stumble halfway up the stairs and begin to sing, "It was on the Isle of Capri that I met her." He only seemed to know one song and would intersperse his singing with, "That Snookie's a good little kid. Snookie's all right." He would then condemn himself, sob out loud and fall asleep. We children, of course, were awake during his whole performance and I could hear Mother tell Father what a terrible influence this was on the children.

One Thanksgiving afternoon, after Father had closed the store for two hours so we could eat together, we heard a knock at the back door. It was the lady next door and she wanted to speak to Father. We had set our one table in the den for the holiday and because it filled the whole room, it was difficult for Father to get out. But the lady was insistent. She would only talk to Father. We all got up, moved the table against the piano, let him through, and followed him out. I'll never forget the woman's remark. "I didn't want to upset your family," she said quietly, "but your attic is on fire."

Frantically we raced outside and looked up to see flames shooting out the attic window. While I called the fire department, Father and the boys ran up the stairs where they found Barber Bill drunk and unconscious. In his drunken stupor he had tipped over his little oil stove which caught the room on fire.

They pulled him out and down the stairs before the trucks arrived to put out the fire. As an ambulance took Barber Bill to the hospital, Mother shook her head and muttered, "Even when we close the store, we can't have one peaceful meal."

Reflections

Our early acquaintance with the evils of drink influenced our lives in a dramatic way. We couldn't understand how a person who was our friend, who was intelligent and had a sense of humor, could turn into an incoherent, babbling old man within a matter of hours.

People would come looking for Bill to cut their hair and my father would say, "He's on a little vacation." Sometimes Bill would come into the store sobbing and beg

Daddy to give him money. I can remember the answer, "I won't give you anything to buy more liquor, but when you're ready to eat again I'll give you money for food." And he did.

We children would hide behind the candy case when Bill came in drunk and wonder how long his "vacation" would last this time. Mother would give us little temperance lectures which were very effective with our friend Bill as a living example.

When did you first learn about substance abuse? When were you first aware that a drink could turn a loved one into a different person? Did you grow up in an alcoholic home where you learned very young to cover up the problem? Were you forced to deny the difficulties and spread a blanket of deception?

So many of the couples I counsel have grown up in dysfunctional families and didn't realize the damage their childhood abuse had on their adult relationships. In our CLASS seminars for the training of Christian leaders, an average of 40 percent have experienced alcohol problems in their immediate families. While the statistic is frightening, there is more help available today than ever before. With the formation of Adult Children of Alcoholics and an abundance of material on co-dependency, people can find answers.

If you don't remember parts of your childhood or are not sure whether what you lived through has become a negative influence on you as an adult, read and work through our book *Freeing Your Mind From Memories That Bind*. You can't help where you've been, but you can change where you're going.

Make the tough times count!

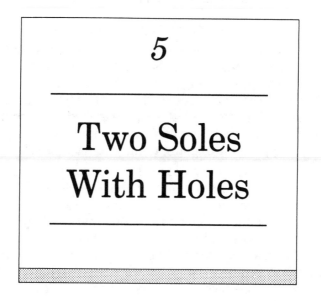

5

Two Soles
With Holes

Once, in desperation, I painted the brown clodhoppers with white enamel paint only to be depressed when they looked bigger in white.

I was not only embarrassed by my sad little drab dresses and my life in the store, but I was often upset over my shoes. Because of our poverty we could barely afford one pair of shoes a year for each of us. They were always too big at the start — we needed room to grow into them — and too tight for the last few months. There never seemed to be that magic moment when my shoes and feet met in harmony.

Besides the sizing mismatch was the fact that my feet were bigger than I was. I wore size 9 in eighth grade. In those days a child's size 9 had to be custom ordered and they only came in brown tie oxfords. I can clearly remember the shame I felt because I had to wear these ugly shoes. Once, in desperation, I painted the brown clodhoppers with white enamel paint only to be depressed when they looked bigger in white. Eventually they cracked and peeled, showing veins of dull brown through the shiny enamel.

Besides the wrong size and the ugly shape and color was what happened when the soles wore out before it was time for the year's new pair. At the sign of a hole in the sole, my mother cut cardboard to fit the shoe and inserted it for our protection. As the hole widened, the cardboard had to be replaced frequently until mother would sigh and say, "Chappie, you're going to have to fix these shoes."

Fixing was a major procedure. Daddy took a package of rubber soles from the nail on the wall where they hung for the customers' convenience. These soles looked like tire treads, black ugly rubber with waffle marks. They came in two sizes, men's and women's, and Dad had to cut them down to create a children's size. I remember him taking mother's bread board and an ivory handled butcher knife to carve up the piece of rubber to make it fit the shoe. Interested customers would watch and make comments like, "The kid sure has big feet" and "Why don't you buy her new shoes? It would be a lot easier."

Once the new sole was carved to the correct size, give or take a jagged edge here or there, it was time to rough up the bottom of the shoe. Included in the set of soles was a "rough up" tool that looked somewhat like a little cheese grater. My brothers were assigned to scrape this vigorously across the shoe sole until it looked as if a dog had chewed it up. This mock destruction was such fun that they fought for the tool and attacked each shoe as an enemy.

When the shoe was gouged up enough, Dad would squeeze the cement out of the tube included in the set and spread the glue across the sole with a knife as if he were frosting a cake. There was an art to this step because not enough glue would cause the sole to drop off and too much would run over the edge and eat off whatever was left of the original finish. The final trick was to place the rubber treads on to the sticky soles and hold them down tight without gluing yourself to the shoe.

Once the procedure was complete, we were supposed

to let the shoe and glue set for twenty-four hours. But usually I became impatient and would put my shoes on prematurely, causing my socks to be cemented into the original hole. I remember once pulling my feet out and leaving the socks in the shoes for several days because they were firmly attached to the sole by the hole.

But this procedure, which could give Bill Cosby a whole show's worth of material, was only a temporary solution. As the months went by the sole would loosen and the tread would flop with each step. How humiliating it was to be teased about the flip-flop of the phony soles as they came unglued. How I longed for a new pair of shoes more than once a year. How I wished for a fairy godmother who would wave her wand and give me glass slippers.

Reflections

Is it any wonder that I have a closet full of shoes today? When I pass by a shoe sale anywhere in the country, I rush in!

A man came up to me one day and said, "Do you know what I like best about your speaking?"

Expecting some meaningful compliment, I answered, "What?"

With a smile he replied, "Your shoes always match your dress."

I realize that purchasing the perfect pair of shoes to accent each outfit has become a hobby with me and looking at the many different styles and colors on my closet shelves says to me, "You'll never have to glue rubber treads on your shoes ever again." What a relief!

As I look back on the embarrassment of wearing tire treads on my shoes, I realize that most of us have had something glued onto us as children that made us ashamed of ourselves. It may not have been a rubber sole but perhaps you were given a derogatory name by an angry parent.

Perhaps there was some failure that had been repeatedly pointed out so you couldn't get loose of it, or an abuse that made you feel you were wearing a Scarlet Letter on your chest.

When you think back, what was glued on you that you've never been freed from? Until we uncover the phony sole over the hole, we won't be able to

Make the tough times count!

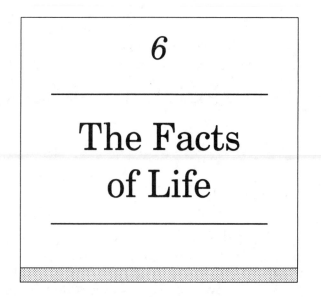

6

The Facts
of Life

The closest Mother had ever come to an explanation of sex was when she casually stated that the lady down the street seemed to get pregnant every time her husband hung his pants in the closet.

In spite of the fun we had with Father, I was still embarrassed about living in a store and wanted desperately to change my circumstances. Not only were my surroundings in need of transformation, but I was also far from the heroine I wanted to be. By the time I was thirteen I knew I was hopeless. I had eaten myself chubby on store candy, and the few dull clothes I owned fit poorly. My feet were too big and my hair was too straight.

I had spent my childhood peering out from under the bangs of a Dutch Boy cut, and when I finally convinced my mother to give me a home permanent, it produced an Afro. When I had to get glasses I knew my life was doomed forever. Dorothy Parker had just told the world, "Men never makes passes at girls who wear glasses." What could be done with a poor, shapeless, frizzy-headed teenager with spectacles? Oh, how I needed a fairy godmother! *If only* I could be beautiful, I could be happy.

Not one to let circumstances get in the way, I decided if I couldn't be beautiful I would at least get organized. Before I entered high school I wrote down my unlikely goals for life:

1. get educated
2. get money
3. get clothes
4. get popular
5. get married

The fact that each goal started with "get" didn't, at that point in my life, seem selfish. I reasoned that a person got only what he set out for, and since I was so far behind, I needed to move twice as fast as others. Furthermore, I felt deprived because I didn't have a regular house like normal people and, since my parents hadn't gone to college, I was disappointed at their lack of knowledge. My brothers, on the other hand, enjoyed the frantic pace of life in the store and even thought double-decker beds were fun.

I was alone in my quest for the grand life. I could see that my only hope was to get out of there and find people who would appreciate my lofty aims. But how could I achieve my goals?

My Life as an Actress

While I was neither an athlete nor a beauty queen, I felt I was somewhat of an actress. This inclination toward the stage started at age three when my father taught me the second chapter of Luke and had me recite it by heart for the church Christmas pageant. Father placed a high premium on articulate enunciation and trained each of us from early childhood to speak fluently.

By age three, my brothers and I had each memorized such statements as, "People who live in transparent domiciles should refrain from hurling geological specimens promiscuously." Before each one of us went to kindergarten, my father taught us a handy phrase to use as a reply when we didn't know an answer: "Not knowing to any degree of accuracy, I dare not assert for fear of erring therein." With this personal coaching from Father, I felt I was ready for the stage.

In the first grade I was cast as the bumbling Cowslip in the Fall Flower Festival. While I had wanted the role of the Rose or the Red Geranium, I was rewarded when the audience applauded my dainty fall which ripped up my crepe paper petals and left me lying on the stage with my panties exposed.

My next major role was Mother Nature in the spring pageant. I wore a long blue gown trimmed in tinsel and carried a magic wand. As the fairy godmother of the world, I was to touch each little child who represented different elements of nature. As I tapped them with my scepter, each seedling was to burst forth in a sequence of spring. Unfortunately, this part never amounted to much. As I turned to transform my little brother, a lowly nasturtium, a trap door in the stage gave way and little James fell in. Somehow, after retrieving a frightened nasturtium, there didn't seem to be much point in going on, and we closed the show.

I next tried to be the "Queen of the May," but because of my weight, I was asked to sit on the base of the Maypole to hold it down while those slimmer forms danced lightly around me.

Even so, my father still had faith in my dramatic possibilities. He paid for weekly elocution lessons and encouraged my participation in every local talent show. By the time I was a senior in high school, I had won the Poetry Reading Contest and had the bit part of Cuckoo in our senior class play, *The Fighting Littles*. As I looked ahead to college, I was determined to become an actress.

In those days the answer to the nation's problems seemed to be in education: "If only people were educated, the country would surge ahead!" I agreed and threw myself wholeheartedly into my studies. Although I took college prep courses in Haverhill High School, I soon realized I couldn't get to college without money.

Working Girl

My first work experience was in Mitchell's Department Store selling chocolates, a heavenly job for a chubby fifteen-year-old.

The chocolates were in bins and I had to scoop them out by hand for each customer. Since the bins were not labeled, I had to memorize each filling by the different squiggles on top. To study them more closely I picked up each chocolate, and since I couldn't put the pieces back because I had touched them, I was "forced" to eat them! The first day I must have consumed a hundred chocolates — everything from lemon to caramel. I ate fewer the second day and by the end of two weeks the smell of chocolates made me ill.

I was a faithful worker and was soon promoted to Gloves. The lady in charge looked as if she had come straight off a cameo. She had snow white hair caught up in the back by jeweled combs. Little wisps of hair framed her face, and she always wore a black dress with a high collar right up to her chin. Tiny silk-covered buttons dotted the front of her dress and a white lace-edged hankie was always attached to her left wrist.

She was remote and serious and seemed to be constantly costumed as if she were playing the role of the old-maid aunt in a Victorian tragedy. While she hardly spoke to me except to give instructions, she became excited over selling gloves. She would work the leather gently over each of the customer's fingers and whisper, "Oh, this leather is so soft you could eat it." She prided herself on being able to spot a customer's size as the lady approached the counter, and she was always right. As much as I wanted to be a success at gloves, I couldn't develop a convincing whisper. I always pulled out the wrong size, and I had no

innate love for leather. I was soon transferred to Books
where there was nothing to eat or stroke.

I loved to read and the book department, hidden in a
far corner of the basement, was a haven for me. The regular
clerk who had been there for years had every shelf organized and alphabetized and there was little for me to do.
I came in each noon from school in time for Mrs. Brown to
go out to lunch, and while she was gone I would read. The
few customers who did come found their own books. I just
took their money and sent it off in the little metal boxes
that shot up to the office on little tracks like elevated trains.
Because I was a fast reader and Mrs. Brown took long lunch
hours, I was able to finish many books.

One day while Mrs. Brown was out, I found a book
hidden under some paper bags under the counter. When I
pulled it out to put it back on its proper shelf, I saw the
title, *Sex Techniques in Modern America*. We didn't have a
shelf for books on sex, so I stuck it back under the bags.

I knew nothing about sex and had learned from my
mother's look of shock at the mere mention of the word
that it was a taboo topic. I knew, of course, it had something
to do with babies and that it was negative. Mother often
sighed over friends who were expecting by shaking her head
and saying, "The poor thing is pregnant again." I began to
wonder why people got pregnant if they didn't want babies.
I wondered *why* and sometimes *how*.

The closest Mother had ever come to an explanation
of sex was when she casually stated that the lady down the
street seemed to get pregnant every time her husband hung
his pants in the closet. This connection was confusing, but
since I didn't want any babies at fourteen I really didn't
care to know. I once asked my mother straight out where
babies came from and she said uncomfortably, "When
you're older, we'll talk about it." I never did get old enough
and she never again brought up the subject.

Up to this time I had never really been interested, but
as I thought about that hidden book I began to get curious.

What was there about sex that required a whole book?

The minute Mrs. Brown went out to lunch the next day I reached for the book. I went to the farthest corner of the basement behind the last row of bookshelves and sat on a high stool. I placed the book on a shelf so I would look as if I were working and began to read.

The first chapter was entitled "The Basics" and was both so shocking and fascinating, I was instantly transported to a world away from Mitchell's. When a customer said, "Pardon me," I gasped in fright, shoved the evidence behind some books and jumped off the stool. After I found what the customer wanted, I hurried back to my hideaway and began again.

As I swallowed up "The Basics," I suddenly lost respect for Mother and Father, realizing they must have engaged in such tasteless tactics at least three times. To illustrate the unpleasant suggestions, the book made absolutely disgusting diagrams that turned my stomach. But sick or not, I was compelled to go on. When Mrs. Brown returned, I put the book back under the paper bags and felt a little uncomfortable for the rest of the day.

The next day I could hardly wait to go to work. I had a new love for my job as I walked swiftly down Merrimack Street, into Mitchell's past Chocolates and Gloves, and down the stairs to Books. Mrs. Brown was delighted with my good humor and my suggestion that she take a long lunch hour.

As soon as she left I grabbed for the book and ran to my stool in the corner. I had been brought up to be scrupulously honest (my mother's instilled standards would have been applauded by the Puritan fathers). Therefore, this hidden, forbidden study was the most indecent thing I had ever done and it added a thrill of excitement to Mitchell's basement. I could hardly wait to get to my post each day, always in fear of being discovered which only heightened the excitement of reading a "dirty book."

While I didn't like the words or pictures I saw, and

sometimes found myself nauseous and sweaty over a sordid thought, I couldn't put the book down. I would come to work feeling like the heroine in a spy story, wondering if I could keep my cover just one more day.

To make it easier to pick up quickly where I had left off, I put in a book mark and was both stunned and scared one day to discover the marker was moved to another page. Had I made a mistake? As soon as Mrs. Brown left for lunch the following noon, I opened the book and the marker had been changed again! Someone else was reading the book when I wasn't around. Who could it be?

There were only two people in the Book Department — frumpy, fiftyish Mrs. Brown and me. What would anyone her age need to know about sex? I felt a little uncomfortable as I read that day and I kept peeking around the bookcase to see if anyone was watching. No one seemed to be around, so I read on, and when I finished I put a new marker in my spot and left the other for my mystery partner.

Could it really be Mrs. Brown, or was there a night watchman or perhaps an early morning clerk I'd never seen? I never did find out, but the elusive mystic and I read secretly in tandem to the end.

From the time I was a young child, I never kept quiet about anything I learned. I once gave clear jitterbug instructions to neighborhood children from a diagram I tore out of a magazine. They all learned to dance even though I never could get my mind and feet together!

Because I liked to share whatever smattering of knowledge I picked up, I called my friends together. Five of us had a girls' club called the L.B.O.E. — Little Bit of Everything. As their leader, I summoned a secret session to preach the truths I had inhaled. Laden with ignorance and distorted thoughts, I began to teach the girls the facts of life. Today it is hard to believe how little we sheltered girls actually knew. But as I continued nightly to dispense sex education to my friends, we all grew up together.

My mother never did attempt to give me any biological

explanations for life and I didn't need to ask. The exposés in this book more than filled my mind and at fifteen, untouched and unsought, I was looked up to by friends as a woman of the world.

A Lesson in Commitment

All through my junior year in high school I worked in Books and by summer I was ready for a new challenge. We high schoolers were feeling patriotic and were geared up to make supreme sacrifices for the highly publicized war effort, but we'd never found an available sacrifice to make. That is, not until my friend Ruthie Clark found one.

Her father worked in a factory and told her of some available summer jobs for girls at Hoyt and Worthings Tanning Factory and we applied. The man who interviewed us showed us a vast room full of women who were smoothly operating big machines and turning out bins of little things that looked like donuts. The man told us these "donuts" were chamois circles stuffed with kapok and were made to fit around the earphones that fighter pilots wore. He gave us a stirring message that made us feel we must seize the opportunity to work in this factory or be guilty of treason. Ruth accepted the job the minute she found it was piece work. Depending on how fast you worked, it was the ideal way to get rich quick. I wanted to sign up immediately, but my father had made me promise I would discuss it with him before taking the job.

I came home all excited over the prospects of making big money while helping to win the war. After I had explained the heroic aspects of the job and the ease with which the women operated the machines, my father told me he didn't want me working in a factory. He said I didn't have the strength or stamina for heavy work and I wouldn't enjoy the people who worked there. He felt I would soon get tired of the long walk from the bus, over the Merrimack River, to the factory, and I would want to quit.

I refuted his words by telling him I was strong and

peppy and loved people. Furthermore, I enjoyed a good walk and I would not quit. Finally, my father made a deal with me. He said if I took the job against his better judgment, I would have to promise not to quit until the end of August. In all confidence and optimism I agreed.

"You must learn to think things over carefully before making a decision," he said. "You'll never amount to anything if you flit in and out of jobs. Once you make a commitment you must stay with it for the allotted time, whether you like it or not."

While I listened to what my father said, I didn't think his caution applied to me. Caught up in the pervasive patriotism of the day and lured by the prospects of gold, I went to work in the factory the following Monday morning.

The supervisor took Ruth and me to our huge machines which looked much larger up close than they had from a distance a few days before. Quickly Mr. Jay explained how to make chamois donuts.

"First, you take a piece of chamois out of the barrel and lay it in this circular mold with your left hand while reaching into the kapok bin with your right." He went on to explain that timed properly, my left hand should have the chamois placed down before my right hand got there with the kapok. It looked simple when he did it, but when I tried, my right hand got there first and I had the mold full of stuffing with no casing.

On the second try I got the chamois there first but I couldn't tuck it in with my left hand. I'd never used my left hand for anything before and it didn't work. I dumped the kapok in my right hand back into the bin and used two hands. Once I got the chamois placed correctly, I filled it with kapok and looked up eager for the next step. Ruth had already made three donuts.

Mr. Jay then showed me how to hold the edge of the chamois with my left hand so that it wouldn't slip out of the mold, pull down a big lever over my head to clamp the donut shut, and at the same time treadle fast with my right foot to sew the whole thing up. I never could quite do those steps all together!

By the end of the first day I completed a grand total of six chamois donuts. The average woman made 120 in an hour! Exhausted, I walked back to the bus stop. It took every remaining ounce of stamina I had to jump off the bus in front of the store, bounce in and tell Father what a great day I'd had in the mill.

The next morning I found Ruth had quit, and I was alone before my big machine with a pile of chamois on the left and a bin of kapok on the right. As I looked at my dim prospects of coordinated success, some of the regular girls walked by, and one asked, "Are you the kid who took all day to do six?" They all laughed at me and said, "You'll never get rich that way!"

I didn't like to be laughed at, so I jumped in and got to work. But when I reached up for the lever, pain shot up my arms and every part of my body hurt. My father was right. I didn't have the strength or the stamina for this kind of work. As I pulled the handle down one girl yelled, "Look, the kid is weak. She needs two hands." This brought hilarious laughter.

While the job was overwhelming in solitude, it was impossible with an audience. To make me feel worse, one overweight girl in a sleeveless print housedress stepped out in front and commanded, "Let's do it in rhythm!" She waved her flabby arms like a maestro and conducted their moves like an orchestra while they all sang, "Laughing on the outside, crying on the inside, 'cause I'm so in love with you." I stood crying on the outside as they popped out donuts in unison on every beat. I wanted to quit.

Just then, Mr. Jay came in and saw me in tears. He yelled and the girls jumped back to their regular routine. In a kindly manner he took me aside and told me I just wasn't going to make it. I sobbed and said, "I can't quit. My father won't let me." He assumed that I had some ogre father who beat me each day before sending me to work, and he didn't know what to do.

"Let me try you on another job," he said with a sigh.

He led me to a counter covered with completed donuts and handed me a large pair of scissors. All I had to do was cut the chamois down close to the stitched seam, and it didn't have to be done in rhythm!

But this job didn't turn out too well either. My right hand became blistered and again Mr. Jay moved me. This time he made me an inspector. My third position in three days! I had to sit on a stool and inspect the donut seams to see if the cutters had cut too close. This titled job of "Inspector" lasted several days until one of the women from the machines spotted me in the inspection room and yelled to Mr. Jay, "How come the dummy got promoted?" He explained that I couldn't do anything else and had to be promoted. This didn't make sense to her, and she called in Sophie, the fat one in the housedress.

"Old Jay has promoted the dummy," she snarled. "We've been working our tails off for years for an inspector's job and this kid walks in here out of kindergarten and gets promoted. What do you think of that, Sophie?"

I could tell Sophie didn't think much of it. She pulled her massive self together and lumbered toward Mr. Jay like a bear. "Look here, old boy. We would hate to slow production and make your plant look unpatriotic, but it's this simple: Get the dummy off the stool and make me an inspector." I got off the stool, and she got on. I followed Mr. Jay into his little office and knew my factory days were over.

As Mr. Jay and I sat and stared at each other, a big, burly man with his T-shirt sleeves rolled up over his muscles came in and asked, "Hey, Jay, ya got anyone who knows how to glue?"

Mr. Jay, looking for a way to get me off his hands, said, "Do you think you could handle glue?" Any job seemed better than having to tell my father I'd failed, so I left with

the T-shirt man. He had "Joe" tattoed on his arm, and I
followed him into a big dimly lighted loft, piled high with
boxes.

"We're backed up, and I need you to get these boxes
labeled in a hurry," he said. Then he showed me each carton
of "donuts" had a label sitting loosely on top. All I had to
do was stick the label securely on each box so they would
get to the right air bases and the waiting pilots. Again I felt
patriotic as I thought of handsome Air Force officers in the
war using these kapok-filled cushions I had shipped from
Haverhill, Massachusetts.

While I was getting sentimental, Joe was setting up a
huge vat of glue. He handed me a large paint brush and
said, "All you do is stick the brush in the glue, wipe it over
the back of the label, turn the label over, firm it down with
your hand, and push the box away."

Joe handed me the brush and I noticed it was already
sticky. As the day progressed, the brush glued itself firmly
to my right hand. At lunch I couldn't separate me from the
brush so I ate my sandwich with my left hand. By the end
of summer I could comb my hair and put on lipstick with
the brush glued to my right hand!

As I pasted my way through the heat of July and
August, I had plenty of time to think over my mistake.
Father was right and I was wrong. I had failed at machines,
blistered at scissors, been pushed out of inspecting and
spent the summer with a glue brush for a right hand.
Father was also right about the people. They definitely
weren't my type. I'm not sure I had a type at that point in
life, but if I did, they were not it.

On my last day of work the women surprised me with
a party on the loading dock where we ate lunch each day.
They gave me a limp handful of flowers from Sophie's
garden and a card with their signatures and a sentiment:
"Congratulations, kid! We never thought you'd make it."

As I sat on the loading dock eating the ice cream, one
girl looked at me in the bright light. "You know," she said,

"you have possibilities. You're not homely; you just haven't got yourself together yet."

I sat wide-eyed with my legs dangling over the edge of the dock as they surrounded me and began to show me how to shape up. I never considered them too stylish, but they sincerely wanted to help me. One had a make-up bag in her purse, and as she took it out, Sophie said, "You know, kid, your features aren't bad if you only knew what to do with yourself." As I sat there in the sun, the women made up my face, plucked my eyebrows and restyled my frizzy hair. Then as they stepped back and looked me over they said: "Not bad. Not bad."

Although I had to agree with my father that these women were not my type, I had become almost as attached to them as to my glue brush. That night I took my flowers home and enthusiastically told everyone what a great summer I had. I never spoke of the lessons I had learned, but I'm sure Father knew. He was just kind enough to never say, "I told you so."

"She Must Be Smart"

Although I had worked hard at Chocolates, Gloves, Books and Glue, I still didn't have enough money for college. But my assorted jobs had taught me one major lesson: I must go to college and become something better than a glue girl. With my future direction resolved, I set out to get a scholarship.

An athletic scholarship was out of the question. I couldn't dodge the dodge ball and was a failure at recess! And I was convinced I couldn't win anything for my beauty. The machine ladies had made that clear. As a child, when I stood next to my little brother James with his curly hair and big blue eyes, people would say, "Isn't he adorable!" There would then be a thirty-second pause while they looked me over and concluded, "She must be smart." If that's the best thing that can be said for you, you better get smart! So I tried.

In high school I threw myself into my studies and never went to the football games or school dances. This direction, however, was not so much a thirst for knowledge as it was the plain fact that no one ever asked me out. Today, my daughters look at my high school pictures and say, "Mother, I can see why nobody ever asked you out."

When I filled out my scholarship applications, I wrote movingly of my dramatic abilities, told of my varied occupations, sent copies of my High Honor Roll record, and listed completely my extracurricular activities: Poetry Club, Math Club, Yearbook, French Club and Drama Club. The combination must have been impressive as I received a tuition scholarship to Massachusetts State College. I was on my way to goal number one: get educated.

Reflections

Did you ever set goals for your life? How old were you when you began to focus on your future?

As I talk to young people today so few have any realistic goals. They assume they'll go through high school and probably continue on to college and then someday get a job. One boy I questioned said, "I don't care what I do as long as I have enough money for a red RX7 and my stereo equipment."

"Don't you need money for rent?" I asked.

"No, I'll just keep living at home."

His casual attitude toward life was so different from mine that I had to think it over. He didn't care to become anything as long as he had enough money to satisfy his desires.

When I was his age we were all hungry for a better life and we knew we had to work hard to get educated if we ever hoped for any measure of success. We had no desire to live with Mother forever and I surely wasn't about to spend my life in three rooms behind a store. My family had no car, no phone, no washing machine and no bath tub. Our total entertainment was one radio. No wonder I set goals and headed out of Haverhill. Little did I realize then that a social problem of the '90s would be adult children who don't want to leave home.

Have you been able to instill values and goals into your children?

What were some of your own goals at sixteen?

Which ones did you achieve?

Did your childhood deprivations cause you to make the tough times count?

As I look back on the lessons I learned from my odd jobs, I am grateful that my father made me promise to stick to my glue job, like it or not. Throughout my life his advice has helped me evaluate a position before accepting it and then to be reliable once I have taken the responsibility.

One summer in an un-airconditioned warehouse by a swamp was enough to teach me a new set of facts of life. I learned not to prejudge people because of their occupation or circumstances in life. The women I looked down upon as uneducated had hearts of gold and became my summer friends in a winter experience.

A few years ago Fred and I went back to Haverhill and retraced the walk I took from the bus, over the Merrimack River, down the dirt road to Hoyt and Worthings. Much to my surprise, the factory was still there and people were still working. The sign on the side of the brick wall was hardly legible and had not been painted since I worked there.

The workers were still eating their sandwiches on the loading dock right where I had eaten mine. I remembered how my feet dangled from the dock and how I ate with my right hand glued firmly to the brush. As Fred took pictures of me looking tearfully at the loading dock, a secretary came out of the office and asked if she could help us. I told her, "This factory changed my life. One summer here gave me the drive to work my way through college so I wouldn't have to glue labels forever."

I look back and praise my father for teaching me to be dependable and for helping me set goals for my future. I could still be in the factory with Sophie. It was a tough summer, but I learned to

Make the tough times count!

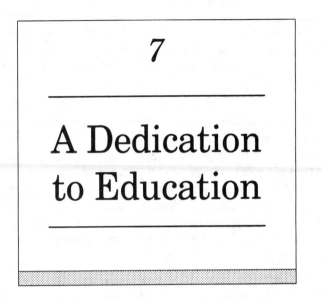

7

A Dedication to Education

I learned that in pouring at a social function, coffee outranks tea and the initials on the silver pot should always face the guest. With such important essentials under firm control, I was ready to meet the world.

In September, 1945, I arrived at the Trailways Bus stop in Amherst, Massachusetts, carrying everything I owned in two shopping bags with rope handles. I had stretched to put together five coordinated outfits and I had even bought two pairs of shoes. I had two itchy khaki blankets left over from my brother's brief stays at Boy Scout Camp, and a bag full of pencils, notebook paper, a Webster's Collegiate Dictionary and assorted high school term papers.

Carrying this inauspicious trivia, I took a local bus to the Massachusetts State College gymnasium where freshman registration was already in progress. After a two-hour wait, I received my schedule and a plethora of information on the glories of Old Bay State. As I looked these over and followed the line of coeds, I found myself in a gymnasium full of girls in their underwear. Before I had time to flee, a gym instructor blew a whistle and barked, "Strip down for your physicals."

As I clutched my printed forms to my bosom in a gesture of self-protection, the woman pointed straight at me and shouted, "And I do mean you." Never before had I undressed in front of anyone. Even with our open store policy, I always managed to wiggle out of my clothes under blankets. The instructor was staring at me. I knew there was no choice. Slowly I began unbuttoning my pink and white striped seersucker suit. My mother had always told me to wear good underwear in case I was in an accident, but I never anticipated this.

As I stood in my cotton panties and a limp unfilled bra in front of hundreds of girls, I forced a weak smile toward the gym lady who was watching me from the security of her warm Massachusetts State sweatshirt. It was then I noticed the line moving past a group of handsome young men in white coats and stethoscopes. When one winked at me I was horrified and tried to cover myself, but I had nothing but my arms, and they just wouldn't stretch far enough.

The man with the wink seemed to be mine. He approached with a thermometer and I heard his buddy say slyly, "You didn't get much of a 8one this time." As I stood unclad in the cold gym waiting for my temperature to go up, the doctor took my pulse, looked me up and down and seemed disappointed.

When the basics were over, the men asked us all to lean over and touch our toes. I watched the others go down first and noticed the doctors focused on the voluptuous girls, who, in this unusual position, were close to falling out of their bras. They singled these girls out as having "bad backs" and asked them to go up and down a few times to see if they couldn't get themselves "loosened up." Obediently the girls exercised.

As I watched the men watching them, I concluded their interest was not in the girls' bad backs. One girl who was detained for further "corrective work" dared to ask where the doctors were from, and we learned they were med students from a distant school who had volunteered to screen the freshmen girls as a sacrificial goodwill project.

Humiliated by these mass physicals, I dressed quickly and left the gym with my shopping bags to find my way to Butterfield Hall. Along the walk I met another girl, Alison, who was also assigned to the same dorm.

When I first saw the path to Butterfield it appeared to go straight up to the sky. *No one short of Jack-and-the-Beanstalk could ever climb it,* I thought. Alison assured me it was possible to make it to the top, and we began a hike that I learned to take in stride at least twice a day for the next year. The boys on campus identified girls from Butterfield by the muscles in their legs. Since I didn't have any muscles to start with, the first few climbs were painful.

After Alison and I arrived exhausted at the front door of Butterfield, I got my room assignment from the housemother. Thankfully, it was on the first floor. I had asked for a private room since I had never had one and was relieved to find I was given a simple single room with a maple bed, desk, chair and dresser. For the first time in my life I had a place for my own things where no one else would touch them.

Alison directed me to the communal bathroom where both of us were fascinated by a series of strange elongated washbasins that went all the way down to the floor. We turned the handles and water ran from the top to the bottom like a waterfall. Neither one of us had ever seen such a strange contraption and we began to discuss its use. Alison said it was a foot bath. We both agreed that after such a miserable walk up the mountain each day it would be nice to rinse off our feet in cool water.

We decided there was no time like the present, took off our saddle shoes and bobby socks and began foot baths in separate units. As we stood there on one foot with the other in the waterfall, the proctor came in and began to shriek with laughter. I had already been embarrassed enough at the physicals and didn't appreciate anyone making fun of me. When she calmed down she explained that Butterfield had been designed as a boys' dorm before the men had gone off to war and the footbaths were really men's urinals. I wasn't too sure what a urinal was but pretended to grasp the idea quickly. With our new information, Alison and I spent the rest of the afternoon in the bathroom explaining to other confused girls that urinals were not foot baths.

Before we went to supper on our first Sunday evening, we were each asked to print our names on our doors. I taped together several pieces of notebook paper and fastened them on my door where I began to print FLORENCE in large black letters. Unfortunately, the dinner bell rang before I had completed my name and when I left to eat I had finished FLO and part of the R. Put together it read FLOP. By the time I came back from the meal, the girls on either side of me had decided my name was FLOP. From that moment on, Flop was my new nickname, hardly the right title for an aspiring actress.

Early Influences

To earn money to support myself in college, I applied for a job and became secretary to the dean of music, Doric Alviani. While I was as charmed by Doric as all the other girls in the college were, I could barely type and I knew no shorthand. I wasn't much of a secretary, but Doric was too kind and compassionate to fire me.

He asked what other things I could do. I volunteered to correct the student papers he had piled on his desk, and I also suggested I could help him direct the college musicals. Although he was doubtful I could do either, he gave me a try. I quickly read three music textbooks and with a little coaching from Doric, I was soon correcting all his quizzes and exams.

Besides working with Doric and unconsciously picking up his unique directional techniques, I studied Shakespeare and drama and attempted to fulfill my ambition of becoming an actress. I joined the Roister-Doister Drama Club and got the part of Ann Forrester in Dr. Frank Rand's version of *First Lady*. The following year a new speech teacher, Professor Arthur Niedeck, cast me in a small role as a type of temptress and then began the impossible task of making me into one.

I remember how he yelled from the back of the hall one night, "Get Flop a pair of falsies. Maybe that will help her out." The costume girl took me out to a back room and in front of several boys stuck two rubber pads in my bra. I slumped back onto the stage, and again the professor called, "Stand up straight and stick your chest out." I did the best I could, but it wasn't good enough. "Get the child another pair," he screamed.

Back I went and got filled out again. This time I walked in as sultry as I could, hoping he wouldn't continue to single out my deficiencies. As I took a deep breath and began my lines, I heard, "Ye gads, she needs another pair." Even with three sets of falsies, I didn't look like anything a man would leave his wife for, and my part was cut to a minimum.

On the closing night as I bowed with the rest at curtain call, I glanced down and noticed the falsies had slipped. I had three lumps: small, medium and large! I don't know how long I had looked like a deformed camel, but I guess if two were good, three were better.

After my failure as a provocative actress, Professor Niedeck suggested I forget acting and try directing. From that moment I changed my ambition and never again auditioned for a part.

As I was simultaneously trained by two outstanding artists, I learned two different styles of directing. Professor Niedeck was precise, natty and detail-conscious. He taught me how to plan every move of every actor before the first one stepped on stage to rehearse. He showed me how to block the action and make a thick prompt book which had every move, sound and light graphed out in different colors.

While Niedeck was meticulous, Doric was flamboyant, colorful, emotional and adorable. He never cared about what he told us yesterday if today's inspiration was better. We hung on his every word and worshipped him as a genius. While he never gave me detailed instructions in directing, he unconsciously taught me that without charisma you could never move the actors to greatness and triumph. I loved his feel for music and flair for the dramatic. As I absorbed the wisdom of these two different teachers, I tried to fuse Niedeck's organization and Doric's enthusiasm. I wanted to direct with command and style.

Another professor who influenced me greatly was a man with the unlikely name of Davey Crockett. He was short but made up for this deficiency with a booming, powerful voice. With perfect control he could raise and lower his tones and roll out his words in resonant cadenzas. He taught me how to breathe, how to project and how to think. He made me study Robert's Rules of Order until making a motion was second nature. He would engage me in a conversation until he found out my feelings on a certain subject and then assign me to take the opposite side in a debate. This training broadened my mind and helped me to be convincing on any topic. "Don't ever let your feelings get in the way of your material," he would say.

As the female delegate from Massachusetts State I wrote a political proposition to present to the 11th Annual Model Congress in 1947. After delivering my moving speech before the congress and judges, I was awarded the title of "Best Female College Speaker in New England." I felt it was only a matter of time before the U.S. Senate would discover me.

Spurred on by my success in congress, I decided to major in speech. Davey Crockett became my official advisor and planned the rest of my college courses. He helped me choose a balance of English, speech, drama, literature, psychology and education, and selected me as the one senior to do honors work in the field of speech. With his guidance and encouragement I kept studying, writing, speaking, directing and hoping to live up to his constant comment, "You'll be a great speaker some day, if you keep at it."

I wanted to keep at it. My father had given me a love for words, my elocution teachers had kept me memorizing poetry, Professor Niedeck had shown me the necessity for order in creativity, Davey Crockett had inspired me to modulate my voice and improve my delivery, and Doric had given my life meaning, color and flair.

Although speaking was my first love and I desired to be dramatic, I was not quite ready for high society. While I had left Haverhill, Haverhill had not left me. As I associated with students and faculty, I began to see I didn't have a feel for social graces. Living behind the store had not prepared me for the elegant life I desired.

Learning to Be a Lady

I reviewed my goals and decided I wanted to become a gracious lady. In between my studies and dramatics, I read books on etiquette and charm and began to file off a few of my rougher edges. As I filled in my gaps in the social graces, I began to feel better about myself. I signed up to take modeling lessons where I learned to do pivot turns, rise from chairs gracefully and frame myself in doorways like Loretta Young. (Although I didn't become a model, the experience gave me the confidence to narrate fashion shows many years later.) I had not planned to join a sorority, but I began to see that fraternal life provided an access to the refinements I needed to know.

My friend Alison had pledged Kappa Alpha Theta and I followed her the second semester of my freshman year. Immediately the dignified housemother saw I had a teachable spirit and spent many hours sharing the specific differences between a woman and a lady. She showed me how to arrange the silver for a tea party and how to set a proper table, two needs that had never arisen while eating in the store.

The housemother also taught me where to seat the guest of honor at a formal dinner or club luncheon and how to introduce people according to protocol. I learned that in pouring at a social function, coffee outranks tea and the initials on the silver pot should always face the guest. With such important essentials under firm control, I was ready to meet the world.

As I helped set the tables for the sorority teas and began to insert ideas into the party plans, I discovered that I had a flair for entertaining. I became good friends with the sorority cook and learned the art of cooking from a pro. Often on weekends I would go to her home and she would show me special ways to make hors d'oeuvres, training me to become a gourmet cook.

Since I was eager to learn everything I could and wanted all the practice I could get, I was willing to assume the difficult job of house chairman in my senior year. I had been the sorority chaplain for two years where my chief function was to memorize and recite 1 Corinthians 13 at the weekly meetings, so I was excited when I was given the responsibility of directing all the physical functions of the house, including parties. Not wanting to do anything in a small way, I began to reorganize and revitalize every phase of sorority life.

One of my master creations was our fall rush party in October, 1948. Since the sororities tried to outdo each other in unusual themes, decorations and refreshments, I decided to turn the first floor of the sorority house into Coney Island. The dining room was filled with concession stands. We had ring toss games, dart boards and the most popular sport, throwing wet sponges at girls' heads stuck through a sheet. For refreshments we served sticky candied apples, popcorn balls that didn't quite hold together and bottles of Coca Cola.

The living room was the most exciting part of our project — we turned that into the beach. We got our boyfriends to borrow a coal truck and go several hours away to the Cape and fill the truck with white sand. We laid newspapers over the rug, and when the boys came back they put the chute through the front window and let two tons of sand pour in. Our guests were impressed with mounds of real sand in the sorority living room and shivered as they looked at us in our bathing suits sitting among the seashells with our pails and shovels.

The real winner was the party favor. At my suggestion, as each guest left we gave her a live fish in a beer can full of water. We had painted the cans black and put KAO on the front in luminous silver paint that shone in the dark. There was no way anyone could forget our Coney Island party as they fed their fish each day and saw KAO before their eyes even after their lights went out. The party was the talk of the campus and we filled our quota of new members.

Unfortunately, in my enthusiasm for the beach scene, I had not given any thought as to how we would remove the sand after the big night. We shoveled and shoveled and vacuumed and vacuumed, but when I returned for my fifth college reunion, the Thetas were still crunching across the carpet!

Reflections

How many of us grew up wanting to be in show business? We hoped someday to be discovered and sent off to Hollywood.

As I look back, I'm grateful for my professors who saw in me an ability to direct and consequently turned me in that direction. Even though I didn't become a leading lady, I can see how valuable my drama training has been in my Christian speaking, how my debating experience taught me to think logically and how my modeling lessons cured my feelings of being uncoordinated and clumsy.

Because I lapped up every word Doric and Professor Niedeck taught me, I was later able to direct musical comedies and teach speech on the high school and college level. I realize now that my time in college was more than an academic experience; it was a turning point in my life. I went in a young girl and came out a lady. My feeling of personal worth grew in four years from insecurity to confidence.

Have there been any turning points in your life? Have you made maximum use of your education? Do you regret your lack of education or training? It's never too late to learn. With adults taking courses as never before, there is no stigma to going back to school. If any deficiency in training has made you feel insecure, sign up for some courses and fill in your gaps with confidence.

It was not easy for me to work my way through college, but I'm grateful today that I'm able to

Make the tough times count!

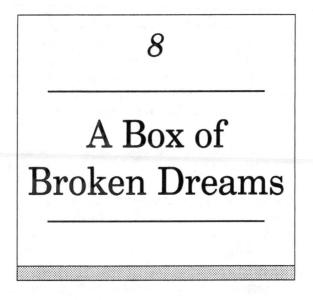

8

A Box of Broken Dreams

Had my dad not chosen that day to show me his box of broken dreams I would never have known about his talent.

During Christmas vacation of my senior year, my father took me into the den one afternoon and told me how proud he was of my achievements in speech and English. He reached in behind the piano and brought out a box of clippings he had kept hidden from the family. They were articles and letters he had written and sent to newspapers. There was even a response from Senator Henry Cabot Lodge to some advice Father had sent him. I asked him why he hadn't shown me these before. He responded that Mother had told him since he didn't have any education he shouldn't try to write. If he tried and failed, we'd all be humiliated.

At that moment I realized, in spite of all my father had taught me, I had never given him much credit for knowing anything. Like my mother, I had always felt that he didn't have the education necessary to be a success. In the past I had downgraded his ability and he had wisely waited until I was mature enough to share his hidden hobby.

Warmly, we discussed our mutual love of English and for the first time he shared that he had always wanted to be a politician. We laughed over how, when I was a child, he had made me sit and listen to political speeches on the radio.

As we discussed these and other subjects, Father brought the conversation back to his secret writing and he told me in confidence that he had sent an article to the editor of *Advance* magazine a few months before concerning the methods used in selecting delegates to our denominational conventions. He had looked each time the issue had come to see if his article had been published.

So far it had not been included and he said, "I guess I tried for something too big this time. Your mother is right. I don't have any talent."

The next day we three children decided to manage the store and let my father and mother take the first day off they had had together in twenty years. We felt we were old enough to handle everything and we joyfully sent them off to Boston. Besides, after working a seventeen-hour day, seven days a week, Father deserved a rest.

About supper time we looked out the window and saw Mother get off the bus alone. When she came in we asked where Father was. "Your father is dead," she said simply. She didn't cry. She just told us the story as we stood by in shock.

They had spent a beautiful day together and as they were walking through Park Street subway station, Father suddenly grabbed his heart and dropped to the cement. She said a nurse had been in the crowd of pushing people and knelt down to check him. She looked up at Mother and said, "He's dead," then slipped into a subway car and was gone. Mother told us how she just stood there in disbelief as busy commuters stepped over Father's form and went their way. A priest came by as a lone good Samaritan and said, "I'll call the police," and disappeared. For over an hour Mother kept watch over the body of her husband as indifferent people pushed and tripped around him.

She then told us how she had sat beside him in the ambulance, stayed with him in the emergency room where he was officially pronounced dead, and then had to take another lonesome ride to the city morgue where the man on duty had her go through Father's pockets and remove his belongings. After all this trauma, Mother took a bus from the morgue to North Station, the train to Haverhill, and then another bus home. She had faced the tragedy bravely and alone. As Mother told the tale, customers came in and listened, and soon we were all crying together.

We kept the store open for the next three days. Mother said Father had told her in the past, "Never close the store except for my funeral." Each time a person came in and asked, "Where's the old man?" we would reply, "He's dead."

The morning of the funeral, as I was going through the mail and reading the day's sympathy cards, I noticed the new issue of *Advance,* January 1949. As I glanced over it I discovered to my surprise that my father's article entitled "For More Democracy" was in print. It had come too late for him to see, and had he not chosen to share his secret ambition a few days before, I would never have looked in that issue of *Advance.*

We would have missed this fulfillment of Father's humble dream.

We did close the store for the funeral. I was the last to walk out with Mother. She leaned over the casket, kissed Father and said, "I love you, Chappie, I love you." Then with head up high, she walked quietly through the crowds of customers and friends who had gathered to say goodbye to an exceptional man.

Reflections

At the time of my father's death I had no idea of any good use I could make of this story. But now I know differently. I was grateful he had shared his heart with me and that I was the only one in the family who knew about his box of clippings.

Later when my mother closed the store, she left the old upright piano behind. Had my dad not chosen that day to show me his box of broken dreams I would never have known about his talent or the article in *Advance*. It was years before I told my mother about the clippings and showed her the article I had framed along with my father's picture. I also mounted the picture of Henry Cabot Lodge and the letter of thanks he had written.

Not only do I have these two framed memories on the wall over my desk for inspiration, but I have used this story as a key example in my book *Silver Boxes: The Gift of Encouragement*.

Have you ever suffered the loss of a loved one? How did you react? Have you been able to use something from this person's life to encourage others? Have you ever felt guilty over what you wished you'd done? I've been sorry that I didn't realize my father's talent sooner so that I could have given him encouraging words, but I am grateful he chose that day to show me his box. One more day would have been too late.

It was extremely difficult for my mother to be left with three children, no money and the store to run alone. I realize now how little I did to help her grieve and to be supportive of her emotional needs. But there were no books on grief in those days and we were told to be brave, put it behind you and get on with life.

My friend Marilyn Heavilin has given birth to five children. She lost two in infancy and one teen-age son was killed by a drunk driver. Because of the lack of under-standing people had about her grief and the thoughtless things well-meaning people said, she wrote the touching book *Roses in December.* God gives us memories so we might have roses in December. The response to this book was so enthusiastic that she followed it with *December's Song* and *When Your Dreams Die.* If you are in a grieving situation or know someone who is, read these tender, helpful books so you can

Make the tough times count!

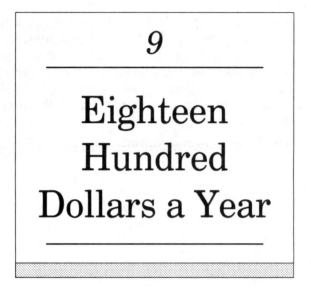

9

Eighteen Hundred Dollars a Year

I amused myself by thinking that I really should go back to Haverhill. After all the work I'd done on myself, it would be a shame not to let the folks at home see how intellectual and sophisticated I had become!

In June, 1949, I graduated from what had become the University of Massachusetts. I had full majors in English, speech and education plus honors in speech. With my B.A. and certificate as a teacher, I felt I had achieved my first goal in life: I was totally educated. Not only was I educated, but I also felt I had become a gracious lady. With these two milestones completed, I reviewed the plan for the rest of my life. I was now ready to pursue my remaining goals: money, clothes, popularity and marriage.

First I needed to get a job. I had received offers from interesting cities, but since my father's death my mother had not been well. She was lost without him and had become emotionally and physically exhausted with the overwhelming responsibilities of raising two young sons and running a business. Although I didn't want to return to Haverhill, I felt for the family's sake I must. I applied to Haverhill High School, and they gave me a job teaching English with the plan that I would also write a speech course and teach it. For this promising position I was to receive $1800 a year.

I amused myself by thinking that I really should go back to Haverhill. After all the work I'd done on myself, it would be a shame not to let the folks at home see how intellectual and sophisticated I had become!

I moved from Kappa Alpha Theta and its parties back to the three rooms behind the store and its customers. I had made a complete circle and I was right back where I'd started. But what a difference! This time I was a teacher.

I was steeped in Shakespeare, filled with multi-syllable words for every occasion and confident in the concepts of classroom teaching. My student teaching had been in high school speech, and the classes were above average, pre-trained, and with the regular teacher sitting in the room. I thoroughly enjoyed my time at Greenfield High School, and I expected my new job to be more of the same.

As I walked into the old red brick Haverhill High School Annex, Room 6, on my first day, I knew more than I thought I would ever need to know. I felt I was at the pinnacle of my intelligence and expectations. As the day wore on, however, I wore out. I discovered first-year teachers get the worst classes, and I was assigned five beauties. I had two classes of "Household Arts English" and soon learned that "Household Arts" was a fancy name for delinquent girls who were deficient in English. I also had two freshman classes and one group of sophomore boys. The five sections had two things in common—they were below average in intelligence and they were determined not to learn. Many of them couldn't read a word over two syllables and they thought a participle was a piece of fruit.

College had not prepared me for this. I had expected to use my large vocabulary and persuasive speech to sway students who would hang on my every word and thirst for more. Instead, I was fighting for survival, surrounded by rowdy kids who were doing time until they turned sixteen and could leave school. What good did it do me to understand calculus and love lyric poetry when these kids could neither add nor read?

As I looked at my household arts girls — dirty, disheveled, and disinterested — I realized they were light years away from understanding the innuendoes of *A Midsummer Night's Dream*. I knew they would laugh me out of the room if I tried to make sense out of little elves dropping love juice into Hermia's eyes as she lay sleeping in her chiffon gown in some shaded glade. Puck was right when he said, "What fools we mortals be." I abandoned Shakespeare and got down to the prosaic facts of life.

Shortly after one of the girls had been expelled for having "cooties," I introduced a hair washing party. I bought a large bottle of shampoo, lined up the girls, gave a speech on cleanliness and then washed each head. It was a humbling experience, but the girls thought it was the best thing they'd ever done in school, and I became their favorite teacher.

The first day I taught the sophomore boys, I walked to class wearing my leftover college clothes and my penny loafers. They all thought I was one of the pupils. One football-type called, "Sit next to me, honey," and several whistled. When they saw I was the teacher they began to laugh, and I was embarrassed. My education classes had been based on the premise that students were well-mannered and wanted to learn. What could be done with a wild group of louts who saw a young teacher as bait to be swallowed? I spent the first day letting them introduce themselves to me and the class. I learned many were veterans and as old as I was.

The text I had to teach was an edited version of *Julius Caesar,* and when I mentioned Shakespeare they groaned. But when I told them it was a man's story full of murders, they became interested. I played the whole thing like a Roman soap opera, with characters named Big Jule and The Brute. My boys actually became excited over the Ides of March and decided they wanted to act out the play. Some even fought over the leading roles. One teacher said, "I don't know how you did it, but those rowdy boys are truly interested in Shakespeare." I smiled.

Step One

I struggled through the year, pushed aside my courses on education and learned to live in the pits. I experienced first-hand the need for discipline and respect and developed a survival plan. Step one: Never let them know how scared you are or they'll jump in for the kill. I had a dramatic chance to practice Step One before I'd even written Step Two.

The school was having a contest to earn money for new band uniforms. Each homeroom had the responsibility to raise money in any way possible. My group decided to have an auction, and I was chosen to be the auctioneer.

In a moment of bravado I said, "Whatever you bring in, I'll auction off." "Anything?" they asked. "Yes," I said.

The day of the grand auction I walked in the front door of the High School Annex and saw my group huddled together whispering. They were normally loud so I knew trouble was brewing. I unlocked the door to our room and they followed in quietly. Those who had items to auction placed them on my desk. All eyes were staring as Angelo put down a corsage box and went quickly to his seat.

As he left, I heard something move in the box. Whatever was in there was alive! The class watched in unusual silence as I began the auction. (Step One: *Never let them know how scared you are . . .*) I sold every item on the desk before touching the box, and when I lifted it, the class in unison drew in its breath.

"This is our last item of the day," I said cheerfully. "Let's see what's inside."

Confidently I lifted off the cover. Staring up at me with bright eyes was a little white mouse. He trembled, and I realized he was as much afraid of me as I was of him.

As the class sat spellbound, I exclaimed, "Isn't he adorable!" Their mouths dropped in disbelief as I reached in and picked him up by the tail. He wiggled, and I felt sick to my stomach, but I held on and asked for the first bid. No one said a word.

"This dear little thing needs a nice home," I said. "What am I bid?" Slowly they began to speak, and soon all were anxious to own the mouse. We sold the pet for $3.50, and I kept him in my desk drawer for the rest of the day. Quickly my reputation as a brave auctioneer spread, and I was accepted into the Teachers' Hall of Fame.

As I overcame my opening jitters and settled in, I found it was possible to teach people who didn't want to learn. It was just much harder. I became creative, simplified my language and learned to laugh at myself. This combination, plus a loving hand of discipline for even the unlovable, brought me respect and popularity.

One day as I was correcting book reports, I found one that started, "Raucous, bold and daring was W. C. Fields." I knew the boy who wrote it had no idea what "raucous" meant, and I doubted he knew much more about W. C. Fields. I put his report aside and soon picked up another that opened with the same line, "Raucous, bold and daring was W. C. Fields." This girl was even less likely to have come up with such a sentence, and as I flipped through the pile of papers I found two more that started with the same line.

They could have copied the report from each other, but there wasn't one in the lot who could have written it.

I decided to check the *Reader's Digest* condensed book of the month in the school library, and there was the biography of W. C. Fields which began "Raucous, bold and daring . . . " Instead of calling in the four plagiarists, I decided to appeal to their honor to come to me and confess.

The next morning I said, "Some of you have cheated on your book reports, but I'm going to give you a chance to make it up to me. Whatever you have done that is dishonest, I will forgive you if you'll come in after school and confess. Since I know who you are, wouldn't it be better to come on your own than to be summoned? Surely you don't want to meet me on the street and have me think, *There is the boy who cheats.*"

The message fell on startled ears, and the class was forebodingly quiet for the remainder of the hour. When the next group filed in, I decided to try the talk again even though I had not found any obvious errors in their reports. Having given my plea once, I found the second time was better, longer and more moving with equally silencing results. I kept it up all day and could have sold it as a television pilot film by the time I had finished my fifth rendition.

When school closed that day, I waited for the four plagiarists to appear, and they did, along with thirty-eight other unapprehended cheats. I was so amazed at the results that I wasn't sure what to do. I quickly realized that if they were willing to turn themselves in, I had better listen and let each one think I had spotted his dishonest work. I called each repentant in separately, told him how proud I was of his willingness to confess and then listened to the most unbelievable tales of creative cheating I could have imagined. I forgave them all, had them write new reports in class and we all became good friends.

Pursuing Goal #3

By the end of my first year, I had collected my $1800 and was one of Haverhill High's most popular teachers. Additionally, I had fulfilled another of my original goals: to get clothes. My living expenses were almost nil as I lived rent-free in the three rooms behind the store with Mother and Ron. Somehow it never occurred to me that I should pay my mother room and board. I assumed that a woman of such humble means whose daughter had risen to such stature should be more than happy to support her. Therefore, with my first $1800 I set out to become well-dressed.

To achieve this goal, I headed each Saturday for "Filene's Basement" in Boston. This is an unusual store where people try on clothes in the aisles, and where every seven days all unsold items are marked down 25 percent. At the end of thirty days, if an item hasn't sold it is given to the Morgan Memorial. Week by week I closely watched a desired item lower in price until, just before it was to be given away, I snatched it up. This astute attention to shopping enabled me to purchase forty dresses, thirty suits, and twenty-five pairs of shoes in my first year and I proclaimed myself to be the best-dressed woman in Haverhill, Massachusetts.

In bringing us up, my mother had always had a conservative attitude on clothes. She believed that when you had only a few dresses, they should be so colorless and nondescript that people would not notice you were wearing the same thing all the time. Consequently, all my life I had been dressed so drably that, put against the wall in any given room, I would blend into the wallpaper and never be noticed.

When I was able to choose for myself, I bought the brightest and loudest clothes imaginable. They had stripes, checks or flowers, and were trimmed with ruffles, sequins or floating chiffon panels. I practiced walking like a model and entering rooms dramatically. Never again was I going to be unnoticed.

During my first two years of teaching, I achieved all but one of my goals. I was educated and refined, my salary was raised to $2200, and I was thrilled when I discovered one of my pupils had made a chart on how many days in a row Miss Chapman could go without wearing the same thing twice. For someone raised in a beige childhood, this was exciting beyond belief. By then I had attained some degree of social prominence, and I was the president of several organizations. I really should have been happy. But what fear begins to creep into the heart of a single English teacher in the hills of Massachusetts?

Reflections

What was your first real job like?

How much did you earn that first year?

What adjustments did you have to make?

Isn't it amazing, when we look back, to realize how little we really knew? I had learned all the textbook answers to teaching but none of them worked with real people. I had taken modeling lessons and knew how to do pivot turns but none of my pupils cared. The only hope I had was to abandon the syllabus and get down to what my mother called "brass tacks." When I stopped trying to be somebody and began to meet the needs of these unpredictable and non-textbook cases, they responded and I received their respect. I had to learn to

Make the tough times count.

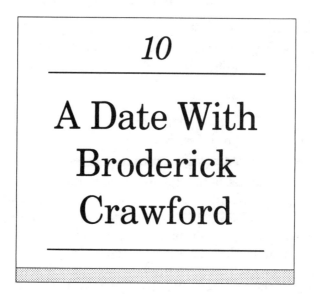

10

A Date With Broderick Crawford

Broderick actually put his arm around me during the performance. I knew he wasn't remotely interested in me, but I hoped my pupils watching in the balcony were impressed.

What fear does creep into the heart of a single English teacher in the hills of Massachusetts? What if I never get married! As I thought of my bleak future without a man, I began to panic.

I had never been popular with the boys. When I was fifteen my first romance with Chauncey DePew MacDonald III lasted one night. Chauncey's father was a friend of my Aunt Sadie and they had mutually arranged for Chauncey to take me bowling while he was home on leave from the Navy. I wanted to look my best and put on my one new outfit—a coral wool homemade dress with a Dutch hat to match, featuring big black velvet bows over each ear. To complete my bowling costume, I wore black patent leather shoes my mother had coated with vaseline so they wouldn't crack.

When Chauncey took his first look at his blind date, even I could sense his disappointment. Years later I realized how humiliated he must have been, showing up at the alleys in front of his friends with a fifteen-year-old girl in a fuzzy wool dress, flippy hat and slippery shoes. Worse than my looks was my lack of bowling skills. After one game where I actually scored eight points, Chauncey decided to take me home.

It was pouring rain as we drove through a dark back road in the woods. Suddenly he pulled the car off to one side, grabbed me, pushed me against the steering wheel and began to kiss me. I hadn't read the sex book yet and my mother's only words on the facts of life came back to me: "Good girls should never drink, smoke or get pregnant." I knew how not to drink and how not to smoke, but I had no idea how not to get pregnant. Maybe this was it.

I pulled away from Chauncey as fast as I could. "What is the matter with you, kid?" he said in disgust.

"Is this how you get pregnant?" I replied.

He never answered and within minutes he had me home. As I got out of the car, still bewildered, he muttered, "The boys on the ship will never believe this one."

A year later I had my second date with a boy named Amos Harrold. He was an artist and my mother thought he was very sweet. While I was grateful he never laid a hand on me, it wasn't until years later when he was discharged from the Navy for molesting his bunkmates that I understood the reason why.

After Amos, I set my heart on a handsome senior class president from a small town near Haverhill. Since I was from the big city, Bing Jordan noticed me when I appeared at his high school functions. We dated for many months and I tested his love by how many nights a week I could keep him sitting with me late enough to miss the last bus and then have to walk two miles home. I was proud that he cared enough to miss the bus almost every night. But when I left for my first year at college, I didn't want to be encumbered by a romance with a hometown boy who had no further education in mind. So I broke up with Bing and went off to Amherst to enter the big time.

I found my first love in a college calculus class. High school math had been easy, but college calculus was beyond my comprehension. I soon spotted a genius who knew all the answers, and I asked him for help.

Frank Rice was a pretty, frail boy who looked like he needed a mother. While he was not my idea of the college hero, he did know calculus, and we had a semester of mutual assistance. I mothered him and he did my math. At mid-term he joined the Navy and to make sure I was faithful, Frank left his best friend, Bill Howard, to take care of me. Bill was 6'4", a track star, and we soon stopped talking about little Frank. Unfortunately, our romance never amounted to much because Bill had to run five miles every Saturday afternoon, and by the time we would get to the frat party and the low lights, Bill would fall asleep in a corner and someone else would have to take me back to the sorority.

When I returned to Haverhill after my first year in college, Bing looked better than I remembered. He had a good job and was willing to spend his money on me. We went steady that summer and all during my sophomore year and were engaged by the following August.

I was excited about the prospect of being a bride until Bing took me out to Georgetown, a suburb of Haverhill, and showed me the old farmhouse he was going to buy where we could spend the rest of our lives together in the wilderness. The thought of plodding through life in the remote reaches of Georgetown quickly brought me back to reality. I returned Bing's ring and went off to my junior year looking for new excitement.

I found intrigue first in my entomology class. The young lab instructor announced that we all had to collect a hundred different insects and mount them in a display box. The thought of bug catching appalled me, and I tearfully expressed the revulsion I felt at sticking a pin through a cockroach. My plight touched the instructor's heart and he volunteered to help me. Every afternoon we leaped together through the Amherst meadows with our nets in search of flying lepidoptera. My collection, full of rare species, was the first completed, and I never touched a single bug. And I got an A! However, once entomology was over, I lost interest in investigating insects and no longer found the instructor intriguing.

Soon my attention was drawn to Melvin Miller, the outstanding student in my speech class. Melvin was tall and handsome, but it was his keen mind and brilliant wit that impressed me. I was overwhelmed that he could take either side of a debate and be convincing enough to always win. Desperately I tried to equal him and was thrilled when the professor chose us as a team. We studied together each evening, held sequestered debates and searched for faulty syllogisms. We were two hearts that beat as one. I was ready to sign on for a lifetime symposium with him.

Because Mel wanted to be a lawyer but didn't have the money for further education, I soon became a one-woman crusade to get him a scholarship to graduate school. I gathered glowing letters from his professors and sent them with his applications. It was hard work but my efforts were rewarded when Mel received a tuition scholarship to Harvard Law School. However, he was still short of money and I pictured myself living in a Cambridge apartment, teaching school to help him become a lawyer. Whatever it would take, I was ready for the grand sacrifice.

At this moment in my young romantic life, Maria arrived on campus. She was an heiress to a Peruvian tin fortune and had gorgeous clothes that made the rest of us seem like rag dolls. The first time she met Mel, she looked up at him and said with her unusual accent, "You are sooo big." She followed him around the fraternity all evening, and two weeks later Mel told me Maria didn't want him to see me anymore. I cried, pleaded and reminded him of how much I had done for him. "You've been a good girl and a lot of fun to know," he said sadly, "but Maria is sooo rich."

When I came back for my senior year, Mel and Maria were engaged and I was heartbroken. I tried to figure out how to hurt him and when I found that Mel's fraternity president sat next to me in lyric poetry class, I set my mind on him. I reasoned that if I could show up at the Phi Sigma Kappa parties with the president, it would unnerve Mel.

Patrick Joseph O'Toole was a fragile fellow who seemed too shy to speak to girls, but I set out to change that. He had been absent from class for a week, and when he returned I introduced myself and volunteered to help make up his missing work. I was so helpful and kind that he repaid me by asking me to the first frat dance of the year. We went to every dance that year, and while Mel noticed I was there, he never seemed jealous.

We all graduated in June. I returned Pat's fraternity pin and Mel married the tin goddess. Thoroughly crushed at my failure to win the man I wanted, I decided to pursue my career without any serious romances.

Dating Life in Haverhill, Massachusetts

In the fall of 1951, when I felt I was close to "perfect," I began seriously to look for a husband. As a child I had been a Cinderella in need of change and I had first become aware of my possibilities that day on the loading dock when Sophie played fairy godmother. All through college I pursued self-improvement as if it might escape. My two years of teaching had given me the money and time to purchase the clothes, makeup and equipment necessary for the final touch, and on November 5, 1951, I knew I had arrived. I had a date with Broderick Crawford!

Broderick had won an Academy Award for *All the King's Men* and was on a promotion tour for a new film, *The Mob.* Since there were no resident movie stars in Haverhill to pair up with Broderick, the committee chose the only dramatic celebrity—me!

I was overwhelmed and went to Filene's to buy a new outfit. Chagrined at not having a Marilyn Monroe figure, I bought a red wool suit and black high-necked sweater, rather than a sequined gown with a plunging neckline, which might have been appropriate for a date with a star.

We met at the ticket booth in front of the Paramount Theater and Broderick didn't seem to get the message that I was his date. Perhaps because I didn't look like any date he'd ever had before! He didn't totally ignore me, but I wondered if he heard my name. To entertain him the committee told me to take Broderick for a spontaneous historical tour of old Haverhill.

I decided to start with the statue of Hannah Dustin scalping the Indians and then go on to John Greenleaf Whittier's birthplace. I had memorized much of Whittier's poetry and felt I could do a dramatic job of combining history with recitation. As I thought up a quick plan, I recalled, "Blessings on thee little man, Barefoot Boy with cheeks of tan."

While I was organizing my steps into history, Broderick turned to go into the theater. "Aren't you coming with me?" I asked, startled. "I'm going to take you to see Hannah Dustin scalping the Indians."

He looked at me and in his movie gangster voice said, "I don't need to see no Indians, honey. All I want is a stiff drink."

In an instant my tour of Haverhill's history evaporated. I followed him backstage where he had a large black tape recorder set up on a simple table. It was the same brand as the one I used in my speech classes and I commented on our similar choices.

"I bet yours doesn't have the same insides," he said as he opened the two doors where the tape reels were supposed to be to reveal a traveling bar.

My eyes betrayed my innocence as I looked at the stemmed crystal, sterling silver jiggers and shakers and an assortment of bottles labeled Scotch and Whiskey all neatly arranged in what appeared to be a tape recorder. I watched stunned as Broderick poured drinks for the committee. I had been brought up to believe that abstention was the path to heaven and I was not about to throw away my salvation for a few drinks with a movie star.

By the time *The Mob* was ready to begin, Broderick was in a better mood and actually put his arm around me during the performance. I knew he wasn't remotely interested in me, but I hoped my pupils watching in the balcony were impressed.

After the show Broderick gave a few words from the stage, then posed with me for pictures for the *Haverhill Gazette*. While our brief encounter wasn't the greatest moment in history, it was the biggest event to hit Haverhill, and the *Gazette* filled a section of the paper that might have otherwise been blank. When the magic night was over, I still faced the dilemma of finding a husband.

In my own opinion at that time, I had perfected myself to such a high degree that there were few men left in Haverhill who were good enough for me. I had over-improved myself and realistically cut my choices to two men who I felt were my equals.

The first one was the local doctor. I dated him and learned he had four things in his favor. He had gone to Phillips Exeter Academy and graduated from Harvard Medical School. His father was president of the most prestigious bank in town, and he was an only child, sure to inherit the family fortune. These were impressive credentials for a husband at that point in my life, but there were two things that disturbed me. He had a strange and unusual attachment to his mother, and he was ugly.

I knew I was supposed to see beneath the surface to the inner beauty, but I didn't have that talent. I had always liked handsome men, so I asked myself, "Could you wake up every morning for the rest of your life and look at him and be happy?"

The answer to this caused me to turn toward the only other educated single man in town: the local priest. He was tall, dark, romantic and looked as if he were about to sing the lead in *Going My Way*. He was bright, witty and articulate, and whenever I saw him at one of the local cultural events, I would look at him and think, *What a waste*.

In those days eligible young girls didn't set their sights on the local priest, so instead I turned my attention toward the doctor. He was so unaggressive that during an entire year of dating, he never once kissed me good-night.

At the end of that year, the doctor decided to stay home with his mother, which is where he is today, and the priest ran away and married one of his parishioners. While the town was shocked, I was disappointed. I had put my efforts in the wrong direction. Who knows — if I had pursued the priest I might today be a Mother Superior!

Reflections

When you think back on some of the dates you had, do you laugh or cry? I shudder at how little I knew about the facts of life and how long it took me to learn. I remember how heartbroken I was when Mel turned me down after all I'd done for him and how humiliated I was trying to be sophisticated and worldly for Broderick.

I look back at my few boyfriends and wonder where I failed. Was I too insecure because of my background? Did I realize at the time I had no sense of style and no money for clothes?

What insecurities did you experience when you began to date? Were you one of those All-American beauties or a football hero? Or were you shy, afraid and easily intimidated? Those dating days were practice for future relationships and I hope we learned from our experiences how to make better choices.

11

Prince Charming

As Fred stared intently out to sea, he suddenly dropped a sentence I never could have predicted: "I'm sure you are a nice girl, but I know I could never marry you."

Discouraged in my search for a husband, I spent the summer of 1951 teaching drama in the woods of Maine. If eligible men were scarce in Haverhill, they were impossible to find in Maine where statistics show there are more cows than people. But one Friday evening, Janice, the sailing counselor, and I went on a pilgrimage to the social mecca of the area . . . the Howard Johnson's in Naples, Maine. This restaurant was so old that it didn't even have an orange roof! It was just a little gray shanty hanging over the edge of a stagnant pond full of floating fudgesicle wrappers, but it was the only place to go to look for men.

All the prestigious girls' camps in Maine made their counselors wear special uniforms when they went off the grounds so that if anyone got into trouble, the local sheriff would know to which camp she belonged. Although I felt I had improved my looks, the uniform did nothing to help me. My camp counselor costume consisted of plain white sneakers, baggy blue slacks, a man's white shirt, black necktie and an itchy navy blue wool vest. Appliqued on the front of the vest was a large white felt pine tree with a big blue letter "T" that stood for Trebor, the name of the camp ("Robert" spelled backwards). Added to this was a heavy canvas crew hat that totally covered my short wispy hair. Janice had on an identical outfit; we looked like a pair of bookends.

After hitchhiking to Naples, Janice and I seductively draped ourselves over a rock in front of Howard Johnson's and began looking for action. As we surveyed the dreary boys passing by in equally unflattering camp uniforms, my glance stopped short. Through the mist, across the bridge over Brandy Pond came the handsomest looking young man I'd seen in the woods of Maine in many a summer. He was tall, blond, blue-eyed, with the build of a football player and the face of a movie star. *This is it,* said my heart. *This is the big moment you've been rehearsing for all these years.*

As I was trying to figure a way to meet this young man, the couple he was with ran over to Janice. They had been old college friends and while the three of them were reunioning, I rose gracefully from the rock, did a pivot turn and in the deepest tone that Davey Crockett had ever taught me said, "Hello."

He answered in a beautiful bass voice that made my studied tones seem weak. As he talked, I fell in love with his voice, and then his light blue eyes, and then his thick blond wavy hair, and then his tanned good-looking face, and then his broad shoulders and arms. Everything on him had been put together in the right places and in the right way.

He told me the couple with him was his brother Dick and his girlfriend Ruthie. As we all went into Howard Johnson's for ice cream, this dream man said his name was Fred Littauer. Littauer, he explained, was the German word for someone from Lithuania. As the others talked about college, Fred told me he was in the Army and was from Larchmont, New York.

The next afternoon he called and asked me out. I was thrilled that he liked me. However, several months later he told me he hadn't asked me out because he had been impressed with me. Rather it was because he needed a date and I was the only single girl he knew in the woods of Maine.

While Fred waited to be discharged from the Army, he began to write letters which I answered within the hour. Since I wrote better than I looked, he enjoyed my correspondence, and at the end of the summer he accepted my invitation to come up to Haverhill for a weekend. I planned everything carefully and begged my two brothers not to say anything bad about me.

The first meal was an unbelievable experience. Just as Fred took his seat near the Coke machine, his plate began to move up and down. Quickly he jerked back and accidentally kicked over the quart of milk my mother always kept under the table. (During each meal she hid the milk so people in the store wouldn't see a bottle on the table and think we were unmannered.)

Fred helped Mother mop up the milk and I investigated and found my brother Ron had installed a "plate lifter" under the tablecloth. He could sit in his chair, squeeze a little bulb and the plate would jump up and down. When Fred wasn't looking, I swatted Ron and pinched him until he apologized. The apology was wasted because just as Fred started to cut his meat, the knife folded back on his knuckles and nicked him. We soon found that Ron had sent for a kit, "Trick Things for Your Table," and had saved them for Fred's arrival. As we tried to laugh and pass over these antics, Fred picked up his glass and as he drank, milk dripped steadily down his tie. Mother declared the dribble glass to be the last straw and sent Ron to bed.

To make up for my meager surroundings, I tried hard to impress Fred with my brains and personality. I even threw in how noble I had been to put my brother James through college after Father had died and left the family with a grand total of three hundred and twenty-eight dollars.

On Saturday we drove to my Aunt Sadie's cottage in Maine. In the afternoon we sat out on the rocks and watched the waves come in. As Fred stared intently out to sea, he suddenly dropped a sentence I never could have predicted: "I'm sure you are a nice girl, but I know I could never marry you."

I hadn't expected a proposal on the first visit, but was stunned as to why he would cross me off so quickly. I asked him how he had come to this devastating decision.

In a slow, thoughtful, business-like manner he said, "I've figured out how many miles it is from Larchmont to Haverhill, how many miles I get to the gallon, and how much gas costs." He then multiplied these amounts, threw in depreciation on the car and lunches, and like a computer came up with a total for one trip.

As I sat dumbfounded, he continued, "If I were going to court you properly," he always did everything properly, not a lot of fun, but properly, "I would have to come up twice a month." He then doubled the original amount and explained. "Frankly, when I look at these figures and then at yours, I don't feel it would be worth the investment."

Disturbed over what Fred had told me, I asked my brothers' advice. "Just forget stodgy old Fred," they said. "He doesn't have a sense of humor, isn't much fun anyway, and can't remember the punchline to jokes."

I followed their advice and forgot about my studied manners, marvelous vocabulary and pivot turns. Instead I went back to the natural way we lived before Fred came along. I decided if I had already lost him I would relax and ignore him until it was time for him to leave.

By Sunday evening Fred asked if he could stay one more day. "Ever since I told you I couldn't marry you, you have begun to shape up, and I'd like to stick around and see if you continue to improve." He stuck around two more days and then in the same business-like tone said, "I've altered my original estimate and I'm going to put you on a three-month probation period." Most girls would have sent him packing, but I had no one standing in the wings and felt a Fred in the hand was worth two in the bush.

My Visit to the Palace

We corresponded daily, and a few months later I was invited to his home for a weekend. I wanted to make sure I was dressed properly so I went to Filene's basement and bought a bright purple knit dress. I had to hunt to find matching suede shoes with grosgrain ribbon woven across the toe. As a finishing touch I bought a bunch of paper violets with long green stems to wear in my hair.

Fred had said little about his family, but I imagined his mother was elegant like that lady who gave me the paper dolls. She probably had lovely clothes and maybe even a fur. A fur—that's what I needed. Luckily Filene's was having a sale on furs and I selected what was called a grey kidskin cape for $99. It had broad shoulders like Joan Crawford wore and I was impressed with how I had put myself together. The purple dress and shoes, the violets behind one ear and the grey kidskin cape.

When the day for the big visit came, I dressed up in my new outfit, took the map Fred had given me in hand, and drove to Larchmont. As I got closer the homes got larger. I was overwhelmed and close to speechless when I arrived at a spacious English Tudor mansion and was met at the door by a German maid in uniform. As she escorted me inside, I noticed a sweeping circular staircase which led into a balcony surrounding the second floor. The huge foyer, central hall and stairs were carpeted in what appeared to be dark burgundy velvet. To the right was a long living room with an obviously expensive oriental rug, elegant furnishings and lamps, silk taffeta drapes and cornices, plus a massive stone fireplace. I had never been in such a home in my life.

There was no one else at home when I arrived and the maid, Anna, not knowing quite what to do with me, took me on a tour of the house. The spacious living room opened at one end into the library which led to a large screened porch. I had only seen home libraries in detective movies, and this one looked like the perfect setting in which to read the will of the murdered uncle to assorted eager relatives. One whole wall was lined with book shelves, and there was a long, comfortable coral couch with Chinese lamps at each end. The mahogany coffee table held impressive magazines and there was another Oriental rug on the floor. Then Anna, in her German accent, directed me to her favorite room, the kitchen, and explained how she rolled out pies and fancy cookies on the big marble table in the center. She gave me a little German tea cake with currant jelly on the top, and I knew she and I would be good friends.

Next to the kitchen on the right was Anna's room and bath and on the left was the breakfast room. I had never heard of a breakfast room before and couldn't imagine having a whole room set aside just for one hour a day. Beyond the breakfast room was an elegant formal dining room with a gleaming mahogany table and Chippendale chairs upholstered in blue-green brocade. I had never seen such chairs, but I could identify them from my college course on home furnishings. The long matching buffet had a shiny silver tea service in the center and sterling candelabra on each end. The wallpaper was a formal fleur-de-lis pattern and over the table was a dramatic crystal chandelier. My mind flashed back to the single hanging light bulb with the frosted glass shade that hung over our only table back in Haverhill. This place was like a fairy tale. I had always wanted to marry a Prince Charming and live happily ever after, and I could see that I was starting at the right place.

The upstairs balcony had many doors opening into the

bedrooms, just like in the movies, and you could look from the balcony right down to the front door. Anna took me into the master suite, which was bigger than our entire three rooms at home. We Chapmans could have all lived quite comfortably in just this one room. There were two stately antique beds with blue silk spreads to match the drapes, two long dressers, an unusual dressing table, several chairs and a romantic moire French chaise lounge with soft colored cushions. The only thing missing from this room of my dreams was a fireplace.

As I imagined what life in this room could be, Anna suggested that I get settled and prepare for dinner. We passed several doors and I tried to peek in each one as she led me to the very last room. Anna showed me where I could hang my clothes and returned me to the study. I looked out the French windows to the sloping green lawns where the colored leaves were just beginning to drop from the big oak trees and realized I didn't belong in a mansion with a maid in uniform. Everything was just as I had dreamed, yet as I saw this grandiose home I realized I was still the same little girl from three rooms behind the store. And although I had been grooming myself for such a moment, I suddenly realized I didn't fit.

As a child, when I complained about our sparse surroundings, my mother would say, "Nothing's ever good enough for you. It's too bad you weren't born a queen." I knew her statement was sarcastic, but it always gave me a good feeling because I truly wanted to be a queen. I had been climbing for years to get a home like this.

As I reviewed my past, I realized I had lived a life of "If Onlys!" *If only* I could get educated, I could be happy. I had worked hard in school; I had a B. A. degree; I was an English and speech teacher; but education was not enough.

If only I could be a gracious lady. By the standards of Haverhill I felt secure, but standing in this mansion without even meeting the family, I was doubtful that I would ever measure up.

If only I could have money. Compared to my family and friends, I was rich. My $2200 a year was more than my father had ever earned. My salary gave me enough for clothes, a car and my brother Jim's college tuition. Yet, in an English Tudor mansion full of silver, antiques and oriental rugs, I felt poor.

If only I could be well-dressed. I had thought I was well-dressed, but perhaps I only had lots of clothes. My students loved my wardrobe and kept track of how many days I could go without wearing the same thing twice, but who knew how these clothes would look in New York.

If only I could be popular. Almost everyone in Haverhill knew me, but I was a total unknown outside of town, and I was way outside of town.

As I thought about how I achieved my goals, a wave of fear washed over me. Was it possible to achieve one's goals and still not be happy? I had spent twenty-three years in a determined quest for a dream. I had moved myself beyond my grandest vision, for here I was in New York, in a private room of the most elegant home I had ever seen, resting while a maid prepared dinner. I was excited and scared. What if I blew it? What if my years of preparation didn't quite fit the occasion? What if no one liked me?

As I mulled these thoughts I noticed a long grey DeSoto wind down the drive. The car stopped, and a young boy got out, hurried around the back of the car, and opened the door for his mother. It was my first view of Mrs. Littauer. Like a spy I watched unseen from behind the drapes. She stepped out of the car and walked quickly toward the house. She was wearing a full-length mink coat, and her blond hair had obviously just been styled. She was hardly the typical New England housewife. I was impressed with her fur coat, and I wondered what she would think of my $99 gray kidskin cape I had bought in Filene's basement.

At that point the front door opened, and I heard a most melodious "He-ello-oo—." I never knew "hello" could have so many syllables or sound so much like music. I wondered if I should go to meet her or wait to be summoned. Fortunately the decision was made for me as she called, "Where are you, dear?" Everything she said was like a line out of an opera, lyrical and beautiful.

How often I had dreamed of such a moment, and yet as Fred's mother looked at me, I knew I wasn't a beauty queen, but a kid from the country in a bright purple knit dress with matching shoes that suddenly seemed too loud. Do you know what happens to a gray kidskin cape when it stands next to a full length mink? It turns into what it is: dead goats!

If Mrs. Littauer was disappointed with her son's choice, she didn't show it. She greeted me with a big hug and said I looked "Lovely, dearie, lovely."

I met thirteen-year-old brother Billy as he carried in the groceries. We all ended up in the kitchen with Anna and tried in different ways to help. Mrs. Littauer quickly took command of any situation merely by her presence, and I felt quite insignificant. She looked far too good for a mother and had a figure in her cashmere sweater that my youth couldn't match. Everything about her was bright, charming and dynamic, and I decided she was the kind of woman I wanted to be.

As I tried to stay out of the way in the kitchen, two other brothers arrived. Dick, who managed one of the family millinery stores, was the one I had met with his girlfriend Ruthie at the Howard Johnson's in Naples, Maine. He seemed to have difficulty remembering who I was. Next came brother Steve, a tall, dark Air Force lieutenant with brown eyes. He was the same size as Fred but opposite in coloring. Finally Fred arrived from New York City after a hard day as assistant manager of Stouffer's Restaurant on Fifth Avenue.

When we sat down for dinner, I noticed all the sons stood until their mother was seated and how Dick, as the eldest, held her chair. She sat graciously and regally at the end of the table while Anna in her black uniform and white ruffled apron served the food. In embarrassment, I thought of how Fred had eaten in the store, with my mother jumping up and down to wait on the customers and my brother Ron doing magic tricks during the meal. *Fred must like me a little,* I thought, *or he would never have brought me down here after seeing where I lived.*

The dinner conversation was all business. Dick reported the daily millinery sales and everyone commented on how it's always slow in October. Mrs. Littauer gave the figures for the other stores and comparisons were made. They next moved into an analysis of the stock market and were elated that most of their holdings were up. All I knew about the stock market was the little I had learned from a sophomore economics course.

Occasionally Fred's mother would turn and ask, "What grade is it you teach, dearie?" She seemed grateful that while I wasn't wealthy I at least had a job as a teacher. Occasionally I tried to drop a light thought into a heavy conversation, but my witty comments never seemed to find an open ear.

Throughout the weekend I discovered that what was smooth and sophisticated in Haverhill turned shoddy in New York. The only person with whom I could have any meaningful conversation was the maid.

The Big Question — Finally!

In spite of our differences in background, our courtship progressed properly as Fred had planned. I was so in awe of Fred's family, with their obvious wealth and finesse, that I subdued my behavior and hid my strong will and take-charge attitude. I struggled to learn all I could about the millinery business and stock market. I also observed how Fred's mother entertained, and I tried to become more like her.

While Fred and I never discussed marriage, we did go back and forth twice a month and wrote almost daily. On

October 11, 1952, I came down to New York City on the train and met Fred at Stouffer's on Fifth Avenue to attend a Broadway play. Instead of eating as we usually did where Fred worked, he took me to the Stouffer's by Central Park. Before we left for the theatre, he suggested we ride through the park in one of the horse-drawn carriages with the driver in the tall, silk hat carrying a whip.

Nothing could have been more romantic and I was eager to go. We sat huddled in the cab while the horse with his tinkling bells trotted through the park. Fred handed me a box from the florist. I was excited at the thought of flowers. The last corsage I had received was from Pat O'Toole at the senior prom. I opened the box and saw a large white orchid and another box. This one was green velvet, in the shape of a heart. With trembling hands almost too shaky to open it, I lifted it up and as I did, I gasped. There inside was the largest diamond I had ever seen with three small diamonds on each side.

"Will you be my wife?" asked Fred.

Mrs. Frederick Jerome Littauer, Jr., I thought, and then wondered, *How could I ever leave my brother Ron?* But only for an instant. "Yes, yes, yes!" I said through tear-filled eyes. I had never allowed myself to think of marriage as a real possibility, but now I began to make plans.

Reflections

Are you ever embarrassed when you think of how you looked years ago? Do you laugh at some of the things you wore and how little you really knew?

I had tried to be so smooth and sophisticated and yet I just missed. I had no idea of how Fred's mother must have felt when she viewed me in my violets and dead goats. It wasn't until I had teenagers of my own who brought home strange friends I was afraid they'd marry that I had any concept of the fear she must have experienced.

Can you remember the first time you met his mother—or her mother? What were you wearing? Did you say just the right things or were some of your words jumbled and senseless? On a scale of tough times, meeting the future mother-in-law is not the worst, but didn't you want to run and never come back? I was too far away from home to run and I was so impressed with the English Tudor mansion that I just stood there awe-struck and said to myself, "Florence, this is for you." I watched everything Fred's mother did and I became an eager pupil.

I wanted to be sure I would pass the test.

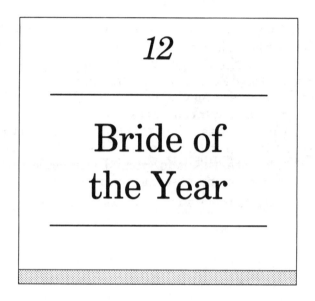

12

Bride of
the Year

*Had they seen me as the sophisticated lady I tried
to be, or did they know that under my wedding
gown was a scared little girl from three rooms
behind her father's store?*

From the moment Fred slipped the diamond ring onto
my finger, I determined my wedding was going to be one
Haverhill would never forget. As a drama teacher in the
high school, I had a captive group of eager students ready
to make a production out of any slice of life. As I shared my
wedding plans, the students instantly volunteered to help,
and they organized the event as a giant-sized senior class
play.

We discussed a possible theme. Because I had always
wanted to be a queen, we decided to make it into a corona-
tion. The art class designed my tatted crown, the woodshop
boys made scepters for the bridesmaids out of gold sprayed
broomsticks, and the metal shop boys created display racks
for the wedding presents. We let it be known that not only
would the gifts be on display at the reception, but each

donor's name would be printed underneath their gift as well. There's no better way to increase the value of the wedding gifts! One would dare not bring a pot holder. Every girl who owned a strapless net dress was in my court. The home economics department planned the royal buffet, the auto shop borrowed a long white Cadillac from the owner of a shoe factory, and the high school band started practicing the Wedding March with my brother Ron at first trumpet.

At this moment in its history, *Life* magazine was doing a series called, "Life Goes to a Party." One of the more imaginative teens in our group wrote to *Life* and invited them to cover a teacher's wedding where the pupils were doing all the work. Amazingly, the idea appealed to *Life* and two weeks before the wedding I received a surprise call from *Life* photographer Yale Joel, telling me he had been assigned to cover my big event.

Poor little Haverhill went into instant redevelopment. At the thought of finding himself in print, the school principal became my best friend and ordered the janitors to polish the brass statue of The Thinker that brooded at the front door of Haverhill High. People I hardly knew asked to come to the wedding and absolute unknowns gave me showers. While my brothers and I were delirious over our own resident photographer, my mother hated every moment of this invasion of her privacy.

"I can't even go to the bathroom without a flashbulb going off!" she complained.

Mother had never shared my feeling for photographs and publicity and withdrew at the sight of a camera. As she withered, I blossomed. In my search for success, I never doubted that I would someday be on stage, but the presence of *Life* magazine was beyond even my confident calculations.

The *Haverhill Gazette* assigned a photographer and reporter to follow *Life's* photographer and reporter. When the *Haverhill Gazette* ran a front page picture of Yale Joel taking a picture of me, I was fascinated to find that my *Life* coverage was being covered! For two weeks *Life,* followed closely by the *Gazette,* recorded my every word and deed. By the time Yale Joel completed his assignment he had taken more than 200 pictures. The community was impressed and so was I.

As the wedding day approached, *Life* hired an electrician to rewire the interior of the church to accommodate their floodlights, the women's guild polished the pews and the janitor repainted the front door.

The day before the big event, Fred and his family arrived in Haverhill. In the frenzied excitement and preparation, I had almost forgotten about my husband-to-be. Suddenly Fred became the handsome leading man in a show where everyone knew their part but him. He had never even read the script! While Fred adjusted quietly to his role, I directed every move of the production with precision.

Choir Room Reflections

Finally the magic night arrived. I drove to the church in a gleaming white Cadillac while the police pushed a path for me through the crowds that filled the square between the big, gray church and our family store. My brothers and I had often played in this street, and now it was roped off for the event of the decade—my wedding.

I smiled, waved at my audience and tried to look like the queen I wanted to be. I held my crowned head high as I walked toward the waiting wedding party in my imported chantilly lace gown with a hoop skirt like those of the Southern heroines I had often read about. My sweeping white silk tissue faille court train was guided by two doting flowergirls who scattered rose petals as they walked. I carried a white silk pillow holding a circle of tatting to match the starched crown on my head. A large white orchid, to be used later as my corsage, accented the pillow which was hung with streamers of sweet peas and stephanotis.

The maid of honor was in turquoise silk and the bridesmaids wore candlelight yellow. They all carried the scepters made by the woodshop boys and decorated with gardenias, streamers and pearls by the home ec. girls.

As I stood that Saturday evening waiting for the Wedding March to begin, I felt I was the luckiest bride in the world. I had gone from living in three rooms behind my father's store to the promise of a large New York apartment; from being a plain unnoticed little girl to being practically worshipped by 2,000 high school students. What's more, I was moving from my humble background into a family which not only had money, but knew how to do everything with class. What more could a girl ask for? All the goals I had set for myself were being realized. I was marrying Prince Charming. I was to be in *Life*. And I hoped to live happily ever after.

I was jolted from my reverie by a phone call. It was Fred's Aunt Edie. She had lost her way and since she had driven all the way from New York, everything had to stop until she arrived.

I slipped into the music room to hide my disappointment and, as I looked around, I remembered how often I had sat on those little chairs while practicing with the junior choir. I had always wanted to be on the director's stool, and that night, all alone, I spread my long lace train over the high chair, then eased myself up on top. As I sat there, I wondered what *Life* would say about me.

Had they seen me as the sophisticated lady I tried to be, or did Yale Joel know that under my wedding gown was a scared little girl from three rooms behind her father's store? Would they feature shots of me in my elegant gown flanked by my flower girls, or would they infer I was a Cinderella whose shoes did not quite fit? I had spent my whole life training for this starring role, and I hoped *Life* would look at me from a positive point of view.

For years I had worked on my vocabulary. Inspired by my father, I had memorized every syllable in *Word Wealth* and was able with ease and nonchalance to drop such gems as *magnanimous* and *mellifluous* into the right slots in sentences. I had learned the value of articulate alliteration and the impressive impact of biblical and Shakespearean quotations. Since my father had taught me Bible verses from the time I could talk, I needed only to brush up on my college Shakespeare to pepper my paragraphs.

I knew that "life's but a walking shadow" and that I might "suffer the slings and arrows of outrageous fortune" as I did "strut and fret my hour upon the stage."

In addition to my mental manipulations, I had worked to beautify my body. No fairy godmother waved her wand, but by diet, exercise and a Peter Pan padded bra, I had produced a commendable figure. With modeling lessons, I learned to walk well, do pivot turns and rise gracefully from my chair. With daily shampoos, I was able to fluff up my limp hair into a promising pageboy, and by proper application of mascara, I emphasized my eyes. I developed an instinct for showing up wherever the newspaper sent a photographer and learned by observation that if I wore a dark dress and stood sideways, I would always photograph slimmer than the rest. All of this self-improvement study had prepared me for this great moment when I would be "Queen for a Day."

As I sat on that high stool in the choir room, my gown flowing out around me, my crown on my head and my bouquet propped up on a music stand, I began to review the path that led me to *Life* and ask myself the question, "Can a simple school teacher from Haverhill find happiness in the big city?"

Aunt Edie finally arrived more than an hour late, having gone to the wrong church. Although the wedding party was a little wilted, we snapped to attention with the first commanding notes of the Wedding March. While the ceremony was short and unimpressive, it hardly mattered. Everyone was watching the photographer and smiling broadly hoping they would find themselves in *Life*.

After the ceremony the guests rushed into the fellowship hall for a drink of fruit punch prepared by the home economics department. The girls had also made tea sandwiches, cookies and a wedding cake. As expected, the labeled gifts were a big hit. The ladies stood around discussing who gave the most silver spoons and wondered why Mabel had sent an obviously second-hand plate.

The receiving line was endless. I had to kiss every pupil I ever had and hug every lady in the church. While the high school band played, Fred and I finally made the grand farewell. The police pushed back the crowds as the long white Cadillac holding Haverhill's "Our Miss Brooks" slowly passed the Riverside Variety Store.

I smiled and waved patronizingly as I had once seen Queen Elizabeth do from her gold carriage. The pupils screamed, cheered and threw baskets of confetti on us and themselves. With Fred's brother Steve at the wheel, we made as royal an exit as had ever been made from the Riverside Memorial Church.

The Honeymoon Was Over (Before It Had Begun)

As we drove into Boston I began to think about the trip ahead of us. The honeymoon had been planned to fulfill my Cinderella expectations. For weeks Fred and I had pored over travel folders. We selected a week in Bermuda as the best place for an ideal honeymoon. The biggest trip I had ever had was a tour of the Massachusetts State House when I was a Girl Scout and the idea of faraway Bermuda was overwhelming. After looking at pictures of petite cottages and azure seas I thought, *If only I could vacation there I could be happy.*

Getting to Bermuda from Haverhill, however, was another problem. After inquiries, Fred came up with an inspiring plan. We would spend our wedding night on a train! The thought of our first night together on a clanking train was hardly romantic. Fred comforted me by explaining that it wouldn't be an ordinary train with cracked leather seats. Rather, it would be a luxury locomotive with real rooms like a hotel. I liked the words *luxury* and *hotel* and romance once again filled my mind.

We arrived in Boston at midnight, drove to South Station and headed expectantly for our lavish suite. As we made our way toward the luxury locomotive, people pointed and giggled. I didn't know why at the time, but as I look back I can see it must have been the way we were dressed. My scarlet poodle-cloth going-away suit with a square double-breasted jacket and two rows of big pearl buttons, fit me as if I were wearing a red box tied with a huge white bow at the neck. To top it off, I wore a white straw hat edged in red velvet. The twenty-inch brim held a fluffy chiffon red rose and streamers down the back.

When we arrived at the gate to pick up our reserved passes, the clerk told us the train we had reserved had exploded and burned the day before. He assured us, however, the substitute train would be almost as good as the one we had anticipated. Disappointed, we entered the train, which may well have been the first Mr. Pullman ever produced, and were escorted to our suite.

When the porter opened the door, my dream of a romantic wedding night was immediately shattered. It was a cubicle less than half the size of our bedroom behind the store. I had expected to be traveling like a queen in a long, elegant car furnished like a European palace with a huge canopied bed. Instead we had an upper and lower berth, narrower than my cot at Camp Trebor. I began to cry.

The bathroom was so small we had to flatten against the wall to get the door shut. And the bedroom with its two bunks was so tiny that when Fred wanted to take a picture of me in my fluffy white negligee with pink satin rose-buds, he had to go into the hall and back against the far wall to get me in focus. Even then he missed the top of my head!

Fred calmed me down, and after agreeing that neither berth would accommodate both of us, he promptly went to sleep on the bottom bunk and I spent the night awake on the top bunk wondering how this could have ever happened to me. *If only* we could have been on the right train, I could have been happy.

Eventually morning came. Fred was alert; I was exhausted. I again put on my bright red suit and big hat and we went to the Hotel Commodore for a 6:30 A.M. breakfast. From the hotel we took a bus to the airport and flew to Bermuda hoping our disappointment was over.

Our honeymoon did improve when I saw the adorable pink cottage we were to stay in at Cambridge Beaches. But it was a little discouraging to find the bed was two couches on opposite sides of the room. Fred rearranged the furniture, put the couches together and our honeymoon began.

The first morning a waiter brought us a huge bowl of fresh strawberries and a lavish breakfast. We ate on our private patio that overlooked the ocean. It was a dream come true! But things were to change.

On our second afternoon Fred decided we should take a bicycle tour of the island. Unfortunately, Fred didn't know how totally uncoordinated I was. Within thirty seconds after renting a motorbike, I drove it straight into a stone wall and bent the front wheel. I had figured out how to start the motorbike but I had no idea how to stop it. Fred's enthusiasm for the trip was suddenly dimmed, but he courageously rented a second bicycle. I managed to drive, fearfully, for the rest of the afternoon.

Fred's idea of a beautiful honeymoon was to tour the ruins of old forts, and the next day we again took off on another bicycle tour. As I turned a corner on a sandy road, my bicycle skidded and fell over on top of me, twisting my right knee. I lay in a pained heap and as Fred turned and looked I could tell he was saddened with my plight, but obviously more annoyed with this delay in his plans.

Graciously, Fred told me he'd give me five minutes to rest and recover before going on. I thought he was cruel and inconsiderate but I had no choice—tears didn't impress him! Valiantly I pulled myself together, got back on the bicycle, and we inspected a few more forts. While Fred read every inscription on every doorway and perused every historical tidbit, I wept silently and wondered how this could have happened to me.

The following day my knee was swollen twice its normal size. When Fred saw I was unfit for the trails, he suggested I stay in bed. Since he didn't want to waste a day, he went off alone on another historical jaunt. I lay in bed all day in misery, wondering if all honeymoons were this dreadful.

On Friday we left for home aboard the Ocean Monarch, a huge ship that was like a floating hotel. I always loved romantic movies where the heroine sailed off on an ocean voyage while her friends wept and waved at the dock. I had read *Our Hearts Were Young and Gay* so many times I could feel the ocean swell whenever I picked up the book.

The ship did not disappoint me. It was greater than any movie I had seen or book I had read. Our stateroom was magnificent, and even though we were again dismayed to find double bunks, I was delighted with the flowers Fred ordered for our cabin.

Before the ship left Hamilton Harbor, Fred and I strolled hand in hand around the deck and relaxed on striped lounge chairs while dignified British waiters in red coats served us tea and crumpets. I was so excited with this storybook setting I hardly noticed my throbbing knee. However, the moment we cast off and Fred felt that first lurch, he raced for the rail. Within minutes he was deathly ill. He immediately retreated to our cabin and didn't emerge until we landed in New York Harbor.

To make matters worse, we ran into a hurricane with waves as high as the deck. As each wave smashed the wall of our stateroom, Fred groaned that he wished he were dead. Depressed to have my new husband wishing he were dead, and obviously having no fun, I left him alone and went off in search of something to brighten up a dull trip.

That afternoon as I limped around the deck, I met

Tom, a handsome young Englishman whose wife was also sick. As our mates lay below in misery, we sipped tea and watched the huge waves from our deck chairs. All would have been perfect, but my knee became steadily worse and finally Tom took me to the ship's doctor. After the doctor examined it, he reprimanded me for my negligence in waiting so long to be treated. He told me I had torn the ligaments. After draining out a vial of fluid, he bound up the knee in an Ace bandage. Tom took tender care of me and we daringly concluded in jest that we hardy souls should have married each other. Although ladies on ships are supposed to have clandestine romances, I was not about to have one on my honeymoon.

Fred's mother met us at the dock in New York Harbor and was aghast to see what a week of marriage had done to us. Fred had lost ten pounds and looked green. I hobbled stiff-legged down the gang plank while he hung on to the ropes to keep from collapsing.

How to Be a Wife — Fred's Way

After we moved into our three-room apartment in Bronxville, New York, I was hit hard by the realization that after every wedding comes a marriage. Too few brides understand that the wedding is not necessarily the beginning of a great life, but the possible end of one. Our honeymoon had been a disappointment, but my hopes for the future were brighter. Unfortunately, when I returned from Bermuda, I became stupid overnight.

From being the urbane queen of Haverhill, Massachusetts, I quickly became Fred's own private Eliza Doolittle. What had looked so smooth and sophisticated in Haverhill suddenly turned shoddy in New York. While Fred had appeared to accept me just as I was before we were married, he found abundant faults in me as I took on the role of his wife. When our marriage was one week old he announced, "I'm going to put you on a training program. It will help you become a perfect wife. The first thing we have to do is get rid of your Boston accent."

"I don't have an accent," I snapped. "Everybody in Boston talks like me."

"Well, it may sound all right in Boston," said Fred, "but your accent will never be accepted in New York society."

I was crushed. I had thought my diction and intonation faultless. It distressed me that I had to learn to talk all over again. Every time I put an "r" where it shouldn't be (such as *idear*) or left one out (such as *paak* for park), Fred made me repeat the word three times correctly. For a person who talked as much and as fast as I did, this constant correction was unbearable. I soon stopped talking and communicated with Fred only in simple, one-syllable words that contained no r's!

The second lesson was teaching me how to walk. Since I had taken modeling and drama, I thought I knew how to walk quite nicely. When I defended myself, Fred pointed out that my feet turned out at the toes and his mother had always told him one should walk with one's toes straight ahead. Every night he made me practice by walking on the tiles on our foyer floor until I could go ten lengths without my toes lapping over the lines. What an exciting way to spend an evening!

My third lesson was how to answer the telephone. In Haverhill we just said "Hello," but Fred said this was uncouth. I had to pick up the phone and say, "Good evening, this is Florence Littauer. With whom did you wish to speak?" I thought this wordy and ridiculous, but Fred insisted and called several times a day to spot-check my responses.

My fourth and most difficult lesson was cooking. He analyzed every dish and then gave me an instant critique. Fred was in the restaurant business and knew far more about cooking than I did. He explained that one should never put two vegetables of the same color on the same plate. Also one should never put two vegetables of the same consistency together. In other words, I could never serve carrots and candied yams on the same plate, nor mashed potatoes and whipped turnips at the same time.

On one occasion Fred became upset because I gave him a sandwich on a paper plate. He told me he expected china service and then asked, "Where is the watercress?" In Haverhill we were lucky to get a sandwich on a napkin and whoever heard of watercress? If I had been asked to guess, I would have thought it was a little fish, like a sardine. Fortunately, I didn't have to ask. "Watercress," said Fred, "is a leafy garnish of a higher class than parsley; no sandwich should be served without it."

The other rule I found difficult to follow was that I must always preheat the dinner plates and pre-chill the salad plates. Fred made me recite to him, "Hot food on hot plates, cold food on cold plates."

On one of our first Saturday evenings after we were married, I served him hot dogs, baked beans and canned brown bread. I had eaten this tasty dish every Saturday night of my life. But when Fred saw it without even a sprig of parsley, he gave me a discouraged look and said, "What's this?"

"They're franks and beans," I said. "It's what everyone eats on Saturday night."

"Perhaps in Boston," he said, "but I never want to see canned baked beans again."

I cried and scraped the all-brown dinner down the garbage disposal—a part of my heritage ground up before my eyes!

The fifth lesson in my exciting bridal instruction course was on housekeeping. Fred's training in the restaurant had taught him to spot, with one sweep of his eye, every salt and pepper shaker that was out of place, every crooked picture frame and every waitress's bow that was not properly tied.

Likewise when he came home at night, he could, with

one sweep of his eye, see everything I hadn't done properly. He would walk in the front door of our little apartment and immediately straighten the tilted pictures, rearrange the magazines on the coffee table so they were even from each edge and run his finger over the dressers to see if I had dusted. He would point out my sins of commission or omission, and with a condescending smile show me how to do everything better.

One night after watching me wash the dishes, Fred heaved a big sigh and told me I had made forty-two unnecessary moves. I had never heard of anyone counting the moves one made washing dishes, so I threw a big wet sponge at him. He was upset with my unladylike behavior and couldn't understand what had disturbed me.

"I'm sick of your constant instruction," I said.

He replied, "It's only natural for one who is more gifted to share his knowledge with one who is less fortunate."

So there it was—Fred's whole attitude toward marriage: a brilliant man trying to put up with a stupid woman. Surprisingly, in spite of Fred's critical attitude, I was grateful for a home of my own, and each morning I was able to bounce back from the previous day's instructions.

After Every Wedding Comes a Marriage

On May 18, 1953, our copy of *Life* arrived with a five-page spread entitled, "Pupils Help a Teacher Get Married." The copy was positive and complimentary, but there was one problem. Fred's name was never mentioned. I chuckled inwardly. The Littauers, who bought magazines for all the relatives, couldn't believe their family name had been omitted. In fact, the only clear picture of Fred was at the rehearsal, where I was instructing the pastor and Fred was looking down at his hand. *Life* said, "Rehearsing wedding evening before ceremony, bridegroom looks confusedly at fingers."

As I looked over the pictures, I was delighted to see

myself in print. I reread the article.

Pupils Help a Teacher Get Married: Admiring Teen-Agers Take Over Ceremony

When Florence Chapman, a high school teacher in Haverhill, Mass., announced her engagement last winter, her pupils promptly besieged her with offers to help out at her wedding. Miss Chapman, who teaches public speaking and dramatics, accepted their offers and began assigning their duties like homework. For the pupils, who designed the wedding costumes, decorated the reception hall, and helped prepare and serve the food at the reception itself, their teacher's wedding had everything that a class play would have, and romance too. Most of them had never been so close to an actual wedding before. But after it was all over and the bride and bridegroom had departed in a car driven by a pupil, one of the girls confessed, "It was lots of fun, but I'd rather get married more privately."

The wedding was the high point of my life, I thought after reading the article, *but it's slowly going down hill.*

I never stayed down for long and cheered myself on by beginning to make my little home a pleasant place to live, even if it wasn't too pleasant living there.

I had never had the opportunity to decorate anything beyond putting a blue Bates bedspread on my college cot. After papering the dinette in white paper with huge red roses, I decided to make the living room into a sort of opium den. I had never seen an opium den, of course, but I had picked up some ideas from Charlie Chan movies. I had a set of twenty silk padded Chinese paper dolls and used them as a focal point by gluing them to the living room wall at different heights.

After arranging the dolls in groupings, I then underlined each section with strips of black plastic tape. Since we were without living room furniture, I took the odd pieces we had collected from relatives and painted them all in black glossy enamel. I made drapes out of bright red heavy cloth adorned with one-foot-high chartreuse Chinamen burning incense. I was thrilled with the consistent theme I had developed and knew the people in Haverhill would have been impressed. However, the relatives in New York were not. They somehow felt my opium den was not a fitting family image, and when Fred saw my Chinese dolls glued to the wall, he told me he thought the place looked like a first grade classroom. However, I didn't let these words discourage me. I was happy with my results and plunged into decorating the bedroom.

Gratefully, Fred said little about my draping the room in soft pink ruffles and I took his silence as a dubious compliment.

Next I decided to become a hostess. I invited some of Fred's family and friends over to play charades. I had spent days planning the party, and when the day came I made what I thought was an extremely clever dessert.

I bought little clay flower pots that were just the right size to hold my custard cups. I baked a half inch of cake batter in each cup, packed the cups with ice cream, and put them in the freezer. When it came time to serve the dessert, I whipped up a bowl of meringue which I spread in mounds on the cake and ice cream cups. I then slipped them into the oven and watched with delight as they puffed up and browned just perfectly. I then dropped each hot cup into a clay flower pot and stuck a real chrysanthemum into the meringue. For the final touch I placed a sugar cube soaked in brandy at the base of each flower and lit the cubes.

I carried the tray of flaming flower pots into the living room expecting Fred's acclaim. Instead he looked up and said, "What in the world have you done?" One of his sophisticated relatives gave a look that said, "What has the poor, gauche child come up with now?"

As I stood before them in my red Chinese gown, my adorable garden of desserts wilted before my eyes. By the time I served the last one, meringue was running down the pot and the chrysanthemum was on fire. Fred was embarrassed and I went to bed discouraged. As I drifted off to sleep, I thought what a hit my pots would have made back at the sorority.

Early Marital Advice

As the weeks passed I became more and more convinced that Fred and I were just two different people and there was little hope for a successful marriage. I began to ask the other girls in our apartment house how they were doing.

Most told me their marriages were no better than mine. I also learned from the other girls that my puritanical, Victorian morals and New England legalism had no place in the Fleetwood Arms Apartments.

My best friend was Gail. Her wealthy parents had left her in their big home while they had taken a six-month trip. When her parents returned, they discovered Gail's boyfriend, Joe, had been living with her, and their only daughter was two months pregnant. The parents insisted they marry immediately, which they did, and Gail's parents rented them the apartment next to ours.

Spoiled and lazy, Gail came each day to visit me. While I scrubbed and cleaned in a vain effort to please Fred, she sat and watched. Then just before Friendly Joe came home from work, Gail would wash off her makeup, flop down on my couch and pretend to be sick. When Joe came over to our apartment looking for her, she would moan about how ill she was and how it was his fault that she was pregnant in the first place. With a deep sense of guilt, Joe would help her back to their apartment and cook dinner.

I was wide-eyed with this game she played and knew I could never get away with such an act with Fred.

Then there was Thelma. She lived across the hall and was a little older and more worldly-wise than the rest of us. I had never met her traveling husband, but one day as I opened my hall door I saw a man unlocking Thelma's door and assumed it was her husband. I saw Thelma that evening and said, "I finally caught a glimpse of your Tom. He's really good looking." She seemed frightened and asked when I had seen him.

"I noticed him unlocking your door at lunch time," I said.

"Oh, that's not my husband," she said, "that's my friend Alex. He comes over every noon when Tom is out of town."

One night when Thelma knew Fred was working, she called and asked if I would like to come over to her apartment. "Alex has an adorable friend and he needs a date," she said. I told her primly I didn't do that sort of thing, and Thelma hung up in disgust.

Some time later Thelma told me I was naive and needed some broadening experiences. She, with Gail, suggested I have a baby. "A cute little thing around the house will take the pressure off your marriage." They also said a baby would keep my husband so happy he wouldn't have time to inspect my housework.

Fred had mentioned he wanted a namesake, but I wasn't in a hurry. Yet my marriage wasn't getting any better. Perhaps having a baby would remove the constant criticism of Fred's continuous training program. I marvel now that I was naive enough to believe a baby would make life easier. Anyone with an ounce of brains would have known that changing diapers at 2 A.M. would not revive a flagging marriage.

But before we began our program of potential parenthood, Fred was transferred to Cleveland to open a new restaurant in the Westgate Shopping Center. I was disappointed to have to tear apart my first home and pry the padded Chinese paper dolls off the wall, but I was excited about moving to a new state. Perhaps a fresh beginning and getting away from Fred's family was what our marriage needed.

We rented an attractive garden apartment in

Cleveland and I began my decorating all over again. Within a few weeks I found I was pregnant, but by the time I had finished settling into my new home, Fred was promoted. Top management saw Fred as a master of detail and organization. The very qualities that bothered me impressed his superiors! They were grateful he could spot a sandwich without watercress, answer the telephone in a distinctive manner and walk with his feet straight ahead! So they sent him to Detroit to open the new Stouffer's at Northland.

Fred found us a beautiful apartment with a full basement; a first-floor living room, dinette and kitchen; and an upstairs with two bedrooms and a bath. It was almost a house.

Both of us excitedly became involved in our own projects. Fred worked extremely long hours and I decorated again and eagerly waited for our first child to be born. I was to learn later that our relationship was always best when our separate projects kept us apart—there was no time to bother each other!

Two weeks before I was due, I caught a terrible cold that turned into bronchial pneumonia. My condition became critical and the doctor decided to induce labor. However, he neglected to tell me or Fred what he was doing. Early the next morning I began to get sharp pains and I was taken unceremoniously off to the labor room and strapped to the sides of a large, white iron crib. There were at least thirty other women in similar cribs, all screaming in pain.

I had no idea having a baby was a public affair and I was mortified to be lying in agony in front of all these women. I asked the one nurse, who filed soberly through the room giving us all indiscriminate shots, if my husband knew I was in the labor room.

"I'm sure they've called him," she said brusquely.

They had not. While I was delivering Lauren Luise Littauer, Fred was home polishing his shoes. When he arrived that afternoon to see his wife who had pneumonia, he learned to his surprise that he had a daughter and a wife who was upset that he hadn't been present for the birth of his first child.

Due to my infection, the baby and I stayed in the hospital for over a week during which time Fred read three books on motherhood. By the time I got home, he already knew more about how to be a mother than I know to this day.

While I felt I was a semi-failure as a wife, cook and housekeeper, I thought genetically I would be a better mother than Fred. Instead of relieving the pressure in my marriage, Lauren only added to it. Fred now had a whole new training program for me. After two years of marriage, I was firmly convinced that in Fred's sight I was a total failure. It took my very best determination to keep my basic optimistic nature alive.

Reflections

Wouldn't you think that someone who had managed to work her way up from three rooms behind the store to an expensive New York apartment and five pages in *Life* ought to live happily ever after? I surely thought so until I got there.

As I look back with the advantage of hindsight I see that Fred and I got married for some of the wrong reasons. I equated happiness with money, a big house and good looks, all things I had so desperately wanted as I was growing up. I felt if I filled those voids I could be happy, and Fred seemed to answer my needs.

Little did I know that Fred had grown up feeling unloved by his busy parents and had been abused by a maid. Where there should have been love, he had nothing but extreme feelings of rejection. His mother had so domineered his life that Fred was eager to be in control of a female. I see now why he demanded I tell him I loved him whether I felt like it or not, why any light-hearted touch of humor came across as rejection, and why he was determined to break my will and be in control.

Since I felt like the poor girl from the country with no rights of my own, I accepted the situation and did whatever Fred instructed. He was never impolite or rude and he never hit me, but I just learned quickly that in turn for the nice home and money I had to play by his rules.

I once saw a sign in a store, "He who has the gold makes the rules." That's the way we lived. As I look back, I realize that I wanted money and a real home and Fred provided these. He needed love and acceptance and I tried to fill that huge, empty well inside him. But when Fred had business failures and didn't give me money, I stopped giving him the doting love he wanted. How we often marry to find someone who can fill our voids. And then when they fail to meet our every need, we assume we have married the wrong person.

When you think about it, can you see some deep emotional needs that you and your mate were craving to have filled when you married? Did you match up in your areas of emptiness? Have you matured emotionally and grown up together? Or has one of you made progress and the other refused to change? Isn't it amazing how we can look back and see our mistakes that were not recognizable at the time? Fred and I praise God today that He had a hold on us long before we had an awareness of our needs. Marriage isn't easy, but it is possible in retrospect to

Make the tough times count.

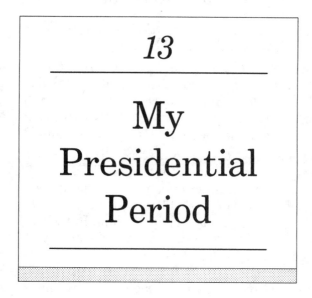

13

My Presidential Period

I had to admit that in those few moments, Ben had gotten closer to my heart and the problem of my marriage than anyone before him.

A year after Lauren was born, Fred left Stouffer's and took a job in New Haven, Connecticut, operating the food service of the Southern New England Telephone Company. He left Detroit ahead of Lauren and me to find us a place to live. One night he called, all excited. He had just rented a lovely home in Montowese and hoped I would like it even though both the living room and exterior were painted black. The thought of a black house depressed me but I had no choice since he had made a month's rent deposit. *We can always paint it,* I thought. Gratefully, when I arrived in Connecticut I found the house was not black, but forest green. Fred is color blind and to him it all looked black.

Life looked black to me as I settled into a lonely house in a town where I had no friends. I began to look for something more interesting than housework and child raising. Since I didn't seem to be good at either, I thought *if only* I had a challenging job I could be happy. I applied to the New Haven adult education program as an English teacher and although there wasn't an opening in the English department, they did have a desperate need for a teacher in a course called Elementary Psychology. The superintendent asked if I could handle such an assignment.

"I don't have credentials in psychology," I said, "but I'm willing to give it a try."

Within a week I read eight books on psychology and skimmed a dozen more. From my instant knowledge, I made up a list of twenty-five subjects of possible study and presented these choices to the class on opening night. Gratefully, the students chose topics like personality improvement and overcoming shyness as opposed to Freud's dream analysis and Sheinfeld's genetics. With my adult pupils' mandate clearly in hand, I went home and wrote a course. In order to teach two hours of class time twice a week, I studied six to eight hours each day. My group was thrilled that I cared enough to tailor the course to their needs.

As the year went on and other classes suffered from dropouts, my psychology class grew from thirty-five to more than fifty. I taught a second semester with most of the group returning and I was hired to teach psychology for a second year.

As I prepared for my second year, the North Haven board of education drafted me to teach a night course for women. The board didn't care what the subject matter was, as long as it appealed to women. I decided to make use of all the things Fred had spent years teaching me, plus a little psychology, and I designed a program called "Gracious Living." I was amazed at how much I had learned from Fred. Who would have thought I would ever enjoy teaching others the things I once hated to learn!

The following year I was hired as a full-time English instructor at North Haven High School. Besides teaching English, I wrote two new courses in public speaking and creative writing. I also directed all the drama productions for the school and in 1958, my version of *The Boyfriend* won the top award at the New England Drama Festival. I was named best director of high school productions in New England. I attended a meeting of the Connecticut Speech and Drama Association and was elected president on my first visit before I'd even joined. On top again, my self-image brightened; I felt I no longer had to worry about what Fred thought of me. The town and even the state had accepted me!

Fred went into business for himself and when his food service company was doing well enough, we decided we should have another child. I was in my second year at North Haven High School when I became pregnant with what was supposed to be my husband's namesake, Frederick Jerome Littauer, III.

I kept on teaching and because I was careful with my weight and figure, no one knew I was expecting. I was also proud that pregnancy didn't slow me down. A-line dresses were in style and I modeled for a fashion show the day I delivered. After the show, my doctor examined me and in amazement said, "You are about to have this baby any minute. Get to the hospital immediately."

I was admitted to Yale-New Haven Hospital at 5 o'clock on October 29, 1958, and Marita Kathryn was born at 6 o'clock without my having one labor pain. The doctor was so amazed at my easy labor that he brought in a whole class of medical students who stood and stared at me throughout the entire delivery.

Doing Something Right

When Marita was six months old I began to escape the reality of my dull marriage by spending as much time out of the house as possible. Now that I no longer worked, I joined several different civic organizations and was elected president of the League of Women Voters in North Haven, Connecticut. While I was giving my full attention to the

League, Fred still talked of having a son. Reluctantly I agreed to try again.

In the fall of '59, I was both pregnant and president, and I decided I needed a maid. *If only* I had a maid, I could be happy. My husband's business was doing well and he felt there would be hope for the home if we had a real housekeeper. We hired Willie May Jones, a dignified black lady who took over my household completely. Finally I had a buffer between me and Fred. Whatever he complained about, I could say, "It's the maid's fault."

Years later I discovered from Lauren that each afternoon Willie May took my two little girls for a ride in her car and dropped into the back room of Joe's Cigar Store in the worst part of town to pick up money she had won playing the *numbers*. I didn't know what the *numbers* were. I just knew she called in some figures to someone each morning. She loved the combination of numbers on my license plate and "played it" frequently. In a year's time she picked up enough money from the man in the back room of the cigar store to buy a three-tenement house and quit working.

However, while Willie May was with us, I took advantage of the freedom and went out daily to save the world. Why should I stay home when Fred was spending every waking moment on his business? In three years he had gone from managing one cafeteria to being president of his own Mealtime Management with eighteen different accounts and a staff of over a hundred. I was happy and relieved that he had a whole staff to boss instead of just me.

He was so successful that one restaurant magazine called him "The Boy Wonder of the Food Service Industry." Fred responded by writing detailed manuals on every facet of his business. He was also asked to speak on the secrets of his success at the National Restaurant Convention in Chicago. But with all this exciting activity, he had little time for his family.

We decided we should expand our house now that financial security was assured and our third child was on the way. Fred began to design what he wanted and together we incorporated every conceivable convenience that any home could contain.

At this point I was called and asked if I could teach a freshman speech class at the University of Connecticut. The person hired had suddenly left town and the dean who knew me from the Speech and Drama Association had confidence that I could do it. I told him I was pregnant, but he said he didn't care if I turned green if I'd just help him out. I was thrilled to go back to teaching two days a week and once again I worked hard to prepare for each class. I kept my weight down, wore loose clothes, and stood behind the lectern so that the students were shocked when Fred arrived to give the final exam and told them I was in the hospital about to deliver.

On February 9, 1960, Frederick Jerome Littauer III was born in another painless delivery, watched this time by a group of student nurses who kept feeling my tummy and saying, "Are you sure it doesn't hurt?" It didn't, and I was thrilled to have produced our Freddie. My husband was even more excited. "Finally, you've done something right."

In March I was re-elected president of the League, and also appointed state budget director for the Connecticut League of Women Voters. In this position I traveled throughout the state to each local chapter, instructing them how to put together a budget — a topic on which Fred felt I was remarkably unqualified to speak.

Since I had always refused to make a budget for our household finances and had difficulty in balancing my checkbook, it was ironic that I would be running around telling others how to do what I could never do myself. Challenges such as the budget job had always fascinated me and I remember the summer I successfully taught archery at Camp Trebor when I was totally unable to get an arrow to the target myself. I did a quick study of the State League of Women Voters' Budget Book and learned enough to present the basic principles clearly.

That same year I was elected president of the Quinnipiac Valley Theatre. While in this position, in the ensuing years, I directed *Call Me Madam, Guys and Dolls, South Pacific,* and *Oklahoma.*

In March 1960 we began the construction of our new addition and in April, on our seventh wedding anniversary, Fred took me back to Bermuda for a one-week second honeymoon at Ariel Sands. I rode the bicycles cautiously and we flew both ways.

A Stranger's Insight

A week after we returned from Bermuda, I left for St. Louis as a delegate to the League of Women Voters' national convention. After Freddie's birth I returned to a size eight and treated myself to a whole new wardrobe. I packed the best of my wardrobe and headed for St. Louis with Ethel Libson, my League vice-president.

The first evening Ethel stayed in our room while I went across the street to the drugstore. As I walked alone through the lobby, I passed a noisy group of men who whistled at me. I was flattered and pleased they found me appealing. Fred had once said, "If there is one thing you don't have, it's sex appeal."

I crossed the street and began to realize I had devoted my life to becoming beautiful, but underneath I still felt like a plain, dull little girl from Haverhill. Fred never let me forget how he had saved me from being an old maid and how grateful I should be for his sacrifice.

As I struggled with my self-image I sensed someone following me. I walked quickly into the drugstore and sat down at the counter. When I ordered an orange juice, a voice next to me said, "I'll have one too and I'll pay for them both." I looked over to see a handsome, well-dressed man seated on the next stool.

Was this a pick-up? In my thirty-two years I had never been picked up. My premarriage romances had been ordinary, and my courtship with Fred so orderly and proper it eliminated any chance of suggestive excitement. While I viewed our marriage as routine and Fred's constant criticism a damper to any emotions, I had been a faithful wife. A strange shiver went through my body as I realized that good little me was sitting in a drugstore far from home with an unknown man who at that moment was paying for my orange juice. The plot was hardly the basis for a movie, but it held a first-time fascination for me.

As his gorgeous brown eyes looked me up and down, he leaned over and said, "I won you for the week."

"You won me!"

"Yes, I won you," he said. "We men are here for a shirtmaker's convention and were standing around the lobby looking for beautiful women. Frankly, the League of Women Voters aren't too appealing. We were discouraged with the flat-footed tweedy types and then you got off the elevator and we all said, 'That's more like it.' When you walked by in your slim silk dress and we whistled, you blushed and we knew we had a challenge. You were the best looking thing we'd seen, so we drew lots for you and I won. You are mine for the week and none of the others will try to take you away."

I was aghast at his explanation. The brightest thing I could think of was, "I'm married."

"So am I," he said. "But that doesn't mean a thing. You're away and I'm away and we wouldn't want to waste the week, would we?"

While I had never been a wasteful person, I thought it might be better to throw away this particular week than to use it the way he had in mind.

I explained what a fine moral person I was and how faithful I had always been to my husband, but this only seemed to increase the challenge. He told me how it was possible to be true-blue at home and yet have fun at conventions. He explained he was a pillar of his community, a member of the school board on Long Island, and a model husband and father. "But what the little woman doesn't know won't hurt her," he said.

There was no way to get rid of this rather fascinating man, and I walked back to the hotel with him. He told me his name was Ben and he had come to sell Donmoor shirts. When we entered the lobby together, his friends applauded.

"Here's the winner," they said. "What a prize! If you change your mind, we'll take her."

I had never thought of myself as a prize and it was a nice feeling. We stood in the lobby and talked for awhile until I remembered Ethel and said, "I have to go to bed."

That statement brought roars from the group and they sent me off in the elevator—with Ben. "I can't invite you in because my friend Ethel is here," I said when we arrived at my door.

"You've got a roommate?" he asked, distressed.

"Yes," I said as I opened the door, stepped inside and gave him a wave goodnight.

Ethel and I laughed over my being the prize in a lottery and I knew that was the end of Ben. However, the next morning Ben was in the lobby waiting to take me to breakfast. I introduced him to Ethel and told him I had to eat with her. Ben wasn't too thrilled to meet Ethel, but asked her along.

After breakfast Ethel and I went to our League meetings, had lunch with the convention, and when I emerged at 4:00 P.M. there was Ben on a couch across from the door. When I looked surprised, he said, "I won you for a whole week, remember?"

I didn't quite know what to do with Ben. I had never been won before. I didn't dare leave Ethel's side, so he took us both to dinner and to breakfast the following morning.

That afternoon Ethel went to a different meeting and I came out from the auditorium alone. Ben was ecstatic to find me without Ethel and asked me to come and look at his shirt display. I had been to many restaurant conventions and the displays were always out in a big ballroom with hundreds of people milling around. Certainly there was no harm in browsing through a few shirt racks.

We strolled toward the elevator, and he told me how much money he made a year in shirts. We got out on the second floor and walked toward what I assumed was going to be a ballroom. As I looked for the crowds, Ben unlocked a door labeled Donmoor Shirts, eased me into a room and shut the door behind him. There before me was a rack of shirts in his bedroom! As I gasped, Ben smiled, put his arm tightly around me and whispered, "I never thought I could pry you away from Ethel."

He eased me onto the edge of the bed and my back went rigid. "Relax," he said, "I'm not a rapist, just a nice average guy with a little free time on his hands. I wouldn't consider doing anything to you that you wouldn't enjoy."

The phrase was well put, but I was scared to death. How could I get out of the room unscathed and yet not appear like a dumb country kid? At the time it seemed important that I didn't appear unsophisticated by screaming. As these thoughts raced through my mind, Ben began to ask about my husband.

"Do you really love him?"

"I guess so," I said.

"You're not sure?"

I realized I was not. What was love, anyway? I was a dutiful wife but had to admit things were better when I didn't see too much of Fred. Maybe I didn't really love him. I never allowed myself to think of failing.

"Does your husband make you happy?"

"He provides for me very well. We are building a big addition to our home and he just bought me a beautiful black cherry Lincoln with leather interior."

"I didn't ask what you owned. I asked if your husband makes you happy. Do you get excited when you see him coming home?"

"Scared is more like it," I sighed. "I'm scared at what he's going to find wrong. But things are getting better now. I have a maid to do the housework and Fred is so busy that he doesn't come home until late at night."

"That doesn't sound like much of a marriage to me," said Ben. "You're each running around doing your own thing and not caring much about each other. You're so wrapped up in your big house, your maid and car, you don't even know you're miserable."

"I am not miserable. I have everything," I snapped defensively.

"Everything but love and contentment," he said. "You're as tight as a drum. I bet you keep yourself so busy climbing your social ladder you don't have time to think about how unhappy you are inside."

Ben had touched a raw nerve. My doctor had often told me I was an uptight person trying to appear happy. *Is it possible I do all these superhuman feats to prove to myself I'm happy?* I thought. I had never been too reflective and felt uncomfortable trying to analyze my motives. "I must be happy. I've achieved all my goals in life," I reassured myself out loud.

"Happiness is not achieving goals. It's being loved," said Ben softly. He whispered the word *loved* and gently pushed me down on the bed. Lying there confused, I looked up into his compassionate eyes and suddenly realized where I was. Virtuous me was alone in a hotel room with a strange man who was showing a warm interest in my marriage. Immediately it struck me that Ben didn't care a thing for my marriage. He had hit a sensitive spot and I had almost fallen for his line. I had to get away, but I didn't know how to retreat gracefully.

Here was a man who seemed to understand me. Oh, how I longed to be understood. Fred was so sure of himself, so businesslike, so proper, so serious, so busy, but Ben was a man who took it easy. He was fun to talk with. He cared about my inner feelings, and he was taking time out of a busy day to talk of love. The contrast overwhelmed me. I was in the wrong place but I was too content to leave.

"You don't know what you're missing," said Ben. "I want to help you find yourself." What a sweet thought. He wanted to help me.

The phone rang and brought me back to reality. While Ben took a shirt order, I got up and went to the door. Ben didn't try to stop me. "You'll be back," he said. "You need my help."

Maybe I needed his help, but I knew I wouldn't be back. Yet I had to admit that in those few moments, Ben had gotten closer to my heart and the problem of my marriage than anyone before him. None of my friends had ever seen beyond my exterior. Whenever Fred mentioned that our marriage wasn't as it should be, I always scoffed and told him I was content and the problem must be his. In my pursuit of happiness I had deceived myself and refused to believe my fairy-tale desires had not been totally fulfilled. But Ben had seen through me; he had hit a vulnerable spot.

I didn't go back. Ben followed me for the remainder of the week but never once did I leave Ethel's side.

On our last evening, Ben took Ethel and me to dinner. About 10:30 he called and invited me to his room after Ethel had gone to sleep. "Come on down," he said. "It's your last chance for happiness. Don't throw it away."

I thanked him for dinner, but I said firmly that I had no intention of ever seeing him again. Then he begged me to come so he could "save face" with his friends. I hated to ruin his reputation with his fellow shirtmakers, but I was more concerned with my own reputation.

"I may have won you for a week," he said, "but you didn't turn out to be much of a prize."

Fred met me at the plane and looked more handsome than I had remembered. He was impeccably dressed in a navy suit and striped tie, and his blond hair had touches of silver. Many women told me I was lucky to have such a handsome husband. And I was. *If only* he could love me just as I was, without all his instructions, I knew I could be happy.

I was glad Fred brought the girls. Lauren at five-and-a-half was a serious child who constantly wanted my attention. Marita was an eighteen-month-old bundle of bubbling energy who was always doing something she didn't want me to see. Both wore matching yellow organdy dresses with yellow bows in their hair.

I was proud.

That Elusive Happily Ever After

After my trip, I immediately got to work on the new part of the house. *If only* my house could be a showplace, I could be happy.

We finished the addition, complete with a twenty-by-twenty-foot bedroom, and to fulfill my childhood dreams, we topped it off with a huge fireplace and stereo speakers under our throne-type bed.

When the house was just the way I had envisioned, I began a round of lavish parties and exclusive social lunches. I opened my home for every imaginable purpose — board meetings, cast parties, the League of Women Voters tea — and crammed between all this activity, I decided to try to match my husband's skill at tennis.

I began by buying several adorable tennis dresses, a good racket and an hour of instruction. I learned where to plant my feet, how to move my body and how to swing the racket. *At last,* I thought, *here is a sport I can handle.* But in the second lesson, the teacher introduced the ball.

I could do professional pivots and swing in style, but could not quite connect the racket with the ball. Even when the instructor threw the ball right at the racket, I missed it. The instructor became discouraged faster than I did, and after six lessons said, "Mrs. Littauer, the best thing about your tennis is your attitude. It's great, but attitude alone won't win tennis games. I suggest you try another sport."

I never did try another sport; I just sat every weekend watching Fred win his matches. Once during a long tournament I was bored so I began reading a magazine. Fred left the court, stormed over to the fence and told me to put the magazine away and pay attention.

Week after week, year after year, I sat with Linda, his partner's wife, while we both pretended to love tennis. We clapped at the right times and hardly dared converse for fear of annoying the men. We stood by them when their pictures were taken and went to the dinners when they were honored. We were perfect country club wives, masking our true feelings. Fifteen years later I met Linda after her divorce and we confessed how miserable our tennis era had been.

Each weekend as I sat looking through chain link fences, I began to question the direction my life was taking. Ben had started me thinking when he told me I was unhappy and miserable. I denied that possibility, but as I sat bored, forbidden to read or talk, pretending to be interested in a little white ball, I wondered if I wasn't deceiving myself.

I knew I should be the happiest woman alive. I had achieved my goals. I had gone to college and become a teacher. I had closets full of clothes and enough money for cars, fur coats and exotic vacations. My house was a showplace. I had a maid, two well-dressed little girls and finally a son to please my husband. It was true that Fred's critical and negative nature bothered me, as did the knowledge that I would never measure up to his ideal of perfection, but I was not going to be defeated. For the first time in my life I had everything I wanted and I was determined to be happy forever.

Reflections

As I look back on this period of our marriage I realize it was a recess for both of us. Fred was wrapped up in his business and I was the professional president for every group in need of a leader. He was too busy and successful to feel rejected and I was so happy with the money and the lifestyle that I finally had confidence in my looks and social status.

I did not realize at that point that while Fred and I could communicate intellectually and socially, we had no relationship on an emotional level. We functioned totally in our minds. No wonder when Ben began to communicate on a feeling level, even for all the wrong reasons, I started to respond. Although we did nothing but talk, he did awaken me to the emotional vacuum in my marriage.

In counseling couples today I find many who are right where I was at that time. They are not fighting or unfaithful. They are intellectual, even spiritual, giants, but nothing's going on between them. I've had some tell me that they are so spiritual they don't need any real romance in their life. I shudder when someone shows a pride in sexual abstinence and I remember Ben's words, "You don't even know you're miserable."

Whenever we are functioning in a marriage relationship without heart, we are open to temptation. I've talked with Christian leaders who sincerely believed they were so like Paul that they needed no emotional communication — until that day when some weepy little lady threw herself upon him or some Ben touched a long-neglected chord. Suddenly feelings long suppressed came pounding on the pillow. At that point in my marriage I felt the best I had in years and yet I see now how vulnerable I was because I was functioning on a polite, intellectual level without realizing my emotions were sitting patiently below the surface waiting to be called forth at a moment's notice.

Where are you today in your marriage relationship? Are you a time-bomb waiting to go off? Would a good offer cause you to chuck it all and run away?

A well-known Christian radio personality in the midwest fell in love with his secretary. When he came to me in desperation he admitted he'd been too busy to pay attention to his wife who'd grown hard and cold by neglect. He knew if he continued with the secretary his whole denomination would turn against him and his ministry would be over. As we agreed intellectually and spiritually I asked, "If she walked in here right now and said, 'Come with me to Tahiti and start life all over again' what would you do?" He burst into sobs and said, "I'd go. I'd go."

A loveless marriage only lasts until someone lights a spark. If you're sitting in a placid relationship right now, these indifferent days are tough times. Do all you can humanly and prayerfully to communicate on a deeper level. Avoid temptation.

Make the tough times count.

14

Two Tragedies

I was faced with a tragedy that I could do nothing about. I had to learn that there were things in life money and willpower couldn't fix.

The fall of 1960 was a whirlwind of activity for Fred and me. Fred spent every working hour directing his business while I socialized, played bridge, rehearsed *Guys and Dolls* and saved the community. We got together on weekends at the Farms Country Club and concentrated on contentment and success. We were the image of what the world wanted for winners.

Although I didn't spend much time at home, I began to notice my beautiful son Freddie wasn't looking well. His china-blue eyes seemed glassy and he stopped smiling. He was seven months old but when he tried to sit up, he lost his balance. I would prop him up with pillows and try to tell myself that he looked just fine. Soon he began to scream in the night and when I would go in to him, his body would be stiff, his back arched and his fingers rigid. I would do everything I knew to comfort him and after a while he'd relax and go back to sleep.

After this had gone on for several weeks I took him to our pediatrician, Dr. Richard Granger, a personal friend. After a thorough examination, Dr. Granger called in a specialist and together they tapped Freddie, with no response. They rang little bells that he didn't seem to hear, and they flashed lights in his eyes that he didn't notice. With each test they became more concerned until finally they asked me to call my husband.

Fred was in the midst of a business conference and expressed annoyance that I had disturbed him. "The doctor wants you to come to his office and get your son's report," I said.

"I can't possibly leave work," answered Fred. "You get the report and bring it home."

By the time I got back to the doctor's office, I was in tears. It was hard for me to realize that Fred didn't care enough to be with me at such a difficult moment.

"Fred is not able to come," I said to Dr. Granger. "You'll have to tell me alone."

Tenderly, Dr. Granger put his arm around me and said softly, "Florence, I don't know how to tell you this, but your child appears to be hopelessly brain damaged. You might as well get your mind set to put him away, forget him and perhaps have another one."

Brain damaged? Put him away? Forget him? Have another one?

I stood there in shock, refusing to believe Dr. Granger's words. There's nothing in life that's hopeless, that somebody can't fix.

I pleaded, "Can't you fix him? Can't you do something? This child is my husband's namesake. We can't let anything happen to Freddie. Do whatever it takes. I'll get the money."

"Florence," said Dr. Granger, "this is one thing your money or your willpower can't do anything about. I'm afraid your Freddie is hopeless."

Dealing With the Hopeless

The word *hopeless* had never been in my vocabulary. I was determined to save my only son. But as I drove home late that afternoon with Freddie lying beside me in a baby seat, the word *hopeless* reverberated in my brain. I went to bed without eating and waited for Fred's return. He came in about 8 o'clock looking for me and dinner.

"You won't want dinner when you hear what the doctor said about Freddie. It's his brain; it doesn't work. He can't see, he can't hear, he's hopeless."

Confused and distraught, Fred said, "Somehow we'll get him fixed." He tried to comfort me, but every time Freddie screamed, I screamed. I was close to hysteria.

The next morning Fred called Dr. Granger for his advice. "We can't give up," he said. "We've got to save Freddie." Dr. Granger suggested a neurologist at Yale and we made an appointment for the following week. This time Fred left work and went with me.

The examining doctor gave Freddie every conceivable test. When he was ready to read us the results, Fred turned on his tape recorder. We wanted his exact words forever; but the words the doctor spoke were words we never did listen to again.

"He is blind. He is deaf. His brain does not work. He is hopeless. He's going to get worse and he probably won't live long."

I sat there holding my Freddie and Dr. Granger's words came back to me, "He's hopelessly brain damaged. You might as well put him away, forget him and have another one."

But how could I put this child away? How could I ever forget him? No, I could not run away from this problem, but I could have another baby.

The following week I asked Dr. Lach if he thought it

would be safe for me to have another child. "After studying the reports on Freddie, I find no obvious cause for the baby's problems. It must have been some freak of nature that would probably never happen again."

We discussed every possible aspect of my situation and concluded the chances were one in a million that the brain damage would occur in another child. We assumed it was a one-of-a-kind situation and that it would be best for me to have another child as soon as possible.

Once I was pregnant, Dr. Lach enrolled me in a special program that Yale was conducting for expectant mothers who had already produced a brain-damaged child. I went through my interviews and tests and the results were all optimistic. The thought of a new baby gave me a touch of hope.

During the nine-month wait, I had time to re-evaluate my life. I began to realize I had always put my faith in me, in my own power to achieve things, and I had been quite successful. But now I was faced with a tragedy that I could do nothing about. I had to learn that there were things in life that money and willpower couldn't fix. When I had been discouraged in the past, I had cheered myself up by reviewing my accomplishments, but now my talents and achievements no longer made me happy.

As I paced the floor, clutching Freddie tightly to relieve the terror of his ten to twelve convulsions a day, it hardly mattered that I walked over plush carpeting. At night when he screamed and I jumped up, it made no difference that my bed was elevated on a platform and constructed like a throne. When I rocked him in the living room, I was no longer impressed with my custom-woven drapes that matched my Bjorn Winblad mural. What had been so important before was now trivial. When you're holding a dying child, the drapes and the wallpaper no longer matter. My only hope in those lonely empty nights was that my next child would be normal and I could put this nightmare behind me.

Christmas approached, but there was little to be joyful about. I was pregnant, scared and I tried not to think about the chances of another problem child. As little Freddie's convulsions grew worse, a visiting nurse came in each day to give him shots to ease the severity of his spasms. For the sake of our girls we tried to have a normal Christmas season. Fred and I maintained that Little Brother would get better, for neither one of us could openly face the truth.

We had always taken pictures of the children and sent them, with a summary letter of our year, to friends and relatives. In December 1960, we tried to do the usual thing. We dressed the three children up in their Christmas finest, propped Freddie in a jump seat and hoped he would look normal.

At the best of times, taking pictures of three children is difficult, but this effort was almost impossible. Freddie kept falling over, bumping his head and crying. Each time he cried, Lauren, who sensed how sick he was, burst into tears. Marita would push him and say, "Sit up, Freddie. Sit up." A lump came in my throat as I watched this sad effort.

The whole idea was a mistake, but Fred was determined. He had all his camera equipment out and was going to take a picture, no matter if they were all crying. And soon they were. Freddie had a convulsion and screamed, Lauren got upset over his pain and sobbed, and Marita got mad because I wouldn't let her push Freddie. When all were crying, Fred captured the mood of our Christmas on film.

For some strange reason I decided to use the picture of three crying children for our annual newsletter with this caption, "The Littauers hope your New Year will be a howling success." I never hinted in the letter that we had a problem, and I closed the message with this paragraph:

> For all of you who have tried to take pictures of your children for a Christmas card, we dedicate ours as the ultimate in Christmas photos. After three sittings, 200 flash bulbs (of which half never worked), and a bottle of aspirin, we gave up on some lovely smiling photo which looks so

casual and easy on other peoples' cards, and settled on the most typical pose of all. It shows how we felt after a fretful and frustrating day before the camera. We hope you'll think the whole thing is a scream as we did.

And so at the close of another year the happy, smiling Littauers wish you all a Merry Christmas and a most harmonious and prosperous New Year.

How could I have even written "the happy, smiling Littauers?" I had pursued happiness so passionately, I couldn't admit I had failed.

Sitting on new chairs at a new table in our newly expanded home, eating turkey served by a maid in uniform, we had the most miserable holiday in our lifetime. Fred and I picked at our food and gave each other presents that we hardly cared to open. While Marita was too young to understand our burdens, Lauren realized there was no Christmas spirit. As she opened Freddie's presents for him, she looked up and said, "Is Freddie ever going to get better?" I couldn't face her straight questions and felt tears welling up within me.

"I don't know," I choked.

"'I don't know' means no," she said as she hung her head sadly.

From that moment Lauren knew there was no hope, and while we never again verbalized it, we understood. When Freddie screamed in the night, I would run in to find Lauren already there, patting him while tears dropped on his rigid form. Few words passed between us, but we spent many silent hours uplifting each other by our presence. I began to realize what a deeply compassionate child I had in Lauren and in our time of mutual anguish we became close friends.

Fred found it just as hard to admit defeat. His defense was to work harder and not come home to view the convicting evidence. I continued my League and theater work and never told anyone but the closest of friends that I had a problem or was pregnant. I kept hoping for a secret solution.

My in-laws had long been members of a religious group that professed healing powers and, while I had resisted their strong suggestions to visit one of their practitioners, I finally gave in. Fred brightened at the thought that a miracle might take place and with his mother's help, found a learned gentleman who agreed to take our case. He had an elegant suite of offices on Park Avenue in New York City and each Tuesday afternoon of a long, hot summer, Fred and I would board the train from New Haven to take instruction in religious healing. From the beginning, the man made it clear the problem was mine, because unlike my husband, I was not a believer in their principles.

"When you can look at your son and say in faith that he is perfect, he will be perfect," said the man.

Each weekend I would go home and recite, "He is perfect. He is perfect," but with the first convulsion I would lose my faith. When I returned, the practitioner would gently chide me for my unbelief and repeat the prescription.

One week the gentleman came to our home and prayed over our child, but there was no change. When I was about eight months pregnant I refused to take any more trips to New York. Fred was disappointed in me and the program and I was weighted down with guilt. The fault had been clearly laid on me.

On August 14, 1961, Dr. Lach had me checked by the team of experts at Yale who had been observing and testing me throughout my pregnancy. They felt the time was right for me to deliver and began monitoring the heartbeat of my unborn child. They tested brain waves by inserting electrodes up to the baby's scalp, then wiring both me and the baby to a big machine. With a little help my labor started and the machines began to record. I watched, fascinated and frightened, as little marks went up and down on charts to indicate both heartbeat and brain waves.

"These lines are all normal," they said. "Your baby is

going to be just fine."

I had another easy delivery, except this time the audience was smaller, just the team from this special program. My baby was born and we all rejoiced that I had a son. They removed the clamps that had been on his head during delivery and quickly tested his reactions.

"You will have no problem with this one," said the attending nurse. "He checks out perfectly normal."

When Fred was allowed in to see me, we wept for joy. We finally had our son. I named him after me: Laurence Chapman Littauer. I could hardly wait to get home and take care of my new baby.

When I arrived home, Freddie was gone. My husband had put him in a private children's hospital in northern Connecticut. I could never have made such a decision myself, and it wasn't an easy thing for Fred. He told me his whole life seemed to drain out of him when he placed his Frederick Jerome Littauer III into the arms of an unknown nurse in a home full of other hopelessly retarded babies.

Fred had redecorated the nursery and I brought little Larry home to a room stripped of any memories of our Freddie. We did all we could to forget the past and start over. I gave up my community positions, my charity presidencies — and put my hope in Larry.

Dark Times

On Valentine's Day, 1962, as I was preparing a party for Lauren and Marita, the phone rang. It was a nurse from the children's hospital calling to tell me my Freddie had died of pneumonia. Compassionately, she explained that a child without the ability to think doesn't know enough to cough, and so Freddie, with badly congested lungs, had choked to death in his crib. I was overcome with guilt. *If only I had kept him home, this wouldn't have happened,* I thought. I called Fred at work and he broke down and cried, "My Freddie is dead." He had clung to a hope that someday his namesake would be healed.

I shall never forget that private funeral held in a cold stark room of an old mortuary in Colebrook, Connecticut. I wore my black seal coat and still shivered as an unknown minister read a few uncomforting verses over the open casket that held the remains of our Frederick Jerome Littauer III. There were no flowers; there was no music. Just Fred and me, alone in our grief. We had told no one that our boy had died, and we stood in silence as we wept over our departed son. No longer was he beautiful, but bruised from banging his head on the crib rails during his frequent convulsions. No longer was he the hope of my husband, but the end of a bad dream.

A week after Freddie's funeral, when Larry was just six months old, I went in to pick him up from his nap. I called to him but he didn't respond. He had a blank look, his eyes were dull and I feared the worst. I grabbed him up, shook him and cried, "Smile, Larry, smile." But Larry didn't smile. Immediately I wrapped him up and rushed him to Dr. Granger's office. I literally shook with fear as I waited for Dr. Granger's answer. He gave Larry the same tests he had given my Freddie. "I don't know how to say this, Florence, but I'm afraid Larry has the same thing."

His words fell on me like a death knell. It was a repeat performance. I drove home on the same streets from the same doctor. Larry lay in the same car bed I had used for Freddie. I had to tell my two daughters the same story: They were going to lose another brother.

I woke up each morning hoping it was a bad dream, but it wasn't. Like his brother, Larry began to convulse, stiffen and scream, and he no longer smiled. These were lonesome times. Fred couldn't bear to come home, and I couldn't bear to go out.

One day a friend called to ask if I knew that Lauren was arriving at school each morning in tears. When Lauren came home I asked her if this was true and she told me the children on the bus teased her every day. They would say things like, "Lauren's brother is no good. He won't ever walk; he's an idiot. He's a moron." As they said these things to her, she would begin to cry and they would laugh. By the time she got to school, she was a wreck.

When I asked her why she hadn't told me of this problem before, she said, "Mama, you have so much sadness on your mind. I didn't want to make it any worse."

I called some of the boys' mothers and instead of sympathy, I received defiant replies. They insisted their children would never say such things, and furthermore they didn't appreciate my accusations. I was shocked at their rebuffs and drove Lauren to and from school for the rest of the year.

Larry continued to get worse, and Dr. Granger made an appointment for him at Johns Hopkins Metabolic Research Unit in Baltimore, Maryland.

Dr. Robert Cook, director of the research unit, operated on Larry and I tried to prepare myself for the results. I asked Dr. Cook, "Is there any hope?"

Gripping the arms of the chair, I braced myself for his reply: "Come now, Mrs. Littauer, you know better than that." I did know better than to ask, but I was searching for some last unexpected ray of hope. There was none. To my horror, I learned my son had no real brain. Where there should have been gray matter and convolutions there was only a round ball, an inert mass.

I brought Larry home with a bandaged head and an empty mind; a child who no longer knew his mother. When our two daughters saw their second brother destroyed, swollen and vacant, they too were depressed. They cried when he cried and our home became a house of perpetual mourning. To save the emotional balance of our two girls and myself, we decided to put Larry in the same hospital where his brother had died just a few months before.

The doctors said he wouldn't live beyond the age of five or six. But they were wrong. He lived to be nineteen. When he died, he was the same size he had been when he was one year old. He had never grown, and for the eighteen years he existed in that private hospital, I never awoke one morning without the startling realization that I had a dying child. *If only* I could have a perfect baby boy, perhaps I could begin to rebuild my life. But my husband didn't care if he ever saw another baby. The desires had reversed. I was now the one who needed a new boy to replace my sons. After months of discussion, Fred finally consented to adoption.

After waiting a year, we drove to Danbury, Connecticut, where the licensed adoption agency brought out an adorable three-month-old baby boy with dark, curly hair and huge brooding brown eyes. As we looked at him, he seemed to analyze us. The three of us stared at each other while the case worker explained that he had been tested and appeared to be very advanced for his three months. We brought him home on my husband's birthday, February 19, 1964—a present for the whole family.

We had a joyful celebration and the party game was naming our new boy. He had been called Jeffrey at his foster home, so we all decided to put Frederick in front of that and have a new Freddie. A new child, we thought, would cheer us up.

But the memory of two failures haunted us. Unfortunately we wasted our suffering. Rather than bringing us closer together, the tragedies had wiped out whatever feelings Fred and I once had for each other. We were numb and began to look for new ways to amuse ourselves and escape the past. *If only* we could really forget, perhaps we could be happy.

Reflections

Statistics show that of couples who have experienced the birth of a retarded baby or the death of a child, 90 percent end up divorced. Since we had two abnormal sons and ultimately two deaths, it is truly a miracle that our marriage lasted at all. I look back now in disbelief that these tragedies happened and that we all survived.

I recall how hurt I was when Fred's mother did a genealogical check and announced that no one on their side had ever been brain damaged. Even my mother said, "Don't let anyone know about the boys. They'll think it's your fault." Additional guilt was heaped on me by the faith healer as well as friends who said, "If you were really a good mother you'd have kept the child at home."

I remember how hurt I was when friends stopped coming to see me. I thought they had abandoned me, but I realize now they just didn't know what to say. Lauren has written a most helpful book, *What You Can Say When You Don't Know What To Say,* helping people who want to be supportive to others in pain but just don't know how.

I wish I'd known what to do with the pain of grief, but Fred and I pushed our feelings underneath and tried to get on with life. There were no seminars in those days, no support groups for grieving parents, no books that showed how you could work through your pain and later make the tough times count.

We thought the children would get over it and forget, so we didn't talk about the loss of their brothers. It wasn't until years later that they told me of their hurts, and I was ashamed of myself when I read Lauren's chapter "The Forgotten Griever."

Have you been through difficult situations—a death, divorce, depression—and felt no one cared? People stayed away or took sides. No one seemed to know what to do with you. If you have, you can know how I felt in those heavy, hurtful hours.

Frequently, people ask me—or sometimes even tell me—what was wrong with my sons. Yale-New Haven Hospital and Johns Hopkins couldn't come up with any label except some kind of a degenerative brain disorder. After Lauren married and while Larry was still alive, we had some additional testing done at Loma Linda University Hospital in hopes of giving our daughter some genetic information. They fed the data into computers and found no other cases that matched Larry's pattern. On the amniocentesis he came out as normal, showing that the flaw was not in the chromosomes but in the genes.

We wish we had answers to the questions, What was it? and Why did it happen twice? Why was each child beautiful and normal until six months old? Why did their brain power seem to shut off at one point and never go back on? Fred and I have had to learn that there are some things in life that defy explanations.

These were tough times—I'd hit the bottom after my years of trying to reach the top. As I look back now I could never say that I'd like to go through it all again, but I can say that those two tragedies showed me for the first time that there are things in life money and willpower can't do anything about.

As I look back on these double depressions, I realize that it was suffering through these dark years that gave me a compassion for others with problems. It is because I've been there that I can comfort those who give birth to abnormal babies or who lose a child in death. No one can say, "I know how you feel," if they've never been there. My book *Blow Away the Black Clouds* traces the steps I went through to get out of my depressions and gives hope to those in similar situations.

Never would I say losing my sons was a positive experience or I'm glad it happened, but I do have a heart for people with hurts that I did not have before.

By the grace of God, I have learned to make beauty out of ashes. I have learned to

Make the tough times count.

15

Good Time Charlie's

I dressed Lauren and Marita in matching dresses and I wore a bright red knit dress with a large brimmed white felt hat trimmed with a bunch of geraniums and streamers. I wanted to make sure they knew there was a new family in church. I'm sure they knew.

Forgetting wasn't easy. Everywhere I looked, there were reminders of my sons. When I rocked my new adopted Freddie, the motion brought back the hours I had spent in that same chair trying to soothe my dying sons. He was in their bed, he wore their clothes, he played with their toys. How could I ever forget them and move on?

Staying at home depressed me and I began to think about getting out. This time I no longer cared to be president of anything and found myself floundering for direction. There was no obvious avenue open for me.

Fred rarely came home. His food service business had expanded into four states, and he hid himself in his work. Defeat depressed him as much as it did me. We were programmed for success and we had failed. Our answer to defeat was to work harder and try to pretend these traumas had never happened.

One day, driving down North Haven's Washington Avenue, Fred noticed a "For Lease" sign on an old red building. It was a typical red New England barn with a second-story balcony around four sides. Fred felt it had great possibilities for a restaurant and arranged with the owner to see it.

"I think you're already too busy to begin looking for new fields to conquer," I said as we walked into the damp, empty barn.

"I think it will be perfect for a Roaring Twenties nightclub," said Fred, ignoring my comments.

I had learned that once Fred got an idea, there was no stopping him. I felt I might as well join him in this new business venture. As Fred became excited over this project, we found we had a common goal — something to work on together.

While Fred drew the designs, brought in carpenters to panel the walls, built a dance floor and stage, and made tables around the balcony, I visited antique shops and hung the treasures on the walls. Fred scouted out banjo players and singers, and I put together a group of young dancers who had been my drama students at North Haven High School. We created Twenties costumes with fringes and pearls and the girls began practicing the Charleston while workmen hammered around them. I found a bar that had been taken out of an old saloon, and Fred designed a modern kitchen for the limited food menu he had planned to supplement the beer and baskets of unshelled peanuts that would be on each table. The barn was soon transformed into a club and we decided to call it "Good Time Charlie's" with Fred as Charlie!

On opening night we invited every town dignitary and friend we could find and were pleased the following morning to find we had received coverage in the local newspaper.

"It being a hot night last Friday, the *Chronicle* decided to go to a party at 'Good Time Charlie's, the new Roaring Twenties-type club opened up by Mr. and Mrs. Fred Littauer on Route 5 in North Haven. And what a night it was as these pictures show!"

The full-page spread displayed dynamic Holly Westin singing in her sequins, the band bursting with banjos, the Charlie girls flipping their fringes in the Charleston and the guests, including me, enjoying every minute of a raucous night.

Fred loved playing Charlie and became a different person when he donned his red striped shirt and black armband. He was able to forget the past and play in the present.

At first, I loved the glamour, clientele and activity at Charlie's. It became my new social center, a big home where I was the charming hostess. For awhile this movie-star era gave me an avenue of escape, but when I tried to make a suggestion to Fred, he told me to be quiet—it was his business, not mine. I had thought it was *our* club, but when I realized Fred didn't want my ideas, I began to lose interest in playing second banjo to Good Time Charlie. I grew tired of dressing up every night to be ignored by Fred and decided to abandon Fred to his Charlie girls. The most humiliating aspect of my departure was that Fred never seemed to notice I was gone. Again, I was alone.

About that time I noticed that a new professional theatre was about to open in New Haven and, true to form, I was soon involved in celebrity lunches and speaking at service clubs and churches. I became the paid director of volunteer services and I coordinated the activities of all who wanted to give time or money to the theatre. Life was again exciting and I blotted out my pain.

But underneath, I was lonesome and empty. I saw very little of my husband and I didn't like to go home much more than he did. The maid I had wasn't much of a cook, so eleven-year-old Lauren prepared dinner every night. A marriage counselor would have told us our life was headed in the wrong direction; however, we never asked one. We didn't even ask ourselves how we expected to hold a home together when Fred was out every night with his Charlie girls and I was running around in circles with a group of young actors. Instead of facing reality, we looked the other way and continued in our opposite directions.

Meeting Jesus Personally

About this time my sister-in-law, Ruthie, seeing the downward direction of our lives, invited me to attend a Christian Women's Club luncheon. A few months before, Ruthie had told us a preposterous story about how she and her husband Dick had watched Billy Graham on television. When he invited them to ask Jesus Christ to come into their lives, they got off the couch and knelt to pray in front of the television. They began to talk about Jesus as if they knew Him, and we branded them fanatics.

The last thing I wanted was for someone to tell me I needed religion. I had always been a good person, gone to church, taught Sunday school and given my time to charitable organizations. I was not interested in anything labeled "Christian Women's Club" which I expected would be full of somber, senile ladies in black dresses praying in a corner.

I kept refusing Ruthie's invitations, but she was persistent and I could see she wouldn't quit bugging me until I went once. The next time she asked me, she explained that the Christian Women's Club was to be held that month in the Old Mill Restaurant in Darien and that they were going to have a fashion show. I thought if these religious ladies liked clothes and ate in fine restaurants, they couldn't be too weird, so I decided to go.

On the specified day in August, 1965, I got dressed in a ruby red Ceil Chapman ensemble with spike heels to match, carried a new Lord and Taylor cut velvet handbag and wore a turban hat of satin and velvet with a large brooch on the front. I wanted to make sure those saintly ladies knew I was not one of them. And I'm sure they knew.

When I arrived at the Old Mill, I was impressed with the beauty of the surroundings and glad the luncheon wasn't in a stark social hall of some old church. At least the atmosphere was positive.

When Ruthie introduced me to the ladies on the club board, I was amazed that some of them were dressed as stylishly as I was. Much to my surprise, they seemed quite pleasant. I hadn't been prepared for bright, sharp women and didn't feel quite as confident and superior as I thought I would. The restaurant tables were elegantly decorated and in front of each plate was a place card: a flag on a toothpick stuck into a decorated marshmallow. I looked at mine and saw it had someone else's name. I whispered to Ruthie, "They have the wrong place card in front of me."

She returned, "It's not supposed to be your name. It's a prayer favor."

I had no idea what a prayer favor was and so I asked. "It has the name of a missionary on there," Ruthie explained. "You're supposed to take it home and put it by the kitchen sink and pray for her each time you see it."

"But I don't even know her," I said softly.

"That's all right. You can pray for people you don't know."

"I can?"

I looked around and saw ladies stuffing the little marshmallows into their handbags. I was not about to put a gummy marshmallow in my new handbag even with a missionary sticking out of it. But I didn't want to look unprayerful so I wrapped the little favor in a napkin and hoped it wouldn't melt all over the bottom of my bag.

As I waited somewhat apprehensively to see what was going to happen, an adorable girl began the meeting with the blessing. The fashion show was exceptional. I was impressed that the models were from the Christian

Women's Club itself. I had never seen a more attractive group of ladies. By the time the speaker got up, I had completely changed my attitude. In fact, I felt a little in awe of the beautiful, joyful women surrounding me.

The speaker, Dr. Roy Gustafson from the Billy Graham team, was a tall, dignified, white-haired, intelligent and articulate gentleman. Not at all the weak, insipid religious type I had expected.

He caught my attention with a story of a woman who sounded so much like me I thought Ruthie must have given him advance information. He told a Cinderella story of an underprivileged girl who was determined to succeed in spite of her circumstances. After becoming socially prominent and well-dressed, she began to experience problems in her marriage. She was miserable inside, but never once had she let anyone know how she felt. I identified with the story—especially the part about never telling anyone her problems. I was proud that I had never told people about my problems and that some friends didn't even know I'd had the second son.

Then Dr. Gustafson got to the solution for the lady's life. She received Jesus Christ into her heart and asked Him to take away her sins and change her into what He wanted her to be. The lady hadn't sounded at all sinful. In fact, she seemed to be a nice, normal, well-intentioned person like me.

When Dr. Gustafson explained that all of us have sinned because we have fallen short of God's expectations, I became a little disturbed. I knew I wasn't perfect, but what did God expect of me? Then Dr. Gustafson explained that none of us are true Christians until we ask Christ to personally live in us. "Christian means 'Christ in me,'" he said.

Never in all my life had I heard any such statement. I thought I was a Christian because I wasn't Jewish, and my brother was an ordained minister. Then it was as if Dr. Gustafson read my mind. "It doesn't matter," he said, "if your relatives are religious. All that counts is the condition of your own heart. You don't get to heaven because your grandfather built a church."

He explained the need to individually open the door of our heart and let Jesus come in and live within us. The beautiful way he said, "Let Jesus come in," made me feel I should do it. He said we could ask Jesus Christ to come into our lives quietly within our own hearts and no one needed to know. *If I ever do such a thing,* I thought, *I surely won't let anyone know!*

"Romans 12:1,2," said Dr. Gustafson, "tells us what God wants us to do: 'Present your bodies a living sacrifice.' We are to give our whole selves to the Lord, not just our minds or our souls for an hour on Sunday."

Why not? What had I to lose? "Holy, acceptable unto God which is your reasonable service." Was I acceptable? I had always had perfect attendance at Sunday school. Would that do it? But then he said, "We don't become acceptable by our own works, but by God's grace—His willingness to take us as we are." As he spoke I was disappointed that my religious background didn't seem to count for much.

"Be not conformed to this world." We were not to make society our standard. It was a little late to tell me that, me the great social leader of the community. "But be ye transformed by the renewing of your mind." I sure could use a new mind. I worked hard to forget the memories of my boys. Was he telling me God could give me a new mind? "That you may prove what is that good, and acceptable and perfect, will of God." If God had a will for me, it surely had been far from perfect: two hopeless sons and a preoccupied husband.

"It doesn't matter what your past interests and gods have been," continued Dr. Gustafson. "If you willingly present your body to the Lord and ask Jesus Christ to come into your life, He will transform your mind and show you His plan for your future."

I knew he was speaking to me. I just hoped Ruthie

didn't know I was touched. *Lord Jesus,* I said in my mind as Dr. Gustafson began to pray, *I have tried to run my life the best way I knew how, and I've failed. I ask you to come into my life and take it over. I ask you to make me into what you want me to be. I present myself to You. In Jesus' name I pray. Amen.*

I had come into the meeting with my worldly veneer firmly in place, yet I left stripped to insignificance. Dr. Gustafson asked all those who had prayed with him to raise their hands while all eyes were closed and before I knew it, my hand was up. I was shocked. I wasn't the type to get emotional and start waving my hand. Yet, I was definitely there with my hand up and it felt right.

Pastor Frost

Nothing unusual happened in my life after that prayer. I began to think nothing would. What I didn't know was that Ruthie and Dick were praying for us. In fact, Ruthie and her next door neighbor met every morning to pray for our family. And Dick, after meeting Sherwood Frost, a young pastor from our town, asked him to visit us. Dick explained we weren't attending church and were in a spiritual vacuum.

So one Friday afternoon, as I was hurriedly heading out the door, I ran into a handsome man on my front step as he was about to ring the doorbell. "I'm Sherwood Frost, the pastor of the Evangelical Baptist Church," he said cheerily, "and thought you would like to come and visit next Sunday." I didn't like the sound of "evangelical" and blanched when he told me they met in an elementary school gymnasium. I was in a hurry and tried to discourage him from talking, but he didn't seem to sense my urgency.

"Do you believe in the Bible?" he asked.

"Some parts I do, and some parts I don't," I said.

"God didn't ask us to be judges of His Word," he said, "but to believe it all or forget it and stop playing at being a Christian."

I had never heard anyone say that before but I knew that was exactly what we had been doing. Fred had been brought up in one of the cults, and while I had never been interested in their doctrine, I had gone with him for ten long, dull years. After the sorrows of our sons, Fred substituted tennis for church on Sundays and for a time I went back to my childhood denomination. But that only lasted until one night at the bridge table when the minister had too much to drink, got angry at his wife and threw the rule book at her in a rage. Fred said to me later, "If that's supposed to be my spiritual leader, I don't need religion." We quit church completely and gave up on God.

However, Pastor Frost so impressed me that when Sunday came, I decided to go to church. I dressed Lauren and Marita in matching Polly Flinders dresses and I wore a bright red knit dress with a large brimmed white felt hat trimmed with a bunch of geraniums and streamers running down my back. I wanted to make sure they knew there was a new family in church and I'm sure they knew. We sat right in the front row so the pastor would see his visitation program had worked — and I'm sure he noticed.

When it was time for the sermon he asked us all to take out our Bibles. I'd never been to a church where they used Bibles or where the people had to do work. I thought that was the pastor's job. What does he have to do all week but study a few verses, make up a sermon and deliver it on Sunday? As I was thinking this, I noticed people were taking out Bibles from under their chairs and out of their handbags. I looked around, bewildered. The pastor pointed at me and said, "If you don't have a Bible this week, bring one next week."

I was humiliated that he had pointed me out as the only dummy in the group who didn't know enough to bring a Bible. *I don't have to come here and be insulted,* I thought. *I just won't come again.*

What I didn't realize is that when we commit our lives to Jesus He doesn't send us an imitation Moses with a big tablet commanding, "Thou shalt not have any fun anymore." Instead He begins to change our desires. When the next Sunday came I got up and got dressed for church. I wore a more subdued dress and no hat. My daughters had asked Fred if he'd come with us and much to my surprise he agreed.

As I started out the front door, I remembered the pastor's words, "If you don't have a Bible this week, bring one next week." I had no idea where I had a Bible. I knew I owned some because when we were children each time we won a contest we'd receive a Bible, but at that point I couldn't remember what I'd done with them. As I was searching my mind for a Bible, I glanced toward the coffee table and there was a Bible — the kind that you lay around the house to impress your friends with your spirituality.

It was a huge gold Bible, embossed on the top. The pages were edged in gold and it had a red velvet ribbon running through it. I looked over and said, "It sure is a Bible." I picked it up and went off to church with Fred and the girls.

I sat right up front again so the pastor would see that I indeed had brought a Bible. When he asked us to open the Word, I really opened the Word. It went over on the lap of the man next to me.

When Pastor Frost started the sermon he instructed us to underline a verse. *Underline,* I thought, *in this fancy Bible with the tissue paper pages and the gold edges?* The pastor noticed my surprise and stated, "If your Bible is too expensive to write in, get a cheaper one." This was the second Sunday in a row that the pastor had pointed me out as the dummy of the group — me who was used to being president of everything. After the service I asked the pastor quietly, "Where do you buy a cheap Bible?"

He replied, "I'll sell you one for 35 cents." That sounded cheap enough, so I bought a *Good News* Bible with the newsprint cover and that was the beginning of my Bible study. We never missed a Sunday after that and when

Pastor Frost preached, he quoted directly from the Bible and told us clearly what God wanted us to do with our lives. I had never realized before, even though I'd been brought up in a church and could recite many Scripture verses, that the Bible was supposed to apply to me today.

Encouraged by the pastor, I started to read the New Testament in the *Good News* version. The first verse that spoke to me personally was Matthew 6:3 which says, "When you help a needy person, do it in such a way that even your closest friend will not know about it."

I had always helped the needy. From that moment at the charity Christmas party when I was seven, I knew it was better to be the one on stage giving out the gifts than the poor sad soul with his hands outstretched. But the verse said not to help needy people from a stage. It said to give in such a way that even my best friend won't know about it. *But what fun would it be to give if no one knew about it?* I thought. It never occurred to me to be quietly generous. I never purposely tried to show off, but as I thought about it, I made sure my philanthropies were presented at a peak viewing hour. Did the Bible mean my generosity was wrong? Was it possible to be good and not tell anyone? These were challenging questions and were the first theological truths I struggled with.

I was eager to learn and looked forward each Sunday to discovering something new. I underlined every meaningful passage in my Bible and became excited when I found thoughts that applied to me. Fred also bought a Bible and he began to neatly underline special verses as each Sunday he listened and applied the truths to himself.

After attending this little church for a year, Fred responded one Sunday when the pastor gave an invitation for those who wanted to become believing Christians. He raised his hand and committed his life to the Lord Jesus, just as I had done a year before.

The changes in me had been gradual, but it seemed that God transformed Fred overnight from a man who hardly ever came home to an avid Bible student. Night after night he sat at the table in our bedroom and studied. In amazement I watched his whole view of life improve. His superior attitude gave way to an admission that he wasn't perfect, and with all his material achievements, he realized he was a failure as a husband, as a father and even as a man.

One day he came home and said, "I'm closing Good Time Charlie's. I just don't feel right about that place anymore." Charlie's was making money and Fred had never shut down a winning enterprise, but that very night he locked the door on his former life.

A few months later the school tripled the rent on the gymnasium and the church held a prayer meeting at the pastor's home to seek God's solution to this financial problem. It was Fred's first prayer meeting. As they prayed, Fred thought about Charlie's. Why not make Good Time Charlie's into a church?

Within two weeks we turned our nightclub into a church. The band stand became the pulpit, the chairs were lined up on the dance floor, the empty bar made space for a classroom, and the kitchen was used for church suppers. Many people were curious to attend a church that had once been a nightclub and the attendance grew. To many it became "Saint Charlie's." Fred was the Patron Saint and I the Mother Superior!

What a time of fellowship we had at St. Charlie's. As excited new believers, we were in church every time the door opened. We became instant leaders and encouraged our friends to try a different, fun-kind of church, one that met in a night club. The piano that once played ragtime swung just as well on gospel songs, and did we ever sing! The pastor preached better, the hymns sounded better, and the people glowed with the joy of the Lord. We almost had as many people out Sunday evenings as we did in the mornings, and after the service we would have homemade cookies and cakes and sit at the tables around the balcony.

We were like one big, happy family.

While the ministry of St. Charlie's was the beginning of our spiritual growth, we soon learned that being a real Christian is not just going to church and being a nice person. It is a total commitment of a life to the Lord and a willingness to let Him direct your path. At first I wasn't sure how to let the Lord direct me. It was depressing for me to stay home, but I began to feel this was what I should do. One day Lauren said, "I hope I never have to grow up and get married and be miserable like you."

I was stunned. "What do you mean?" I asked.

"Well, you're always complaining," she said.

"I am not," I said. "I'm a cheerful person. Just ask my friends."

"I don't have to ask your friends," she said, "I live with you. You may not think you're complaining, but when you do the dishes, you always say how much you hate dishes, how Daddy's always late and how you were made for better things than this."

I couldn't believe I'd ever said such things, but I soon became aware that I muttered around the house with everything I did. While the pressures of our sons had relaxed, and I was in church as often as I could attend, I was still unhappy. I tried to be the life of the party outside of the home, but inside my children saw me as a bitter, angry, complaining woman. I didn't know quite what I was supposed to do with me.

Reflections

As I look back on my life in the '60s, I realize now that I was depressed. Because I didn't know how to handle depression I denied its existence and pushed down my anger.

I have learned that many of us don't know how to take a good look at our problems, label them for what they are and work to overcome them. Since I had always labored in my own strength and there was nothing I could do to restore my sons, I had given up and had tried to find challenging activities to occupy my mind so I wouldn't have to focus on my grief. I'm sure what I did was better than a nervous breakdown, but it was no long-range solution.

Some of you may have suffered a death in the family and have not been allowed to grieve. Friends and other family members have said, "Aren't you over it yet?" Or perhaps you have a spouse who hasn't grieved as you have and you don't think he cares. Many of us don't realize that different personalities grieve differently. Marilyn Heavilin's chapter "The Rose of Uniqueness" from her book *Roses in December* explains how to view a person's grief according to his or her natural temperament. Don't condemn your spouse if he or she reacts to death in a manner quite unlike your own.

I wish someone had told me that it was all right to cry. I regret that Fred and I never shared our grief together. Instead, we put it aside and pretended it never happened.

Today I meet so many people who have stuffed their defeats, depressions and abuses down inside them. They didn't know what else to do with them, so they swallowed them like a large pill. And that pill is still stuck in their throat causing headaches, nervous stomachs and undiagnosed pains. They don't want to be sick, but they just don't know how to get well.

Some of you may be like me — good moral people who don't deserve what's happened to you. Perhaps you've gone to church where everyone looks happy, even saintly, and you've thought you're the only one who hurts. Perhaps the pastor has only pasted platitudes over your problems and you've been afraid to mention them again. It isn't the pastor, the people, the pulpit or the pews that make a difference; it's the presence of the Lord, active and alive in your heart, that can change your life.

If you have any doubts about the power of the Lord in

your life, ask Jesus to come in as I did that day at the Christian Women's Club. It's not the end of your problems, but it is the beginning of your solutions. And it will start you in the right direction so that someday you will be able to

Make the tough times count!

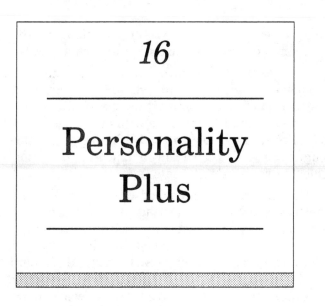

16

Personality Plus

There was a section in the book about the strengths of the Sanguine temperament. I could hardly wait to show Fred how much fun I really was.

Early in life I developed a talent for straightening out other people. Innately I believed I could spot faults in others and improve them if they would only listen to me. My mother called this my Cinderella complex—always ready to transform any damsel in distress.

I had grown up as the oldest child in a family of three and felt I was a born leader. When my father died, I simply took control of my family. My grieving mother, who was weak and exhausted, allowed my strong will to reign, and no one questioned my authority. It was the same when I taught school. My pupils doted on my every word. Not until my marriage had anyone ever suggested I needed help.

Meanwhile, Fred had been brought up believing he was God's perfect child and there was no such thing as sin. His mother encouraged this belief and told him he was

God's gift to women. Both of us entered marriage expecting the other to be grateful for receiving such a prize.

The result of this unreality was a constant battle of the wills. I thought everything should go my way, and Fred insisted it go his. I submitted on the surface, but underneath became more rebellious with each passing year. Dr. Lach once said to me, "In the beginning you fooled me. I thought you were as cool as you appeared, but I now know inside you're tied up in knots."

By the time God reached down and picked up the imperfect pieces of our marriage and began putting them back together, we were almost too antagonistic and apathetic to care. We each hoped the other would recognize his faults and improve. When we both asked the Lord Jesus to come into our lives and make us what He wanted us to be, we were at the bottom. We knew we were failures, and wanted to improve, but we were not sure how to begin.

As we groped for direction in our new Christian life, a friend gave us the book *Spirit-Controlled Temperament* by Tim LaHaye. I found myself on page thirteen: "Sparky Sanguine, the warm, buoyant, lively and 'enjoying' temperament. When he comes into a room of people, he has a tendency to lift the spirits of everyone present by his exuberant flow of conversation. He is a thrilling storyteller because his warm, emotional nature almost makes him relive the experience in the very telling of it."

Oh, how I loved to talk and oh, how I thought everyone but Fred enjoyed listening! Before marriage, I had been considered the life of the party. My brother Ron and I were frequently invited to social affairs just because we were hilarious. Often we rehearsed comedy lines on current topics of interest so that when someone brought up a subject, we would have a stock routine.

In adult life I did the same thing, often varying the story to fit the audience. Once Lauren, after hearing me regale my mother's church circle with one of my tales, said with a sigh, "That's the fifth time I've heard that story, and every time it has a different ending." Quickly I took her into the bedroom and told her she was never to make comments about my stories in public. My brother and I had always agreed we would support each others' tales, no matter how far they might travel from the truth.

Fred, who I thought had no sense of humor, called this lying. We called it "colorful speech."

As I read more of Sparky and his "disarming effect on many of his listeners," I was more convinced than ever I had married a dullard who couldn't appreciate my sense of humor. Fred just liked the straight facts. Before we were married he used to think I was amusing, but after twelve years of my fun and games, he groaned every time I repeated a story.

There was a section in the book about the strengths of the Sanguine temperament. I could hardly wait to show Fred how much fun I really was. But then I read the chapter on Sanguine weaknesses, and it sounded as if Fred had written them about me.

"His life is spent running from one target to another, and, unless disciplined, is not lastingly productive." Fred often pointed out that I seemed to run in circles, make a big production out of every little thing, and accomplish nothing at the end of the day. I felt I was a super achiever and had perfectly good reasons why my days looked incomplete. I never really listened to Fred, and I certainly never thought I was wrong.

Tim LaHaye went on to point out that the Sanguine temperament "can go overboard and become obnoxious by dominating, not just the major part of the conversation, but all of it." While Fred never called me obnoxious, he had for years told me I talked too much. "God hasn't appointed you official gap-filler in every flagging conversation," Fred said frequently. At dinner parties Fred often kicked me under the table when he thought I was too domineering. He also waved negatively from across the room if he heard my voice above the crowd. I barely tolerated his judgmental attitude and constant interruptions, and in twelve years it never once struck me I might possibly be obnoxious.

As I continued to read, I began to wonder if these verbal gifts I'd been so proud of may have a negative side. Did Fred have reason to be disturbed about me?

Fred also began to read the book and identified himself as a Melancholy. "Mr. Melancholy has strong perfectionist tendencies. His standard of excellence exceeds others." Fred began to realize that it was a positive trait to have high standards, but his wife couldn't live up to them, and his well-meaning instruction only made our marriage worse.

"He does not waste words like the Sanguine, but is usually very precise in stating exactly what he means." How true! Fred could say in ten words what took me a half hour! He opened his mouth only when he had something to say. I'd never thought of this as a strength, but the book said it was.

"Mr. Melancholy will be found to be very gloomy, depressed." Fred never seemed to be genuinely happy. No matter what I did, he would find something wrong with it. This attitude made me feel our marriage was hopeless. I gave up trying, and when I gave up, Fred became depressed. In retrospect, I see that living with me, a perpetual comedy act in search of an audience, was enough to send any serious man into a depression!

It was easy for an objective observer to see where each of us was wrong, but it took a miracle for us to begin to see ourselves as others saw us. We prayed for the ability to examine ourselves and began taking steps to break the judgmental patterns we had established in our lives. One day it dawned on me that just because Fred didn't see things as I did, he wasn't wrong; he was just different. As Fred and I looked further into the book, we found "Rocky Choleric. He is hot, quick, active, practical and strong-willed."

These adjectives belonged to both of us. After years of

his criticizing me and my deflating him, our reactions were perched, ready to go, preprogrammed for hostility. Additionally, we both wanted to run the family our way. Fred wanted everything organized and charted out ahead. His idea of a great day was one in which he knew where he was going to be from 7:27 A.M. to midnight. He would get the children organized into a routine with tabulations of their activities on the wall.

I, on the other hand, preferred a day where if I didn't feel like doing anything, I didn't. When Fred went out of town, I would gather the children together and announce, "The ogre is gone. Now we can have some fun for a change." We'd sleep in late, ignore our duties, eat simple food and stay up late at night. I would keep reminding the children of what a great time they were having with fun-filled Mother and when Fred returned they would tell him, without my suggesting it, what a wonderful week they'd had while he was gone.

We were both strong leaders going in opposite directions, and the children didn't know which one to follow. "All we like sheep have gone astray," so far astray that as I look back, I'm amazed our family has been put back together. We were playing roulette with each other's emotions, and each thought it was the other's fault. It took a supernatural power to take our battles and bitterness and begin to change them to love.

We each started to pray, as the book suggested, that God would help us to accentuate our strengths and eliminate our weaknesses. When we did, God began a mighty miracle in our lives that resulted years later in my actually falling in love with my husband and giving him the genuine affection he'd been craving.

When I began to accept Fred unconditionally, he stopped caring whether the vegetables on the dinner plate were of a different color and texture and he ate whatever I gave him with pleasure.

Why had no one ever told us to look at ourselves first?

Or perhaps someone had told us and we hadn't listened. Gratefully, God began to show both of us that we would never know true joy until we began to put our own interests aside and aim to please each other. We had so much to learn and so far to go.

Reflections

Surely God has a sense of humor. He reached down and took Fred out of Good Time Charlie's and me out of the Long Wharf Theatre and showed us the need for change in our lives. He turned our night club into a church and inspired us to study the Bible in a meaningful manner.

Can you believe that in one year's time Fred and I went from not knowing the Lord to owning a church?

Could I even know as I began to study *Spirit-Controlled Temperaments* that God would use this simple concept of self-analysis as the basis for a ministry I had neither asked for nor anticipated? I didn't know you could take examples from the tough times you'd had and use them to give other people hope.

Without knowing what we were doing, Fred and I became excited over our new understanding and I decided to invite in a few friends and make the four personalities into a parlor game. Little did I know that on the simplest and sketchiest information peoples' lives could be changed. As I shared how I found out I was a Sanguine who wanted to have fun and talk and that Fred was a Melancholy who didn't like frivolity and admired silence, couples began to nudge each other. "That's why you're like that! I thought you were out to get me."

We showed how we both were somewhat Choleric — wanting to be in charge and impatient when people didn't do it right. We used my mother as the Phlegmatic example, someone who caused no trouble and would do anything to keep peace and in her words, "not rock the boat."

The group had such a good time they asked if they could come back next week and learn more. As a Sanguine party-lover I was thrilled they wanted to run it all by again. Once Fred saw how much fun we were having, he decided to organize our class and take the fun out of it.

By the next Friday night Fred had made charts of the strengths and weaknesses and divided us up in groups. I took the Sanguines to the bedroom where we looked at our list and saw the first word was *talkative*. We were so excited to see other fun-loving storytelling people that we all began to talk at once, each one aiming to top the last story. When Fred walked in at the end of the hour we looked up stunned. Is our time up already? My, doesn't time fly when you're having fun!

Fred and his Melancholies had naturally finished their list exactly on time—not early or late but on time. He was depressed when he found out we had never gotten beyond talkative. He had made the mistake of putting the Phlegmatics in the family room with all the couches and when he went to check on them, they were all asleep. We had no Cholerics that night—they probably had important meetings to run. We learned by our second meeting that the four personalities concept was valid and when used as a simple measuring stick it could be the catalyst to a changed life.

Even I couldn't have dreamed at that time that I would later become friends with Tim and Beverly LaHaye and that I would go on to write *Personality Plus, Your Personality Tree, How to Get Along With Difficult People,* and *Personalities in Power*—all an outgrowth of that initial parlor game. I had no idea that the marriage problems Fred and I had would sound humorous to others and that our examples could encourage others and give them hope.

We were beginning to learn to

Make the tough times count!

17

Dying of
Heart Attacks

I never did seem to have a name. I cried and thrashed and they watched the dials, assured that if I died the machine would tell them.

Before Fred and I got far in our new Christian life, we were stopped short. In April 1966, Dr. Lach decided to put me in the hospital for some exploratory work. After minor surgery, he explained that while there were a number of things wrong, none were serious, and he scheduled a major operation for May 11.

One afternoon as Fred was leaving to play tennis, I noticed he looked flushed and took his temperature. It was 100 degrees, but he refused to miss his match. The next day the doctor took tests which showed Fred had rheumatic fever.

During his month-long recuperation, Fred had time to read the Bible and one day found this verse in Solomon 1:6: "They made me the keeper of the vineyards; but mine own vineyard have I not kept." Fred meditated on this and began to realize he was the keeper of many vineyards. He watched over his food service business, was the president of Rotary, the country club tennis champ and finance chairman of our church. Yet this verse convicted him that he had failed to keep his own vineyard.

One Sunday after church, Fred shared how he had listed all his responsibilities and arranged them in order of importance. As he reviewed this list, God showed him he hadn't put me and the children first in his life.

"Business has always been most important, followed by tennis and civic activities," he said. I thought, *It's about time that came through to him!*

I had never been able to forget how neglected I had felt when the doctors told me about my first son's fatal condition and Fred had been too busy to come. As I began to dig up past negatives, Fred asked me to forgive him. I was stunned! In all our years together, Fred had never once told me he was sorry. I sat on the edge of the bed and cried in disbelief. His willingness to put me first came at a most crucial time as I was getting ready to leave for the hospital.

The surgery was to be a routine hysterectomy with some other repairs. However, when Dr. Lach began working on me, he came up with eleven other problems. Later he told me, "Nothing below your waist is where it was." What I expected to be a quick recovery was excruciatingly painful and endlessly slow.

Fred was still weak from his month-long bout with rheumatic fever, but he came to see me twice each day and cared for me in a new and tender way. We spent more quiet time together than we ever had before and reached a new depth in our relationship. He seemed genuinely interested in me and wanted me to come home so badly that he convinced Dr. Lach to let me leave before the catheter was removed. By the time I got home from the hospital, still connected to the little tube and plastic bag, Sophia, our new Greek maid, was in firm control of the house. "Just don't expect me to play nurse," she said. Fortunately my mother was there to care for me.

On Memorial Day good friends invited us for a family cookout and I begged Fred to let me go. Fred helped me to the car and the children were thrilled to be finally going somewhere. The cookout was the first fun I'd had in weeks. We ate hamburgers and out-of-season fresh corn and tomatoes from the agricultural experimental station where our friend worked. I lay on their chaise lounge basking in the joy of being among friends, out of the house and free of pain.

Hanging Between Life and Death

But when I got home that night, I began to experience new pain, this time in my chest. Nothing had been touched above my waist and I assumed I had indigestion from all I'd eaten at the party. At 2 A.M. I was jolted awake by a severe stab in my chest. As I sat up, a second pain gripped me. Fred awakened as I began to cry, and I became violently sick to my stomach. "I'm dying!" I screamed.

After Fred talked with Dr. Lach on the phone, I overheard him tell my mother, "The doctor thinks Florence may have a blood clot from the operation lodged in her heart. He hopes he can save her." My mother burst into tears as she remembered her sister who had died of an embolism after a similar operation.

When Lauren saw Grammie cry, she began to sob, "Don't leave us again, Mommy, don't leave us!"

I'll never forget the sight of Lauren and Mother standing in the driveway, clinging to each other in tears and Lauren crying, "Mommy come back! Don't die!" as the ambulance attendants lifted me onto a stretcher.

I didn't want to die, but I knew I was going to. I couldn't breathe. The attendant put an oxygen mask over my face and I began to relax. When I arrived at the hospital, Dr. Lach rushed me into X ray and then gave me a shot. As I passed out of my pain, I heard Dr. Lach tell Fred, "She may not live until morning."

When I next opened my eyes I saw a circle of white

masks. Was I in heaven or a hospital? I had no idea. One of the masks had Dr. Lach's eyes. He had stood over me all night.

The X rays showed no blood clot, and the doctors decided I must have had a heart attack. I was moved from Emergency to the Cardiac floor where almost every patient had a beeping monitor above his door. In the weeks that followed, I heard many monitors stop and saw the rush of nurses followed by weeping relatives as the body was wheeled out for the last time. The fear of death invaded every room.

I was still uncomfortable from my operation and now fought to recover from my heart attack. In addition, a team of doctors came to see me every morning. I didn't mind their visit, but they stood around with their clipboards and looked me over as if I were a plastic model. They all seemed fascinated that a thirty-five-year-old woman, who hadn't moved a muscle in weeks, could have a heart attack.

"If we can keep her from having another attack, we will be able to save her," one doctor said with the detachment a dentist would have in trying to preserve a baby tooth.

"Let's keep her feet up and see if that helps," suggested one intern. They cranked up the end of the bed and I felt as if I were standing on my head. No one asked how I felt. They discussed my medication and agreed I should have my blood thinned. This was accomplished by inserting a needle in a vein by my right elbow and strapping my arm to a board.

After several days of standing on my head, half groggy, with my stiff arm, I again felt the pain and pushed the button for the nurse. Quickly she sent for the cardiogram machine and my team of experts. When they arrived, they never looked at me, but instead became fascinated with the machine as my pain increased.

"Watch the dials!" said one. "She's having another one!" I never did seem to have a name. I cried and thrashed and they watched the dials, assured that if I died the machine would tell them.

The attack passed and the group left with the machine. The next morning when they came in, they seemed surprised to see me. "She's a hardy girl," they said. I kept wishing someone would say, "Mrs. Littauer, *you* are a hardy girl. Well done." But to this team I was only a case with a chart and a machine.

When Fred came in to visit that afternoon, a doctor told him I had had another heart attack and they were going to increase my anti-coagulant drug. "If she continues having these heart attacks, she will not live long," he said. "You should make plans for the care of your children in case they end up with no mother."

No mother, I thought. *No mother.* I had waited years to have a normal son and now that I had adopted Freddie, he was to have no mother?

I continued having one or two heart attacks a week. Each one would bring the nurse, the machine and the doctors, and each attack produced the same proclamations of imminent death and increases in my medications.

As the weeks passed, I became depressed. My tongue would no longer form words and my mind couldn't hold two thoughts together. I was too weak to eat and began to hate food so much I felt sick whenever I heard the shuffle of the tray girl's loose loafers. Day after day they set down food and picked it up untouched. No one ever noticed I hadn't eaten. I was so emaciated that my mother looked at me as if she were already at my funeral. After seeing me drugged and dying she begged Fred to do something. Fred pleaded with the doctors and they finally agreed, "If she can last a week without a heart attack, we'll let her go home to die."

At that point, going home to die seemed good. I prayed for a week free of attacks and the Lord answered my prayer. I passed a long, dull week and the doctors decided they would let me leave, but not without a few tests.

A Hospital Nightmare

I was tested for a number of things in my tilted bed, but one day I went for an unforgettable adventure. A tough nurse's aide was assigned to get me out of bed for the first time. I had been off some of the drugs for three days and I could talk slowly. The aide helped me sit up, then plunked me in a chair.

"Don't you dare move out of that chair," she said sternly. "You're very sick. The man next door disobeyed me and when he got up to walk by himself, he fell. He whacked his head right here on the edge of his bed, split his skull and bled all over the place."

Even if I could have moved, I wouldn't have dared disobey this frightening woman. Shortly after she left me sinking into the chair, an orderly arrived with a stretcher and told me to hop on. I explained I could no more hop on the stretcher than I could fly. He groaned, grabbed me under the arms and eased me onto the stretcher. As he pushed me down the hall, past the nurse's station, I noticed it was twelve noon. It was refreshing to see some other area than the square room I had lived in for almost five weeks. The orderly rang for the elevator and we landed in a basement.

"Where are we?" I asked.

"In the corridor that leads to underground tunnels which end up in other buildings," he said.

As we started down into an obvious tunnel, the boy spotted another orderly coming toward us with another unfortunate lady on his stretcher.

Immediately my boy yelled, "Chicken!" and charged forth, racing me in the direction of the other stretcher.

Just as we were about to crash, he swerved. "You're the chicken!" called the other boy as he whizzed by.

When I recovered, I asked him why he had tried to kill me. "We just like to play games," he said with a laugh. "It gets dull wheeling old people around all day."

How ironic if I survive the heart attacks and die in a stretcher crash in a tunnel, I thought.

We arrived at the radio isotope building and my friend parked me in a hall and left. As I lay looking at the ceiling, I noticed that the fluorescent light fixture directly over me was hanging by only one wire. *Maybe I'll be killed by a lethal light fixture,* I thought.

I called to a passing doctor and pointed out the hanging tubes. "Oh, that's been like that since Christmas," he said. "Don't worry, it won't fall."

But lying alone in the hall, there wasn't much to do but worry. Soon a nurse came by and read the instructions the orderly had tucked under my feet. "You're to have a liver scan," she said. "I have to shoot this solution into your veins."

She found a vein on the top of my right hand, put in the needle and injected the liquid. Unfortunately she missed the vein and shot the solution into my hand. As I looked aghast, my hand immediately turned green. "Don't worry," she said, "it'll go away some day." It never did; the skin is still green around a large damaged vein on my right hand.

After the nurse succeeded on my other hand, she pushed me into a cool room and inserted me and the stretcher into a huge machine. It was July and very hot in the hospital and this one air-conditioned room seemed like heaven. I was exhausted from my stretcher ride, the chicken game, the fear of falling light fixtures and the blown-up vein. As soon as she pressed a few buttons and turned out the lights, I went off to sleep.

The next thing I remember was someone turning on a light. It was 4:30 P.M.!

As I tried to collect my senses, a night watchman walked around the room and jumped when he saw my head sticking out of the machine.

"What are you doing here?" he asked.

"I have no idea," I said. "Someone just pushed me into this room and left."

"You shouldn't be here," he exclaimed. "This building is closed."

"What do you want me to do?" I asked. "I'm strapped in this machine, too weak to move."

He ran out the door, made a frantic phone call, and I heard him say, "I just found some lady in the radio-isotope machine. No, I don't know who she is or how she got here. Just send someone to get her and quick. I don't want to be responsible for any of your people."

The watchman came back and looked at me. I looked at him. What was there to say to each other? In about five minutes a doctor arrived with an orderly. The doctor grabbed my wrist, read my name bracelet and told the orderly I belonged in 602 of the main building. Without so much as a hello, the doctor pulled a few switches that released me and the orderly wheeled me away.

As the orderly pushed me by the nurse's station, the head nurse called over, "Who have you got on that stretcher?"

"I don't know," said the boy, "just some lady from Room 602."

"That's the one that's missing!" she said happily. "She's back. She's back!"

I soon learned no one knew where I had been. When the nurse's aid returned and found me gone, she thought I had disobeyed her and wandered off. She reported my bad behavior to the head nurse. The cleaning woman was assigned to find me and she emptied the waste baskets in each room twice trying to locate me without letting anyone know a patient was missing.

At 4 P.M. the security office had tried unsuccessfully to reach my husband, so they called my mother to say they had lost me.

"How could you lose her?" Mother asked, almost collapsing.

"We really don't know," they said sheepishly. They had run out of searching ideas when I was calmly pushed out of the elevator at 5 P.M. in time for dinner.

Learning to Live Again

The next day the doctor team arrived with good news. "Your test results are all in," one said, "and you haven't been having heart attacks at all. Instead you have the worst gall bladder we've ever seen and now we're going to take it out." They all stood smiling proudly, impressed that after five weeks of treating me for the wrong problem, they could now remove my gall bladder.

Instead of being happy, I began to cry. I was ready to go home to die. I had prepared my mind for it, knowing that as a Christian I would go to heaven. Now life meant staying in the hospital and going through another major operation.

When they tested my blood it had been thinned so much it wouldn't coagulate. They quickly removed the needle for the anti-coagulant and changed it for another with a blood builder. Next the doctors told the nurse to take me off all tranquilizers and drugs and let me level off before the next operation.

I can now appreciate what a drug addict goes through in withdrawal. I became shaky, nervous, hot, cold, sick, wild – and I couldn't shut my eyes or sleep all night. I felt as if I were going insane. I asked for something to help me, but the nurse said, "Our instructions are that you are off all drugs."

After three days of withdrawal and blood building the doctors said I was ready.

The gall bladder operation was much more debilitating than it should have been. With the addition of new pain killers and medications, my ability to think was again shattered. The television faded in and out with my fantasies. I couldn't hold a book or focus on a phrase long enough to understand its meaning.

During the second evening after the operation, my private duty nurse made the mistake of not adjusting the flow of my intravenous fluid. While I was unconscious, the liquid poured into me at five times its normal rate. When Fred walked in to see me, he thought he was in the wrong room. My gaunt face was fat, my scrawny hands were stretched to their limit, and the nurse was asleep in the chair. Fred quickly awakened her and sent her home, deciding he could do better. For a week he slept on the hospital floor, jumping up each time I stirred or cried. He fed, bathed, and loved me in a way I had never known. I could hardly talk but my eyes said, "Thank you."

Before I left the hospital, the surgeon pulled out my drainage tubes and I felt as if all my intestines were being removed in one long rope. Fred took me home and I began a long, slow recovery.

I hadn't seen a mirror in weeks and was shocked at how I looked. My blond hair had grown out half brown and lay limp and shapeless on my head. My cheeks were sunken, my eyes never more than half open and I had lost more than twenty pounds. My hip bones stuck out and the skin on my legs hung in folds.

For someone who had spent her life working to be beautiful, the view in the mirror was the ultimate depressant. Fred kept reassuring me I would recover and look good again and often showed me how smooth and soft my feet had become with all this rest. I stared at my feet as the only improvement I could see and had Lauren paint my toenails. As I focused on my toes at the end of the bed, those ten small spots perked me up and I began to care about living again.

Reflections

If anyone in today's litigious society had the series of blunders that were committed against me, they would sue the hospital for gross negligence and misdiagnosis. But we grew up feeling doctors were one step below angels and so we just accepted what had happened and tried to get me back on my feet.

One of the greatest problems was the withdrawal from the eleven drugs a day I had been on for five weeks. Tim Hansel, an author-friend who has an amazing sense of humor in spite of constant excruciating pain from a near fatal fall off a mountain, told me of the time when his pain pills had ceased to work and the doctors had taken him off all medication. "I never suffered so much in my life," he said. "I was climbing the walls in agony."

My heart went out to him, and my prayers also, as I remembered the pain of my attacks and the withdrawal anguish I went through. I can't think of any good that came out of my five weeks of blunders except that I now have a personal appreciation for pain and an understanding of addiction that I might not have learned in any less painful way. I now have a compassion for anyone addicted to anything. I no longer say, "Well, just don't do it anymore."

This new attitude is a result of daring to

Make the tough times count!

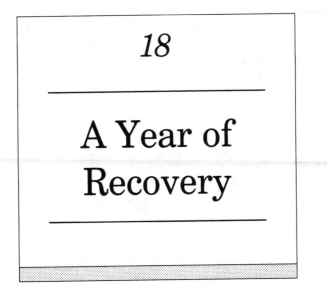

18

A Year of Recovery

I prayed I would be able to do dishes without reviewing Fred's wrongs, but a thirteen-year-old habit is difficult to break.

The unnecessary excess of drugs to prevent my supposed heart attacks had put my mind in neutral. When I read a page, I couldn't focus on what it said. Often I would start a sentence and forget what I was trying to say, and when my friends came for bridge, I could no longer remember what cards had been played.

I would go out of the house but my physical strength diminished rapidly. I would go to the supermarket and be too tired to finish my list. Months after I should have been well, I would find myself standing in the middle of a department store looking for a place to lie down. I had to tell myself to get moving and my mind would push my weary body home.

As I tried to coordinate my mind and body, I realized I hadn't read my Bible in months. In the hospital I had been too limp to hold a book and too confused to care. Pastor

Frost had visited me frequently and I knew my new friends at St. Charlie's were praying for my recovery. As soon as I felt I could concentrate, I started attending a Bible study at the church.

My "What Ifs?"

One day as I was worrying about whether I would ever again be able to speak in public, I read 2 Timothy 1:7: "For God hath not given us the spirit of fear; but of power, and of love, and of a sound mind."

I began to see I was still full of fear. I had spent the majority of my life in an "if only" anticipation—*if only* I could get my circumstances in order, I would be happy.

When I committed my life to Jesus Christ, He showed me that carpeting and cars were not the answer. He also showed me that I was part of my marriage problems and I began to move toward a life of faith in Christ instead of in me. But I had only taken a few baby steps in the Christian walk when I was stopped short and put on the sideline for months. Now I was emerging in fear. My "if only" had been replaced with "what ifs."

What if I could never really concentrate?

What if my memory never returned?

What if I couldn't speak again?

What if my haggard face didn't improve?

What if I couldn't regain my strength?

As these questions filled my mind, I reread the verse and saw that God had not given me the spirit of fear. I began to analyze my "what ifs." What was I truly afraid of? As I thought about this I was startled to realize my fears were all about me. *What if* I never could make me great again? My fears were not about war or famine or home or business. They were not about Fred or the children. They were about me. *What if* I couldn't rise again or meet my expectations of myself? As I concentrated on my fears about my own personal future, a disturbing thought flashed through my mind: "What difference does it make?"

What difference did it make whether I rose like the Phoenix from my mental ashes? Did Fred care if I got back on the stage? Were my children hoping I'd run off on the club circuit again? Had the League fallen apart without me? Had the theatre ceased production? Was there any great cry for my brilliance? The humbling answer was, "No!" Then what difference did it make whether I ever got going at top speed again?

I had to face it — I had never allowed myself to live a normal life. I had kept myself on an ambitious race for superiority. I had won, yet I ended up a failure. Now that I had been stopped and taken off my treadmill, I was afraid I would never again reach new heights. The fear didn't come from God, it came from me. I was afraid I couldn't accept me as I was. I wasn't directing anything. I didn't like me as a plain person. Stripped of titles and positions, I no longer felt I amounted to anything. I began to seriously reflect on the barrenness of my busy life. Before, I equated busyness and success with happiness. But I learned I could cry in a Lincoln Continental and shiver in a seal coat.

As I thought about myself I realized I had better accept myself just as I was. I didn't have a lot of energy, but I was no longer deathly ill, and for that I was grateful.

"For God hath not given us the spirit of fear, but of power." Whose power? His power. It surely was not going to be my power. My days of strength and leadership were apparently over and I was not willing to accept that all I needed was the Lord's power in my life.

"I can do all things through Christ which strengtheneth me" (Philippians 4:13). I had heard this verse in church but never claimed it for myself. Now I realized that once I was willing to give up my own plans, Christ would give me the strength to do what He wanted. But was I willing? I decided I didn't have much choice. It would no longer be my way, but His.

As I reflected more on 2 Timothy 1:7, I thought about

how I equated progress with love and realized I loved only those who pleased me. What an ugly thought! But I was not yet willing to face its full implication and went on to what had first attracted me to the verse: "a sound mind."

I needed a sound mind to get back into my old routine. As the thought hit me, I realized I had just decided, for the first time, not to push myself into new projects but to relax and wait for the Lord's strength and direction. It was going to be hard for me to let the Lord lead in my life.

Learning the Definition of Love

As I continued to read and study the Bible, I tried to apply the words of Scripture directly to me. One of the most difficult passages for me was the thirteenth chapter of 1 Corinthians. I had memorized this entire thirteenth chapter when I was chaplain of my college sorority but never thought about its meaning for me. I struggled with verse six: "Love does not keep a record of wrongs." I saw what it said and what it meant, but how did it apply to me? Before I had finished phrasing the question, the answer came: *You have a big record in your mind of all the things Fred has ever done wrong.*

What does that mean? I thought.

It means you don't love him.

Me not love Fred? I've lived with him for thirteen years. Of course, I love him.

I was trying to convince myself in the same strong, conclusive manner I had always used on others, but this time I couldn't. I had to open my mind to the possibility that I didn't love Fred. It was an unattractive thought for a model wife and I held court with myself.

Do you have a record of wrongs against the accused?

Only of things he's done really *wrong, Your Honor.*

Where do you keep your records?

Oh, only in my head, Sir.

How long have you kept this record?

Thirteen years.

How do you keep it fresh in your mind?

I rehearse it every day. You see, when I put my hands in dishwater, it triggers a switch in my head and I begin to review the list.

Very interesting. Then you do not love your husband?

Of course, I love my husband.

That's impossible, because our book says, "Love does not keep a record of wrongs." You have testified that you have a record of wrongs; therefore, you are guilty of not loving your husband.

Guilty as charged, Your Honor.

Once I admitted I was guilty, I had to make reparations, and I decided to start with the evidence: my record of wrongs. I prayed daily, sometimes hourly, that God would remove the list from my head. I prayed I would be able to do dishes without reviewing Fred's wrongs, but a thirteen-year-old habit is difficult to break.

As I continued to pray, the list began to disappear. But if Fred displeased me, it started all over again. Then a new thought came to me. When people give up smoking, they often chew gum to replace the habit. Perhaps I needed to fill the habit vacuum with something new; perhaps I should start a list of "rights."

I began by copying Philippians 4:8 and tacking it on a cabinet door where I could see it while doing dishes.

>Whatsoever things are TRUE,
>Whatsoever things are HONEST,
>Whatsoever things are JUST,
>Whatsoever things are PURE,
>Whatsoever things are of GOOD REPORT;
>if there be any VIRTUE and if there be any PRAISE,
think on these things.

As I began to think on these things, I started to replace my negative list with some positives. Fred had always been true-blue to me. He was scrupulously honest, and certainly just and fair, and clean and lovely to look at. People in town spoke well of him; he was of good report. These were virtuous traits and I should have been willing to praise him, but because he rarely praised me, I was not about to go first. What a rebellious spirit! I won't be nice to you unless you're nice first. How childish!

Yet at the time I didn't consider myself childish. It took time, and as I studied the Scriptures, gradually I became more pliable and ceased searching for goals. I began to replace my record of wrongs with things worthy of praise, and as I became willing to be set on the sidelines forever, the Lord Jesus began to restore me. As I prayed, He worked. While I was weak, He was strong. As I studied His word, He rebuilt my mind. "God hath not given us the spirit of fear; but of power, and of love, and of a sound mind."

Reflections

In retrospect I see that God had to allow me to become weak so that He could become strong. Are there some points in your life where you have been ill or depressed and felt there was no hope? I can understand how you feel. I've been there. Have you found a verse that fit your situation so well you knew God wrote it just for you?

This time on the sidelines was a transition period for me where I finally learned to give up on myself and let the Lord take control. I'd been forced to accept my lack of power to change the fate of my babies, I'd been drugged into obedience in the hospital, but as I tried to re-enter the mainstream of life I was ready once more to take charge. A Choleric-out-of-control is depressed. As I look back I see that God would have kept me weak for years if I hadn't learned to give Him the control of my life so that He could show me how to

Make the tough times count!

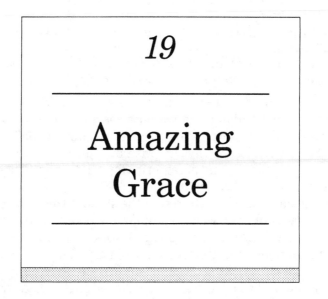

19

Amazing Grace

While we were too new in the Christian life at that point to understand what they saw in us, we realize now that they looked at us and thought, "If only this couple would get turned on for the Lord. What an impact they could have."

Once I accepted the fact that I might never get better, I began to get better. Once I ceased setting worldly goals, I was given a reward. Once I gave control to God, He began to bless my life.

In March of 1967, less than a year after my hospital siege, a friend called to say she had a job commentating fashion shows for a local store. They had booked two shows on one day, and she wondered if I would be able to fill in for her. I had always loved clothes and kept up with current fashion. Even when I was too weak to read, I flipped through *Vogue* and *Glamour*. I said yes and then wondered if I would be able to handle the job.

I still had trouble with my memory, my words sometimes got mixed up, and I often got lost in the middle of a sentence. Did I dare stand up and speak? I decided the Lord had opened this opportunity and would give me the strength to perform. I was excited about getting back on stage and began to prepare for the big day.

When it was time to choose the clothes for the show, I took Lauren along and we both learned from my friend how to "pull a show." While I had done some modeling and had commentated many club fashion shows, I never had to choose the clothes and accessories for each model. Together Lauren and I picked up the sense of selecting and coordinating the outfits and on the day of the show at the New Haven Country Club, we were ready. We had pulled the show, coordinated the accessories and reworked the lineup. I was to be on stage and thirteen-year-old Lauren was to direct the models and see that they got out on time and in the right order. To give the show an added touch, I had written a review of the season's fashion in verse.

The show went smoothly and the audience loved my poetry. Diane Brown, public relations director for R. H. Macy's in New Haven, observed the show and when it ended she told me how pleased she was with my work.

"Would you consider being the commentator for all the Macy's shows in Connecticut?" she asked. "I was impressed how smoothly the lineup moved."

"Oh, that's because Lauren was working backstage," I replied.

"We'll take her, too!" said Diane.

During the time Lauren and I worked for Macy's, Fred expanded his business to New York and decided to open an office there. When he checked rental prices, he found he could get an apartment for the same amount as a decent office. Fred met me one day when I was at Macy's in New York and took me to see an elegant new apartment building called The Churchill.

He had selected an apartment overlooking the East River with a clear view of the United Nations Building. The view was breathtaking, and I was enthralled with the thought of a second home, a retreat in New York City. While Fred intended to use it for business, he told me to decorate it any way I wanted. "You've improved so much as a wife," he said, "I want to give you the best."

Nothing inspired me more than decorating a new home. This time it was extra special — Fred was also interested. Even though he said I could decorate it in any style, I wanted to please Fred for a change, and we shopped together.

As we divided our weekends between our two homes, we found our family time improving. Every other week we would leave on Friday for New York and spend the weekend in close fellowship in the apartment. We toured the city with the children and took horse-and-buggy rides in Central Park. Afternoons we wandered through the toys at F. A. O. Schwartz. For the first time in our married lives, Fred actually spent two days a week in our presence.

I was so deliriously happy with the attention he gave us, I couldn't do enough for him. I noticed that as I began to put his desires first, he started to enjoy my company. On Sunday mornings we would go to the Calvary Baptist Church where Dr. Stephen Olford would inspire us to improve our Christian lives. As we drove home on Sunday evenings, we would sing hymns and rejoice that we had each other.

Amazing Grace

While we spent much of the summer of '67 in our New York apartment, we settled into our Connecticut home in time for school. When we returned to church at Good Time Charlie's we were introduced to Grace Mintz, a bright, attractive girl in her early thirties. Grace had big green eyes, a radiant smile, and our family was immediately attracted to her.

We became acquainted with Grace and discovered that she had been a member of our church before we joined. She was divorced and was bringing up two little girls alone. We hadn't seen her before because she had been working as a secretary in the lay division of Campus Crusade for Christ in San Bernardino, California.

None of us in our little church had ever heard of Campus Crusade, but Grace began to change that. She made plans for a Crusade-sponsored Lay Institute for Evangelism in Connecticut and began promoting this among the pastors in our area. She wanted Fred and me to help her, but we were afraid of anything with such a heavy title as Lay Institute for Evangelism. Although we politely avoided promoting the Institute, Grace cheerfully kept us posted on her progress.

With no real help from anyone in the church or community, she single-handedly scheduled the Institute and visited almost every pastor in the New Haven area plus many in Bridgeport, Milford and Hartford. Few were willing to help. Undaunted, she arranged for a downtown New Haven church to lend her their social hall, and she persuaded Mike Hopping, a dentist from Atlanta, Georgia, and his wife Joyce to come and share their testimony. Throughout all of Grace's efforts to put on this Institute, Fred and I remained indifferent and had no intention of attending. We were a little reticent to get too religious.

As the October date approached we planned to spend that weekend in New York, but then Grace asked us if we would do her a big favor.

"Since you have the largest and the nicest home of anyone in church," she said, "I wonder if you would consider having Mike and Joyce Hopping stay with you while they're in New Haven."

She knew how to appeal to me! I was flattered to think my home was the best and quickly said I would be glad to take care of her guests. The Friday evening of the Lay Institute arrived, and Fred and I still had not planned to attend, even though the speakers would be spending the weekend in our home.

At dinner that evening, Fred said, "I really don't think it's polite to have the speakers stay here and for us not to show enough interest to go and hear what they have to say."

We both concluded it would be embarrassing for Grace to bring the Hoppings to our home that evening if we hadn't gone to the program.

While Fred felt we ought to show interest out of moral obligation, I was afraid to attend. I didn't want to get involved with anything that had to do with "evangelism." Grace had said something about knocking on people's doors and sharing your faith, and I panicked at the thought that she might expect me to do the same. Fred said we should go, and I said only if he got a babysitter. The first girl he called said yes. My heart sank, but I had no choice.

Grace was delighted to see us that evening. "I just knew you would come," she said confidently. I wondered how she had this advance knowledge since we had just decided ourselves within the hour. Grace ushered us to the front row of a dingy basement room. I assumed she wanted to make sure we would pay attention, but I was very uncomfortable.

I pictured the Hoppings to be old, gloomy, pious people, but was pleasantly surprised to meet a young, attractive, dynamic couple. They shared the story of their married life and humorously pointed out their failures. Their experiences sounded just like ours. As they shared their Christian testimony and the changes the Lord had brought to their home, I began to see that Fred and I had a long way to go. We were impressed with their message and their inspiring example.

After the session, we took them home and sat up until 2 A.M. asking questions about how we could live out Christian principles in our daily lives. They gave us simple, factual steps to help us improve our marriage. They made it clear that once we invite Christ into our lives, He truly dwells in us and uses our bodies to do His will. We learned that, while a decision for Christ is a one-time commitment, we depend upon the power of the Holy Spirit to give us an abundant Christian life. We must appropriate the Holy Spirit's power daily and ask God in prayer to give us the strength and desire to do His will.

"Jesus came that we might have life, and that we might have it abundantly," they said.

I had been afraid that being a Christian would be dull, and I was relieved to see this personable couple had found an exciting relationship with Jesus Christ. Although God had already been working in our hearts, Mike and Joyce Hopping gave us a new understanding of how to live and enjoy a Spirit-filled life.

Fred and I had no intention of going to the Institute on Saturday. Fred had a full day of work at the office, and I had to prepare dinner for the Hoppings that night. The next morning, however, Fred got dressed and went to the meeting. He told me later that after listening to the Hoppings, God had spoken through them to him about his life.

After a gourmet dinner that had taken me all day to prepare, we again talked late into the night, questioning our guests and paying close attention to their answers. While we were too new in the Christian life at that point to understand what they saw in us, we realize now that they looked at us and thought, *If only this couple would get turned on for the Lord. What an impact they could have.*

Years later we often thought of others in the same way, but at that time we had no idea *we* were considered "baby Christians with growth potential."

The Hoppings encouraged us to take the week-long lay training offered by Campus Crusade in Arrowhead Springs above San Bernardino, California. There seemed to be no possibility of our getting to California for a week of Bible study, but the Hoppings emphasized that this experience would be extremely helpful in getting our Christian life underway.

On Sunday afternoon, the fifty people who attended

the Institute were scheduled to go out into the community to witness. The idea of ringing doorbells and trying to convince perfect strangers they needed to invite Christ into their lives frightened and appalled me, and I stayed home. Fred, however, was braver than I and went off with a partner who had just committed his life to the Lord at the Institute the day before. They were to give the "Community Religious Survey," as they had been trained to do, to anyone who would listen. While I stayed home and prepared dinner, Fred knocked on doors.

At the third home Fred found a man raking leaves in the yard. When Fred asked if he had time to answer some questions on a survey, the man said, "I was just looking for an excuse to sit down." He was most hospitable and invited Fred and his partner inside.

Fred asked him all the questions on the survey, shared the "Four Spiritual Laws" gospel presentation, and at the conclusion asked, "Is there any reason why you would not want to pray and receive Christ into your life right now?"

"No, there isn't," said the man. "I would like to do this."

Fred was so shocked that he swallowed twice before leading the man in prayer. The man's name was Bernie Roop, and he began attending St. Charlie's. The last we heard, Bernie and his wife are still members of that church. Fred came home that afternoon excited that God had used him to reach a man who was ready and willing to commit his life to the Lord.

Sunday evening we stayed up late with the Hoppings again, and on Monday Fred took an unprecedented weekday off and took them sightseeing, then to their plane in New York. Every minute of our time together was filled with an insatiable desire for direction, and God used the Hoppings as Christian role models for us.

A Turning Point

The following month, Grace had a new plan and invited Hal Lindsey, who was then a traveling representative for Campus Crusade for Christ, to come to our little Charlie Church. Grace again asked us to keep the speaker in our home. That night we sat up again until two in the morning plying Hal with questions and, like the Hoppings, Hal insisted we go out to Arrowhead Springs to take the lay training.

Since Grace, the Hoppings and Hal Lindsey had all strongly suggested we go to California for Christian training, we began to consider the possibility. Grace provided us with information on activities at Arrowhead Springs, and in January of 1968 persuaded us to go. We took our pastor and his wife, Sherwood and Ruth Frost, and Grace asked some local businessmen to send three other Connecticut ministers to go with us.

We arrived in Los Angeles and took a little helicopter to San Bernardino. The shaky craft flew so low I could see the people on the ground, and I was frightened. A week later a helicopter crashed, and the service was discontinued.

The drive to Arrowhead Springs was beautiful. I was amazed at the tall palm trees, lush green lawns and bright smiling pansies in January! I was also impressed with the size and grandeur of the hotel. I was surprised to learn that Elizabeth Taylor had spent her first honeymoon on the sixth floor of the Arrowhead Springs hotel, then a resort for the Hollywood stars.

Our room was tastefully decorated, and later we all ate in the Candlelight Room, an ornate ballroom with a huge crystal chandelier in the center and candles doing double duty against the mirrored walls. I was overwhelmed. I had assumed that any religious retreat would be stark and barren, and we might expect to be called to prayer at four in the morning by a little monk with a tinkling bell.

I also expected a sparse diet and simple cots covered with khaki Army-surplus blankets to quicken our spirituality. I had presumed the staff would be seriously dedicated people who dressed in simple pilgrim style, carried large Bibles and seldom smiled. How wrong I was!

We spent the first evening in the Little Theatre, a former movie hall for the Hollywood set. Instead of watching risque movies, we sang hymns, listened to a fantastic pianist and enjoyed the rich fellowship of people in love with the Lord. After the singing and welcoming introductions, Dr. Bill Bright spoke to us.

I expected a big powerful man to leap on the stage and barrage us with a dynamic message. Instead, a short, unassuming man came quietly to the lectern and gave us a low-key talk on the founding of Campus Crusade for Christ. He told us how he began his ministry while operating a candy business and how it had grown from a handful of students at UCLA to an international organization with a staff of over 2,000.

"Campus Crusade is a worldwide movement," he said, "totally dedicated to one goal: to help fulfill the Great Commission of our Lord by taking the claims of Christ to the millions of students in every country of the world. Our special emphasis, though it is not our total thrust, is on the college and high school campuses, because we believe it is here that the main source of untapped manpower waits to be challenged and trained to help change the world."

He then said we were to be trained as laymen in order to go back to our own communities and become Christian leaders. We would receive biblical instruction plus helps in witnessing, teaching others and living the Christian life.

He concluded his quietly persuasive message by telling us to go to our rooms without saying a word to anyone and write down a list of all the sins in our lives. I knew this wouldn't take me long and I went quietly off to our room with Fred. No one said a word as we went through the lobby to the elevator. I had never been in an absolutely mute crowd before; it was a little creepy.

By the time we got to our room the silence was killing me, and as we shut the door, I opened my mouth to speak only to have Fred raise a finger and shush me. I could see he was genuinely moved and intended to follow through with the assignment.

He sat down at the desk and began to write. As I didn't want to appear too saintly, I also got out a piece of paper and sat on the edge of the bed. I expected to have difficulty writing bad things about me, but as I began to write, it was as if another hand took control and put down one fact after another.

An hour later Fred and I concluded our lists and were soberly ready for step two: prayerfully read over your list, confess that these are your sins and ask God to forgive you. We each did this quietly and then together went to the wastebasket where we slowly tore our lists in pieces and threw them away. This was to symbolize God's forgiveness, His cleansing and the promise that He would never again remember our sins.

By the time we completed this act, both of us were in tears. God had shown us sins in our lives we had never even thought of before. With almost no effort we had written pages of faults. It was hard for me to tear up a part of myself, even a bad part, but I did it. We threw our sins away and received God's forgiveness, and for the first time in our lives we were truly repentant of our newly admitted sins. We realized how we had hurt each other and apologized for our selfish lives.

That night was a turning point in our Christian experience. We had humbled ourselves before the Lord and one another, and God was ready to help us grow. I have learned since, the Lord is not pushy. He will not begin a work in a life until the person has been willing to look deeply into himself, pull out his sins and humbly confess them. When we are willing to be cleansed, He will forgive us of our faults and start to build a new life.

The next morning we could hardly wait to share our experience with others at the breakfast table. Later in class we memorized the "Four Spiritual Laws," an evangelistic pamphlet written by Dr. Bright to help the inexperienced share their faith with other people. It states simply: (1) God loves you and offers a wonderful plan for your life. (2) Man is sinful and separated from God, thus he cannot know and experience God's love and plan for his life. (3) Jesus Christ is God's only provision for man's sin. Through Him you can know and experience God's love and plan for your life. (4) We must individually receive Jesus Christ as Savior and Lord; then we can know and experience God's love and plan for our lives.

Once we learned how to use the Four Laws, we found out we were all going witnessing on Wednesday. When ringing doorbells was mentioned at our Lay Institute in Connecticut, I stayed home, but this time I was excited. I went off with a feeling of anticipation and a handful of "Community Religious Surveys" and the "Four Spiritual Laws" booklets.

When we arrived in West Covina, I thought I would have Fred to lean on, but our leader paired me with Ruth Frost, our pastor's wife. We were assigned a certain street and told to go to each house and ask if they would be willing to take a survey. If they were interested, we were to ask them the printed questions and share the Four Laws. When the reality of this process hit me, I wondered why I had come. Ruth was even more afraid than I, and we began to hope no one was home. But we looked down the long street and knew there was no chance that everyone would be on vacation.

Slowly we went to the first house. I rang the bell and a huge Great Dane jumped to the fence and looked down at us. I had never seen such a dog. He was as big as a horse! He barked ferociously, and Ruth and I clutched each other in genuine fear. Slowly we backed down the walk. There was no one home at the second house and the third had a teenager watching soap operas who had no time for us. The fourth home had a lady who was very pleasant, answered all the questions and said she would read the Four Laws later.

At the fifth home a sad lady came to the door and let us in. She was willing to take the survey and gave brief answers which indicated she had some religious background. We sat at her kitchen table and went over the Four Laws, explaining that God loved her and had a wonderful plan for her life. She didn't seem like the type to want any wonderful plan, but I proceeded anyway.

At the conclusion, I asked if there were any reason she would not like to pray to receive Christ right now and read the prayer at the end of the book with me. Instead of answering, she began to recite the prayer and finished the first line before I could join in. By the time we said "Amen," she was in tears and I was in shock. This event was the first time anyone had prayed with me to receive Christ.

"Does this mean that when I die, I will go to heaven for sure?" she asked.

I assured her she would. "The Bible tells us in John 3:16," I said, "that God so loved the world that He gave His only begotten Son, that whosoever believeth in Him should not perish, but have everlasting life."

"I asked my pastor this question," she said, "but he told me there was no way to know until I die. I've been worried about this and just last night prayed that God would send someone to tell me about heaven."

I was overwhelmed to realize that God had sent me, a totally inexperienced believer, to give this woman the assurance she was seeking. I know there were bells ringing in heaven and in my heart—a new believer entered the family of God.

As this dear lady didn't own a Bible, I spent the rest of the afternoon introducing her to my New Testament and showing her how to study it. I've often wondered what I told her, I knew so little. Later I mailed her a *Good News* New Testament from Connecticut. A year later she wrote to tell me her house had burned down but she had saved her handbag and her Bible.

The next evening, as I was getting ready for bed, Fred showed me a little pocket New Testament.

"This Bible is really exciting," he said. He studied every minute he could find and began to pray for wisdom and knowledge. In six months Fred went from knowing almost nothing about the Bible to being able to find verses on any subject at a moment's notice. I couldn't believe how quickly he learned and how rapidly his whole personality changed. The more he studied, the more pleasant he became. One day a friend of ours said, "What's happened to Fred? He seems almost humble."

Revival in New Haven

By the time we returned from California, Grace had already planned another project. She had prayed for a second area-wide Lay Institute for Evangelism in New Haven and had gathered together a group of interested pastors. They asked Fred to be the chairman. Fred and I had seen the practical influence of such a conference and wanted to reach as many people as possible.

Fred and I also determined that if we were in charge of a Lay Institute, it was going to be the best. We were willing to spend as much time and energy as possible to insure a large audience. Since Fred had the weight of his business obligations and I was working for Macy's and keeping up two homes, we decided to look for someone to take care of the children. Through an ad in the Heidelberg newspaper, a German friend chose Gudrun Pitchel as our new mother's helper.

I pictured Gudrun to be a big, husky German girl straight off the farm, but when I met her, I was surprised to see she stood only four feet eleven inches, weighed ninety pounds, and was a size three. Gudrun spoke little English, and I knew no German, but from a note from our friend we learned she was twenty-four years old, was a professional dress designer and seamstress, and had taken the job to learn English. When I looked at her petite form next to mine, I thought I should be taking care of her. I wasn't sure how to communicate with her, but gratefully, Gudrun picked up English quickly. She was absolutely adorable, and we soon adopted her as one of the family.

She was a compulsive housekeeper, loved to make me clothes and adored the children. Fred and I were delighted with her service and gave ourselves wholeheartedly to the upcoming Lay Institute.

We arranged to have Arlis Priest, the director of public relations for Campus Crusade, as the main speaker. We rented the ballroom of the Hotel Taft in New Haven and encouraged Mike and Joyce Hopping to return. Grace asked Dave and Carolyn Petersen, a young couple from Syracuse, New York, to speak to the teen and college groups. Our biggest job was promotion — we were praying for 400 people.

Fred and I began speaking to any club, organization and church that would have us. The month before the Institute, I spoke thirty-seven times in thirty days. On the opening Sunday afternoon, the ballroom in the Hotel Taft was jammed with an overwhelming 700 participants. We didn't know how they all heard about it, but were excited to see what the Lord had done.

Instead of the number falling off during the week, it increased. By Tuesday we had outgrown the ballroom and moved to the First Congregational Church on the Green in New Haven. During that exciting week many people received Christ and hundreds learned for the first time how to appropriate the power of the Holy Spirit in their lives. It was the beginning of a revival in New Haven.

The following week Fred attended the President's Prayer Breakfast in Washington, D. C. and sat next to Dr. Bill Bright. When Dr. Bright discovered Fred was in the food service business he asked Fred if he would be willing to come to Arrowhead Springs for a weekend and evaluate their food service. They arranged for Fred and me to come out on Memorial Day weekend.

Fred spent a day examining the food services and concluded that Campus Crusade was faced with an impossible situation. They had a new facility close to completion which was to feed and house 800 college students, but the new kitchen was totally inadequate for such a crowd. The new area, called The Village, was almost a mile away from the main hotel and was scheduled to handle 1400 people.

Fred gave his report to Dr. Bright and suggested that Campus Crusade get out of the food service operation and bring in an outside company. There were no available services in the San Bernardino area, and Fred agreed to bring some of his staff from the East to run the food service for the summer.

We flew home, Fred packed his clothes, and he left for what we expected to be a two-week period. But when he arrived back at Arrowhead Springs, he discovered the problem was greater than he had imagined. After working eighteen hours a day, seven days a week for two straight weeks, Fred called to tell me he didn't think he would get home that summer. He suggested I close our home, pack up the children and Gudrun, and spend the summer at the Arrowhead Springs hotel.

We moved into three rooms on the third floor, and while Fred worked in the hot kitchen, the children and I had a wonderful, relaxing summer. We ate in the Candlelight Room and swam in the same pool where Esther Williams had made many of her movies.

The Desires of Her Heart

Our good friend Grace Mintz also spent that summer at Arrowhead Springs, and through our mutual influence, five more people from New Haven came out for a Lay Institute in August. By that time, Fred and I had taken staff training and were accepted as directors of the lay division for the state of Connecticut.

One afternoon Grace came to me and shared an unusual story. The previous year she had worked with Campus Crusade in Phoenix, Arizona. During that time she prayed constantly for God's guidance in her life. One night she was awakened from a sound sleep at 3 A.M. She said she felt the presence of the Lord and an inner voice saying, *Grace, go home to Connecticut and organize a Lay Institute there.* She debated with the Lord in prayer for the rest of the night.

"But Lord, how can you use me? I'm divorced. People won't accept me; I'm just a lone woman. Anyway Lord, I just want to meet and marry a nice Christian man to be a father to my girls."

As Grace gave her excuses, she suddenly seemed to hear the Lord say, *Grace, go home to Connecticut and work for me there for a year. After that, you'll be married.* A peace came over her and she never doubted she would one day be married to a Christian man.

Grace finished out her year in Phoenix and that summer went to Arrowhead Springs to attend the Institute of Biblical Studies before returning to Connecticut.

While at Arrowhead Springs, she heard Hal Lindsey speak on the topic, "Any Old Pot Will Do."

"If we're willing to be used," he said, "God can use us. It doesn't matter what our backgrounds, spiritual experiences, or our talents might be."

At that moment Grace realized it didn't matter what her qualifications for Christian service were, it mattered only that she be willing. She left the auditorium that night saying, "God is able to use any old pot or any old person who is willing to be emptied of self and filled with the Holy Spirit."

Grace became excited about what God was going to do with her in Connecticut, and she soon met four young women from Connecticut who all agreed to pray fervently for their home state. They also prayed that Grace would be able to reach out to the Christian communities. Their specific prayer requests that summer were: (1) There would be two Lay Institutes in Connecticut during the next year; (2) Twelve people from Connecticut would come to California for training; (3) One couple would be raised up to join the Campus Crusade staff.

We never knew about Grace's covenant with the Lord and as she shared that God had answered all these prayer requests, I was stunned and delighted that Fred and I had been part of her covenant. It was amazing to me to realize that all the things that appeared to just "happen" that year in our lives had been part of a divine plan. Because Grace had been faithful and believed God for impossible things, our lives had been changed. Two Institutes had been held in New Haven, exactly twelve people had come to California, and we had joined Campus Crusade staff.

As Grace and I rejoiced over these answers to prayer, she hesitated a moment and said, "There is one other request that hasn't been fulfilled. I also prayed that God would give me a Christian husband and father for my two girls."

She told me she had claimed Psalms 37:4: "Delight thyself also in the Lord; and He shall give thee the desires of thine heart."

She hoped the Lord knew that the desires of her heart included not only revival in Connecticut, but a husband.

"Grace," I said as I put my arm around her shoulder, "maybe the Lord is still working on that. Let's keep praying for the desires of your heart."

The following week Grace left for Connecticut, thankful for the prayers but disappointed her personal desires seemed to have been forgotten.

None of us knew God was already working on Grace's desires. During a Lay Institute at Arrowhead Springs in August, Grace had met Amy and Pat Booth, a couple from Dallas. They had taken a picture of Grace and shown it to their friend, Tommy McClain, an ordained minister and real estate investor. Tommy had recently lost his wife after an agonizing bout with cancer and was left with two sons to raise alone. When the Booths showed him Grace's picture and told him about her cheerful personality and sincere Christian commitment, he became interested and began to pray for the Lord's direction. About the first of September he felt led to call Grace from Dallas.

After talking on the phone several times that week, Tommy suggested he fly to New York, meet Grace and get acquainted.

"I can't meet an unknown man in a big city," she said.

"Haven't you been praying for a Christian husband?" asked Tommy.

There was nothing to do but admit it and with her faith challenged, she agreed to meet him.

On a Friday evening Tommy flew to New York, met Grace and put her up properly in a separate room. They spent Saturday in New York and Sunday going out to Connecticut where Tommy met Grace's two little girls. He also attended church with Grace at Good Time Charlie's and met the pastor and Grace's friends. Before he left Sunday evening, Tommy told Grace to pray about their future, and commit it to the Lord. A week later Tommy called to say it was clear in his mind that Grace should come to Dallas. After meeting Tommy's children, and the parents of Tommy's deceased wife Kathy, they knew the Lord wanted them together for life.

Thirteen days after they first met, Grace and Tommy were married. Grace had been faithful, had delighted herself in the Lord, had obeyed God, and the Lord gave her the desires of her heart.

In October, Grace and Tommy came back to Connecticut for a belated wedding reception. During the reception the pastor read a letter that Tommy's wife Kathy had written shortly before her death. She knew the Lord was taking her home to be with Him, and had written a thank you letter to the Lord for His sustaining power. She began by quoting Psalm 119:71: "It is good for me that I have been afflicted, that I might learn thy statutes."

It is hard for us to understand. But our understanding will have to be that God knows best. God has a plan. I cannot see it now, but whatever it is, it will be good — for me and perhaps for others. I know He has a blessing for us.

Lord, I so pray that if Your will is to take me that You will be ever so close and real to Tommy and the boys as well as our families. They will need strength. I know your grace is sufficient. Teach Brad and David the tenderness and complete healing power in death so they will never be bitter or question the reason. My wish would be that shortly You would lead Tommy to someone who would give him empathy and understanding. Someone he would love and she would return his love. I know Tommy well enough that he would never consider anyone who would not be a Christian mother to Brad and David and help them through their oncoming trials and frustrations.

And I pray they will completely open their hearts to her and accept her and show her the respect she deserves. Lord, help them to put me in the background and to love this new unity as if it was the first for them. May they not try to mold their new mother into my pattern but love her for what she is. No two people are alike and none of us is perfect. Goodness, the world doesn't need another Kathleen McClain anyway.

No work of fiction, no matter how great, would have equaled the gripping truth of that moment. God took a beautiful woman, rejected by her husband but devoted to the Lord, and moved her and her two daughters from Connecticut to Texas into the life of Tommy McClain. He took a lonesome widower with two sons to bring up, and gave him a new bride. Together as one they began a new life. Later they added a baby girl of their own. They built a lovely home, complete with a gymnasium, and opened it to the teenagers in their community. The McClain home became a center of Christian activity in Rockwall, Texas. Fred and I are grateful to God for bringing Grace into our lives and using her to bring us into Christian service.

Reflections

Once Fred and I had given the Lord control of our lives, He began the refining process and kept bringing Christian leaders onto our path. As Fred and I listened, they all seemed to say, "You two could really amount to something for the Lord if you ever got trained." We didn't even know what training was but we had learned enough to know that if God keeps sending you people saying the same thing, you had better listen.

Fred and I had first committed our lives to the Lord in desperation over the loss of our sons. We had given over control of our egos when we had felt weak and needed strength. We had attended seminars to learn about the Christian life. We had confessed our sins to the Lord. These steps, made in faith, prepared us for the one I never thought I'd do: door to door witnessing.

How great it is to look back and see that "the steps of a righteous man are ordered of the Lord." Our Christian growth is like our physical growth. We start out as babies drinking spiritual milk but step by step we grow up until one day we can walk and even witness. The Lord doesn't call us to any mission without giving us the strength to carry it out.

As I look back now and remember the fear we had of going to a Christian meeting and of witnessing to others, I can have compassion for those who come to our seminars and aren't sure if we will be too religious and serious or if they will be called on to recite some unknown verse. I also remember how different leaders encouraged us to study and get prepared for the call of God in ministry. Much of my life today is spent encouraging others to write, speak and become leaders.

Our amazing Grace lighted our path and we are grateful that she and Tommy, more than twenty years later, are still shining brightly for the Lord.

Have you experienced Christian growth in such a way that you can look back and see the steps as they were ordered by the Lord? Perhaps you've never looked at your life from that perspective. Why not review the past so that you can have faith today that the Lord will use you tomorrow? What is there about your life that you can use to encourage others? Don't waste it!

20

Bungalow One

As I prayed, God quieted my heart and showed me Philippians 4:11: "I have learned in whatsoever state I am, therewith to be content." I knew, for me, He meant the state of California.

When Grace left Arrowhead Springs for Connecticut, we expected to follow her back. We had been accepted as Connecticut lay directors for Campus Crusade, and I could hardly wait to put into practice all I had learned at staff training and move ahead with this new phase of our life.

But one day Dr. Bright called Fred to his office and explained that Colonel Irwin Stoll had resigned as director of conference services and hotel manager. Dr. Bright asked Fred to consider remaining in California to replace Col. Stoll. Surprised at this unexpected request, Fred knew that after three months in a hotel room I was anxious to return to my spacious home, my friends and my own Christian ministry.

When I first committed my life to the Lord at the Old Mill Restaurant, I asked the Lord to transform me into what He wanted me to be. In my own mind I was asking for help from some distant God, hoping He might be able to make me happy since the world had disappointed me. In reality, I switched my "if only" search from the secular disappointments to the Christian hope, but I didn't expect my prayer to alter my lifestyle.

As God began to work on me, my attitudes began to change. I sensed a gradual shifting from my focus on social events to Christian activities. As with everything in life, once I saw a new field I ran straight into it. I told God I was available and then tried to help Him out. I was constantly aiding His direction, which resulted in a seesaw Christian life.

I had already made my plans when Dr. Bright asked us to stay, so I immediately rejected the idea. I had spent years building a sound social reputation in Connecticut and felt I wielded considerable influence in the New Haven area. I just knew God wanted to use me to evangelize Connecticut. I knew also my connections would be helpful to the Lord and I told Him so. I had worked out God's plan for me and it didn't include a move to California. It never occurred to me He might have other plans.

I let Fred know my feelings clearly, but he wanted God's answer, not mine. Fred felt we should weigh each side of the question prayerfully and, in his organized way, he made a chart. On one side of the paper Fred wrote down all the reasons for staying in Connecticut, things like owning our home, having many friends, enjoying social acceptance and not having to move. On the other side of the paper he put the reasons for coming to California: things like leaving our security to trust the Lord, answering God's call to service, living in a Christian atmosphere and adjusting to a different lifestyle.

As Fred wrote these lists and prayed over them, it suddenly became clear to him that to stay in Connecticut was easy and to move to California would be a sacrifice. Fred felt we had lived a comfortable life too long and the

Lord was testing us to see if we were willing to give it all up, leave our family and friends, and go to California. After Fred made this pronouncement, the Lord encouraged him with Matthew 6:33: "Seek ye first the kingdom of God and His righteousness and all these things will be added unto you."

Fred believed if we followed God's sacrificial plan for our lives, we would be rewarded. I was not so sure. Why would God want to take things away from us? I didn't want to leave my home, my friends, my New York apartment, my job with Macy's or my secure life. I was willing to be a Christian leader but didn't want to give up anything to do it. Fred, however, wanted to find God's divine direction and felt sacrifice was a pivotal part of that plan. Fred knew he had received a clear call from the Lord, and I was waiting for him to come to his senses.

Listening When God Speaks

That Sunday we attended the Community Bible Church in San Bernardino, where Pastor John Emmans told the story of Nehemiah trying to encourage the Hebrews to go back to Jerusalem and build the wall. In applying this to our everyday lives, he said, "There may be some of you here this morning who are trying to decide what God wants you to do. The Lord wants you to be willing to go wherever He sends you. Are you willing to move when God says, 'Move'? Would you be willing this morning to agree with God if He were to ask you to move from one end of the country to the other, to leave your friends and family, to leave your reputation and your social life, to give it all up, and to follow God's sacrificial plan for your life?"

When I heard those unwelcome questions, I knew God was speaking to us. I knew I wasn't willing to give up my comfortable life. I also knew Fred was. Pastor Emmans ended his message by asking anyone to stand for prayer if they felt God was speaking to them about a new direction. At that point my husband rose and I slumped down. I knew his decision to move to California had been stamped with God's approval.

While I was upset over the thought of this drastic change, Fred was overjoyed and had a serene peace about him. Nothing I said disturbed him. When I told him he was wrong and I was right, he quietly asked, "Then how come I am calm and confident and you're doubtful and depressed?" I hated to admit he had a point. I was not about to give up my case.

At Fred's suggestion, I made an appointment to discuss my problem with Dr. Henry Brandt, a noted Christian psychologist who was spending his summer interviewing potential Campus Crusade for Christ staff. When I told Dr. Brandt about my indecision, he gave me a way to test whether the move to California was God's plan or Fred's.

It was a little after 4 P.M. when we began our conversation, and I knew Fred was in the hotel kitchen rushing to get supper ready for 1000 students, plus directing some fifty kitchen workers. Dr. Brandt suggested I go down to the kitchen at this hectic moment and ask my husband to sit down and talk with me. I told him I wasn't certain about such a move and didn't want to make a quick decision. I was sure Fred wouldn't have time to speak to me just before dinner, and what's more, he would get upset with me for disturbing him. I also told him Fred had already made up his mind and nothing I said would make him change.

As I gave Dr. Brandt my excuses as to why his suggestion wouldn't work, he said in a firm, but loving way, "You asked for my advice, and I have told you what to do. Now go and do it. If Fred won't see you to discuss the problem, then you will know he is behaving in the flesh. But if he leaves his work, sits down with you and agrees to postpone the decision, you will know the Holy Spirit is in control of the situation."

Dr. Brandt and I prayed and asked God to show me clearly what He wanted Fred and me to do. I left his office and went down to the huge kitchen full of people rushing to get dinner ready, stood on a platform above the kitchen and called to Fred. I expected him to say, "I'm much too busy to speak to you now. I'll talk to you later." Not only did I expect him to say this, I hoped he would.

But when I called, he came immediately and asked what I wanted. I told him I needed to talk to him about our big decision and wanted to do it now. To my amazement, he put down the towel in his hand, took me to a small, private dining room, smiled and sat down. I told him I was not yet ready to move to California, that I didn't have peace about it, and I wanted to postpone our decision for at least another week.

"I'm willing to wait," he said. "I don't want to move against your will. We both must be in agreement before we make the commitment."

When Fred said that, I began to cry. He couldn't understand why his agreeing with me was upsetting until I explained how Dr. Brandt had planned my mission. That gentle, Spirit-led conversation convinced me Fred was making a spiritual decision.

I spent the following week in prayer and Bible study, seeking God's confirmation on our future and waiting for His peace. As I prayed, God quieted my heart and showed me Philippians 4:11: "I have learned in whatsoever state I am, therewith to be content." I knew, for me, He meant the state of California.

Home Sweet Home

Once I had accepted that we were to move to California, I began to wonder where I would live and pictured buying a beautiful hillside home and maintaining the standard of living we were accustomed to in Connecticut. Imagine my shock when Fred told me Dr. Bright wanted us to live on campus at Arrowhead Springs.

"Where?" I asked. "In the hotel?"

"No," said Fred. "We can choose any bungalow we like

and I think you'll want Bungalow One."

I had no idea what Bungalow One had in store for me, but I'll never forget the afternoon Fred took me to look at what was to become my new home. The immediate surroundings were green and lush with little pools and waterfalls in front, but the bungalow was unbelievable.

The bungalows were built in the early '30s and had been used as individual motels by movie stars who came out from Hollywood for vacations. Bungalow One, next to the hotel, consisted of five rooms in a semi-circle set up like a train going around a curve. Each of the rooms had a motel door leading out to the central patio, and to go from one end of the house to the other, you had to go outdoors or go through every room as if you were on a train. There was a raised living room with a little porch in the center of the bungalow, and on each side were two bedrooms facing out on the patio. I couldn't imagine how I could make a home out of this antiquated motel with one living room and four bedrooms.

Not only was the layout peculiar, the condition of the bungalow was dreadful. The original carpeting was still on the floors with several places worn through to the cement. The ceiling was falling in chunks in every room. The bathtubs had been used to develop pictures, and the chemicals had eaten away the finish down to the black, rusty iron. The kitchen was a hot plate on a porch, and the place was infested with spiders. I took one look at this disaster and became homesick for my luxury in Connecticut. "Lord," I said, "when I told you I'd go anywhere, I surely didn't mean this."

But the Lord did mean this. I had to accept this house and try to make it a home. In spite of my feelings, I planned to renovate and decorate what appeared to be a hopeless impossibility.

While Fred worked in the kitchen, Gudrun and I spent our days sitting on the floor in Bungalow One with a pad, pencil and measuring tape which Gudrun called her "inches." Not only did we have to create ideas on how to reconstruct this abandoned building, but we also had to figure out where to put my twelve rooms of furniture. Every time I thought about my furniture, I got homesick and had to pray, "Lord, make me willing to move. You know I have no heart for this." I would then get back to my measuring and planning. The biggest problem was how to use the roomful of Spanish antiques we had bought in Madrid. The huge carved bookcase would overwhelm one of these motel rooms and yet it was my favorite piece. As I mentally placed my Connecticut furniture into this California cottage, most of it just wouldn't fit. What was I to do? I liked decorating challenges but this was too much!

Finally, I gave up worrying about what I had left in Connecticut and started to plan what I could do with what I had before me in California. Since Bungalow One had no kitchen, I had to create one from the porch. Gudrun and I decided to leave the beams on the porch roof in place and paint them in gold, orange and avocado, the hot decorator colors of that time. We ordered avocado appliances and Gudrun created Austrian shades in a flowered print. She sewed each little hoop on by hand and wove the fancy trim herself.

We planned to make the room behind the kitchen into a family room and converted the accompanying bathroom into a laundry room with an avocado washer and dryer. We designed the bedroom at the end of the house to be the master bedroom. The carpenters we hired totally gutted the antiquated bathroom and made a new bath and dressing room with gold and red flocked wallpaper, red sinks set in white marble counters, gold faucets and fixtures, and an unusual chandelier of Victorian ruby glass trimmed with crystals. It became the most dramatic room of the house. The high center room became our living room, and the two bedrooms on the other end of the house were for the children.

Lauren and I found some wild sheets on sale in shocking pink and orange and painted the girls' room pink with orange trim to match the sheets. Gudrun made the sheets into bedspreads to be used on the bunkbeds we brought down from the hotel. When I got married, I had vowed my children would never sleep on bunkbeds, but I had to eat those words as we put Lauren, Marita and Gudrun into one room.

Once construction was underway and the children were registered in school, Fred and I flew back to Connecticut to pack our belongings. As I walked into my cold, quiet home where I had spent thirteen memorable years, I reflected on what the house had meant to me. When we had first bought this shingled New England ranch, I knew it would be my home for life. After a series of apartments and a small rented house, this spacious three-bedroom home seemed huge. We had moved in with an assortment of second-hand furniture and bit by bit had replaced the couches, tables and chairs until almost everything was new.

As our family grew, the house that had been bigger than anything I'd ever hoped to live in, seemed to close in on us and we had added six rooms and a large patio. The house had become almost a shrine to me and yet when I looked at it with no family in it, I realized it was no longer our home. I had lived in it, laughed in it, cried in it and now I was leaving it. I was here to pack up one life and ship it to California.

I had walked into this home with Lauren in my arms. I had added Marita and then Frederick Jerome Littauer, III. I looked at the rocker in the nursery and remembered the hours I had spent holding him, trying to soothe him. I saw the crib, empty at last, and I thought of the babies it had held: Lauren, in Detroit, then Marita, then Fred III, then Larry, and then our new Freddie. That one piece of furniture housed a fluctuating series of joys and tragedies. I would give it away. I never wanted to see it again.

For days Fred and I sorted, packed or discarded every-thing we had gathered in thirteen years of living in one house. I reread the college term papers I had saved and wept over baby pictures of my boys. Fred worked on the principle that if you haven't used something in the last five years, you're not going to need it in the next five. As I cried, Fred filled up the trash cans.

My mother, who had moved from Haverhill to Connecticut to be near us, couldn't believe we were going to move away and leave her alone. Fred's family was sure we had been conned by a group of religious fanatics who were going to lock us up in a monastery and make the children live a drab, spartan existence. Our friends were in a state of shock that the Littauer home, an institution in North Haven, was closing its doors; and Fred's office staff couldn't believe he was going to leave the business in their hands and move across country.

Family, friends and business associates were at best confused and at worst afraid we'd lost our minds. To tell them God had instructed us to move would have confirmed their worst suppositions. Their pleading with us to change our plans made parting almost impossible, since I didn't want to leave North Haven in the first place.

Our church held a commissioning service on our last evening with them, dedicating us as the first full-time Christian workers to be sent out from St. Charlie's.

We stayed in our New York apartment that night and next morning went back to pack the car and take a final look at our home. It was stripped of everything that had made it home; its empty rooms signified the end of an era.

As I carried a box from the basement, I was stopped by some handprints on the stairway wall. I remembered the day Marita poured out a whole jar of bright blue poster paint onto the basement floor. She had put her little hand in the paint and printed it on the wall. The hand by the bottom step was dark and as the prints came up the stairs they became lighter and lighter 'til the top one became a shadow. I remembered how upset I'd been when she had shown me her blue hand and pointed proudly to her work.

Yet, as I stood staring at those little fading handprints, I forgave her and I wondered how I could cut out that portion of the wall and take it with me to California.

By the time I had dried my eyes, Fred was ready to go. He had the trunk and back seat so full that the car was dragging on the driveway. Just as I was about to get into the car, I spotted a large dried flower and bird arrangement on top of the trash and remembered that a friend had given it to me when Larry was born. I couldn't leave it alone there in the garbage, so I plucked it from the trash and laid it on top of the boxes in the back seat. The branches stuck up high behind us and the flock of dead red birds followed us to California.

Four days later, after one of the sweetest times Fred and I ever spent together, we drove into Arrowhead Springs. For the first time we looked at it as home.

What the Lord Really Wants

Before I had finished arranging the furniture in Bungalow One, the Lord added more people to our family. A single girl named Dolores had joined staff and needed a place to live. We added another bed to the girl's room and she moved in. That gave us Lauren, Marita, Gudrun and Dolores in two doubledecker beds in one room. Freddie had the next bedroom to himself for a short while, until Fred's nine-year-old nephew Dwayne came out from Florida for a vacation. While he was visiting with us, his parents separated and asked if Dwayne could stay with us. We put a double-decker bed in Freddie's room and totaled six bodies stacked in layers in two rooms. My life had come full circle; I was now back to the same situation I had left fifteen years before when we all were piled tightly in one bedroom behind my father's store.

My mother had often wondered, "How can I ever bring up decent children in a place like this?" and had then gone on to bring up decent children. Now I was faced with the same question of bringing up decent children in a small space—eight of us in five rooms and a converted porch.

No longer did we have individual rights. It could no longer be my room, my towels, my toys; everything was everybody's. I began to realize how spoiled we were. We had become too possessive of our own things. Before, we each had our own record players and even a stereo that played through our mattress. Here we had one combination record player and radio and had to learn to like the same music. We were unable to get television so we spent our evenings playing games and talking as we'd never done before.

Fred decided we should pray together as a family each night, so we made a schedule. Gudrun and I would have dinner ready at 5:15. While the dinner sat in the oven, we would gather around the coffee table in the little family room. We made up prayer cards with headings on the top line such as Family Needs, Christian Workers and School Friends. We wrote dated prayer requests on each card and the children would take turns choosing a card and then praying for those specific requests. As the Lord answered our prayers, we dated the reply on the card. This scheduled prayer time each evening taught our children how to pray and showed them the reality of answered prayer. At 5:30 we would move to our crowded table on the porch and there never was an angry word.

As I accepted my new life in the old house, God began to fill my mind with Himself. I spent many hours in Bible study and took all the courses Campus Crusade had to offer. As I studied, listened and prayed, God began to train me for a new ministry.

Although I had not wanted to leave Connecticut, I could see after a year at Arrowhead Springs why the Lord had moved us. We could never have been trained so deeply and consistently if we had stayed in North Haven. We were too easily on the top without having started at the bottom. We had become Christian leaders before we knew what the Christian life was about. Fred and I had taught Bible studies in our home before we had studied the Bible.

In order for the Lord to teach us enough to teach others, He had to move us from our worldly surroundings and place us in a desert. I have since learned from Scripture that God frequently sends his children into a desert for training. This is just what He did with us.

While I was willing to give my time to serve the Lord, I never considered that true service demanded a humble spirit. If I thought about humility at all, I would have assumed humility to be a reward for those without talent. I had always been able to succeed at whatever project I embraced whether or not I knew anything about it. Yet I didn't brag about my accomplishments and had always put my efforts into positive, altruistic and now Christian activities. I always felt we should do the very best we could with whatever gifts we had been given. However, I learned, in Christian circles superiority was not necessarily applauded.

I felt I was a good speaker but I was seldom asked to speak. When I did speak and received an enthusiastic response, others who had been around longer were sometimes jealous. Once when I gave what I felt was a moving message, a staff member said, "You have too much charisma. There is so much of you that no one can see Jesus."

I always dressed well because I had a huge wardrobe. I felt I should be a good representative of Campus Crusade, yet one day a staff lady said to me, "You know what I'm afraid of about you, Florence? Someday you might have to wear the same dress twice." I drove a big gold Lincoln Continental and my neighbor would call out to me frequently, "Oh, there goes Mrs. Rich in her Lincoln."

I couldn't understand why, when I had given my life to come on staff, people looked at my strengths as problems. Was I supposed to be a silent soul in sackcloth and ashes riding on a donkey? I had left a twelve-room home for five rooms and a porch. I was willing to work in an organization full of young beauty queens even though I had always associated with older people so I could be the youthful spirit of the group. I had agreed to invest thousands of dollars in a bungalow I didn't own and pay rent to live in it besides. I had graciously played Martha to hosts of visitors who I knew would never be able to reciprocate. And most devastating of all, for the first time in my life, I had joined an organization where there was absolutely no hope that I would ever become president.

I had thought Campus Crusade would want to use my talents, but instead, all my achieved goals in life were wasting away. As I sat lonely and discouraged in Bungalow One asking the Lord why He had done this to me, I began to get an answer: *You needed to be humbled. You must learn I don't need your talents, your money, your cars, your clothes, your houses, your hospitality, your leadership. I can only use you when you have a broken spirit, when you are an empty vessel willing to be filled, when you have gotten yourself and your pride out of the way. I put you in a desert with people who don't appreciate you so you would finally give up.*

I finally gave up. If that's the way it's got to be, Lord, I'll quit. I felt alone, lost in a desert, but Jesus became my friend. I had always loved the hymn *In the Garden* and I used it as my baptism song. I had sung those words, "And He walks with me and He talks with me, and He tells me I am His own," but I never knew how it felt to have Jesus really walk and talk with me. As I isolated myself in my bedroom in Bungalow One, Jesus moved in. I asked Him, "For this I left everything behind?" and He answered, *You didn't leave anything you'll ever need. My grace is sufficient.*

While I thought I had given my life totally to the Lord, I began to realize I was proud of what I had given up. I had presented my body a living sacrifice and then wanted a badge for nobility. I was working for the Lord in my own strength and then looking for the glory. God resists the proud and gives grace to the humble. I wish I could say that humility fell upon my shoulders quickly like a queen's cloak. Instead it has come slowly, in pieces, like a patchwork quilt.

Once I willingly gave up my role as the Christian heroine, the Lord began to show me His new direction for my life. One day the superintendent of Sunday schools in Community Bible Church asked Fred and me to teach an adult Sunday school class. I felt totally unqualified to instruct anyone in the Bible. We told the superintendent this, but he continued to ask. Finally, Fred agreed we could put together a course on marriage since this was where God had already worked His greatest miracles in our lives.

We had never taken a course or read a book on marriage counseling, but as Fred often said, ignorance never kept me quiet! We proceeded to write a course and for our references used several Bibles, a large concordance and our lives. At the end of the thirteen weeks, after dividing the responsibility for teaching and writing between us, our attendance had risen from thirty-five to eighty-three.

News of the course spread and many people from outside the church began attending. We had touched a raw nerve. We improved it as the Lord gave new insights, wrote a weekly Bible study series to go along with the lectures, and by the time we had given the course four times we had an average attendance of 125. This course was the beginning of what became *After Every Wedding Comes a Marriage*.

A New Phase in Our Ministry

Just as the Lord led us to Arrowhead Springs, He led us away. Once I was willing to relax and let the Lord lead, I assumed He would use me at Campus Crusade for life. I pictured growing old in Bungalow One and becoming the sage of the hill, sitting in my rocking chair while young people came to me for wisdom and advice. But again, the Lord had other plans. Fred's Connecticut business needed attention, and because we had depleted our reserve money, we needed to get back to work. At that point we could have located anywhere in the world, but after searching for a place to live, the only place we had peace about was San Bernardino.

One day we found a secluded building lot cut out of a mountain which looked into the San Bernardino National Forest. We prayed and asked the Lord to direct us and give us a sign. A few days later a stock we owned went up sharply and we were able to sell it for a profit which gave us the exact amount we needed to buy the lot. When our offer was accepted, we took this as further confirmation that we should live in San Bernardino. Together, we designed a custom-made house to fit our pie-shaped lot.

With the lot paid for, we were able to get a mortgage for the exact amount of the building cost. Once the Lord had seen that I could live joyfully in a tiny home, He provided us with a big one. He had started my humbling process, and I knew He would help me handle a new home without it going to my head. I was eager to have some space again and Gudrun and I tackled the decorating of a new home with great excitement. What I thought up, she sewed up. She custom-made every curtain, drape, bedspread and pillow in the house.

Our new home was built of brick-colored Mexican slump block. The front entry was walled like a fortress with a redwood drawbridge that led over a recessed pool to a huge castle door complete with big iron hinges. The foyer, living room and dining room were all decorated like a Spanish castle with appropriate antiques. The carpeting was a four-inch white shag, the long Spanish couch was red velvet, and a rich tapestry hung on the rough plastered wall. A Spanish arched window led to a magnificent view of the city below and the olive groves in the canyon.

We designed the family room and kitchen to be large enough to hold groups for the Bible studies we planned to have. The walls were painted brick red to match the massive fireplace and hearth on the twenty-foot wall. There was also a window-wall that looked out to a swimming pool and a direct view of Mt. McKinley.

Running the length of the long house was a hall with doors to each of the five bedrooms. Since we planned to place the family tree in the hall with pictures of our ancestors, we decided to decorate each room in the nationality of our varied backgrounds. We designed our bedroom and bath in ornate English for the Chapman part of the family. The walls were gold with flocked Victorian paper and I had my English father's picture framed on the wall. My collection of jasper Wedgwood gave touches of blue to this English retreat. Our study was Scotch with a plaid floor like my mother's MacDougall tartan and I hung up a clan map of Scotland, my grandfather's picture in his kilts, and my mother's first violin.

Freddie and Dwayne had the Littauer German room done like the courtyard of a Teutonic fort. I stood by the plasterers to make sure they made the walls look like stone. Gudrun designed an awning to go over the two beds which had been custom-made with drawers underneath. The carpet looked like plush red brick, and there were scenes of Germany on the wall.

Marita and Gudrun had a Swedish room after Fred's grandmother Klein and had two built-in beds fronted with Swedish arches filled with ruffled curtains. We did Lauren's room in Early American to commemorate our years in Connecticut. The wallpaper was little purple flowers, the carpet was purple shag, and Ethan Allen furniture lined the walls. Her double bed was canopied with white organdy, and swags of fluffy curtains were at the windows.

What had started out to be a comfortable house had become a show place which later was used for two different home tours. We dedicated our new residence to the Lord and His service on July 14, 1970.

By September 1 we were settled enough to begin thinking about starting a Bible study. I didn't consider myself to be a Bible scholar but was happy I knew more than I had two years before. At that time, Barbara Fain, a gifted Bible study teacher, began tutoring me in the Word. When she was out of town, she would have me substitute for her Bible study classes and this gave me experience.

One day she said to me, "The greatest thing about your teaching is that you are unencumbered by theological training and therefore, not deep enough to be confusing." I wasn't sure if this was a compliment, but at least I knew I wasn't going over people's heads.

When Barbara moved to Atlanta, Georgia, I was left to teach her Bible study class, and when we moved, I brought the class into my new home. On the first day sixty ladies arrived to start "The Survey of the New Testament" with an emphasis on practical applications. As the ladies tried to put into practice the truths of Scripture, their husbands noticed that their wives were becoming more loving and considerate and wanted to know what these Bible studies were about. The women soon asked for an evening class for couples.

This request prompted us to begin our Christian Home series. We printed invitations for the ladies to take home to their husbands and set aside thirteen Friday nights for study groups on marriage. We chose study leaders from among our friends and began to train them. Our plan was to have small discussion groups from 7:30 to 8:30 in different rooms throughout the house. Everyone would come into the family room at 8:30 for an hour's lecture, followed by refreshments. The response was good and we expected to have thirty to forty people who were willing to commit themselves to a thirteen-week marriage improvement course. But a week before our first scheduled class, something unbelievable happened to our new home.

Reflections

When I look back on our move to Bungalow One I can hardly believe we did it. Only the Lord could have inspired us to leave a large, lavish home to camp out in Bungalow One. In retrospect I wish I'd learned humility faster so that the Lord could have spared me some of my humiliating experiences, but He continued to place me in deserts until I learned in whatsoever state I am therewith to be content. As I have shared my Bungalow One story, I've had women come rushing up to say, "I'm living in Bungalow One right now." I've been able to encourage them and show them Bungalow Two will be along any moment.

One great bonus of living in Bungalow One is that every house after that looks spacious and is a refreshing step up. I'm grateful now that I lived next door to Bill and Vonette Bright and that we've kept in touch over the years. I'm glad we met Glen and Marilyn Heavilin at that time and that they have remained friends.

At the Christian Booksellers Convention in Denver, July 1990, Fred and I spoke at the Here's Life Publishers breakfast along with the Brights, the Heavilins and Josh McDowell. I reminisced how we had all been at Arrowhead Springs in 1968-70 when Josh was but a child fresh out of college and how exciting it was to have the seven of us back together at one function after so many years apart.

The Lord does have His hand on all of us who are willing to take His direction — even if it means moving to the desert and living in Bungalow One.

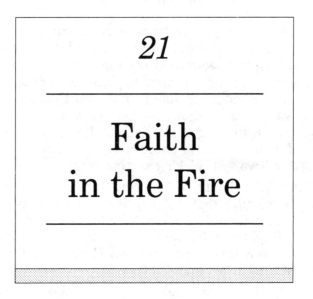

21

Faith
in the Fire

*We were told not to lift our heads and look out the
window no matter what. We didn't know if we
were going to crash into the water or on land—
we just knew we were going to crash.*

Friday the thirteenth began for us at 6:17 A.M. with an
earthquake. As we were jolted awake, Fred turned on the
radio and heard that besides the earthquake, a forest fire
had started in Big Bear, a mountain community twenty
miles away. As the day progressed, so did the fires, fanned
by 40 m.p.h. winds. By 5 P.M. when I put the meat in the
oven for a company dinner, I looked out to see the entire
sky behind Mt. McKinley a bright orange. The radio reports
ominously told how hot hurricane force winds were wildly
blasting the fire out of control, heading it toward homes in
the northeast section of San Bernardino where we lived.

At 6:30 P.M. our little six-year-old Freddie, who had
been listening closely to the radio, called us and our dinner
guests into the living room and announced we were going
to have a prayer meeting. He moved our antique prayer

bench into the center of the room and stood behind it like a little pastor in a pulpit. He opened in prayer, then handed me the family Bible and said, "Mother, read us something from the Bible that tells us we'll be safe from the fire." It was quite an assignment and I struggled to find a verse that would show God would save our home. Then I remembered Psalm 91: "Thou shalt not be afraid for the terror by night; nor for the arrow that flieth by day; nor for the pestilence that walketh in darkness; nor for the destruction that wasteth at noonday. A thousand shall fall at thy side, and ten thousand at thy right hand; but it shall not come nigh thee."

We prayed and claimed the promise that the fire would not come nigh unto us. We also claimed verse 10: "There shall be no evil befall thee, neither shall any plague come nigh thy dwelling."

We then saw God's condition. He states that if we put Him first in times of plenty, He will care for us in times of danger: "Because he hath set his love upon me, therefore will I deliver him: I will set him on high, because he hath known my name. He shall call upon me, and I will answer him."

We called upon Him and waited for His answer. As Freddie stood behind the bench, he pointed to each one of us in order and asked us to pray for our home. He concluded our meeting by thanking God ahead of time for the miracle He was going to perform. I knew then the Lord would save us—if only to reward the faith of this little child.

"The Lord Won't Let My House Burn"

When our last guests arrived at 7 P.M., we chatted over the clatter of fire trucks racing up our street. Before long we were startled by heavy footsteps on our front deck. Two big firemen knocked on the front door. "Prepare to evacuate," they said as I opened the door. "The fire has whipped up the back of Mt. McKinley and as soon as it comes over the top, you'll have to leave."

At exactly 8 o'clock, the first flames fanned over the summit and we left the dinner table to watch as the whole crest of the mountain was quickly outlined in fire. It was a majestic sight. The flames advanced in a straight path from as far as we could see, left and right, heading down the mountainside to the canyon below us. As I stood on the redwood deck watching the approaching fire, a fireman said, "Only a miracle could save this house."

The police made a roadblock at the bottom of the hill and only residents and relatives were allowed through. In order to get up the hill, our friends told the police they were our brothers and sisters. Later the officers said, "I never knew anyone to have so many brothers and sisters." Several friends came up with trucks ready to move us out and some came to take our children home with them. Freddie refused to leave. He wanted to stay and see the miracle he knew was about to happen. Lauren, unaware of our danger, was cheering at a high school football game many miles away, and Marita was already at a friend's home for the night. Dolores was cleaning up from the dinner and Gudrun was cheerfully serving coffee and leftovers to the firemen and friends.

At 9 P.M. Marita ran into the house and gathered up her two cages of pet mice to take back to her girlfriend's house.

"Don't you have any faith?" I called.

"I do," she said, "but the mice don't, so I'm taking them with me."

By this time the whole street was a mass of confusion. Policemen evacuated hysterical women and excited children; people with hastily rented moving vans loaded up priceless furnishings; one woman threw her sterling silver into the swimming pool. A reporter for the local newspaper, Harvey Feit, worked his way up the street through the turmoil to our house. When he interviewed us, he was amazed at the calm and joyful attitude in our home.

"How do you feel about your house being destroyed?"

asked Harvey.

He was stunned at Fred's confident answer. "The Lord won't let my house burn. He gave it to us, and we use it for His work. If He wants it to stand, it will stand."

"Do you share your husband's faith that this house is not going to burn?" asked Harvey. "Yes," I said with an assurance I'd never known before. I could hardly wait to see how the Lord was going to do it.

During the long evening Fred made more coffee and Gudrun poured. There was an air of expectancy as we — family, friends and firemen — sipped, watched and prayed. We had received word from Campus Crusade that their prayer chain had been activated and hundreds were praying for our safety. Our church called to say that its members had been alerted and were also praying.

Throughout our home and on the roof, groups of friends gathered in prayer, and a few strangers who wandered in to watch remained to pray, several for the first time in their lives. A teenage boy, Paul Britton from across the street, asked Christ to come into his heart while standing on our roof holding a firehose. Because of his commitment that night, both his mother and father later became believing Christians and are now involved in Christian work.

About 10:30 the firemen insisted that all women and children leave before the fire reached our home. My friends ran quickly through the house and gathered possessions they thought I might want to save. One friend took all the gold-framed pictures off the family tree. I smiled as one girl went off into the night with my mother's cello under her arm. Freddie, Gudrun and Dolores left in one car and as Freddie kissed me goodbye, he whispered, "I'm sorry I can't stay to take care of you, Mother, but I'll be back as soon as it's over."

At 11 P.M. Lauren ran through the crowd, flung her arms around me and sobbed for joy to see me alive. She had been coming back to San Bernardino on the bus from the football game and suddenly realized the fire was burning "our mountain." By this time the fire had reached the bottom of the canyon nearest us and was starting up. We were all praying as the fire hit the olive trees. We hoped the green groves would slow the fire down, but the olive oil in the trees increased the fury of the fire and sent flames shooting fifty feet into the sky.

As the 60 m.p.h. winds moved the fire in a massive march toward our house, firemen turned on the hoses for the first time. I looked out of the kitchen window and saw an olive tree not twenty feet away burst into flames. A fireman told me I had to get out as the house would probably explode any minute. I kissed Fred goodbye and, with my Bible in hand, walked through the kitchen where a friend was pouring a cup of coffee. I'll never forget his question: "I hate to bother you at a time like this, but where do you keep your sugar?" I thought it hardly mattered whether his coffee had sugar or not, but I stopped long enough to hand him the sugar bowl.

As Lauren and I ran through the smoke to our car, the reporter called, "How does your faith look now?" We glanced back and saw the cliff behind the house flare up in a fence of fire and then, as the smoke enshrouded the silhouette, we could see the house no more. As we drove out of the yard, the firemen lifted the hoses over the car, making an archway to escape. We left, knowing Fred and his best friend Ralph Wagoner were still inside.

Still in the Miracle Business

Twenty minutes later, after a slow trip through the traffic to a friend's home, I called Fred and was relieved when he picked up the phone.

"Praise the Lord," he said, "the house is still here!" He then explained in jubilation how, as the hurricane-force winds whipped up the hill, the direction had suddenly changed, splitting the fire in two, sending half of it up the cliff behind the house and the rest down to the ravine below. For twenty minutes the smoke and flames had enveloped our home as Fred and his faithful friend Ralph watched through the windows and prayed for the Lord to save the house. Harvey Feit told Fred later that as he saw the flames shooting over the roof of the house, he was afraid it was gone. But then the smoke cleared and he said he looked in disbelief as the house came into view—whole and unharmed. God had covered our home with His protective hand.

One fireman later said, "I've never been a believing man before, but I was there and that was a miracle!" The next morning, November 14, 1970, the front page of the *San Bernardino Sun-Telegram* ran this headline: "The Lord Won't Let My House Burn—It Didn't." The story following the headline was the reporter's impression of his evening in our home.

SAN BERNARDINO—Fred Littauer stood looking out the patio door at the jagged line of flames advancing on his new house off the end of Manzanita Drive last night and said: "If the Lord wants this house to stand, it will stand."

At midnight, the Lord, with the help of some fifty firemen who stood fast in the face of forty-foot-high flames, saved Littauer's home. They also saved other homes in the exclusive residential area in the foothills of northeast San Bernardino.

Littauer, 41, who operates the food service for the Campus Crusade for Christ, was unwavering in his belief that his home would be saved despite its vulnerable position.

About three months old, the house on Aspen Drive was on a peninsula jutting toward the approaching wall of fire and the first in its path.

Littauer and his wife, who shared his faith, declined to move their furniture as some others did in less exposed locations.

"I'm not concerned," said Mrs. Littauer, "the furniture can be replaced."

She did take some "valuables" to the car. These included her Bible, notes and tapes she uses in teaching her Bible classes.

Their twelve-year-old daughter, Marita, one of their four children, dashed in, gathered up two cages of mice, and left.

City firemen, first on the scene, had time to prepare. They hooked up their hoses and waited.

At 11:40 P.M. the flames burst over the hill below the Littauer's home. Firemen turned on their hoses and began wetting down the brush on the surrounding slopes.

At the last minute, a crew of U.S. Forest Service firefighters arrived.

Sparks showered the area and thick, gagging smoke drove back the few remaining bystanders. But the firemen stayed, standing in the face of intense heat, and beat back the flames which circled in a giant U around the house and other exposed houses in the area.

At midnight it was over. Littauer looked through his patio door again at the ember-strewn slopes surrounding his home and said: "Good show, but we knew what was going to happen all the time."

The testimony of our faith was there for all to read. There was also a lighter side to the fire. One of our friends who had been there for dinner that night said later, "That was the most spectacular after-dinner entertainment I've ever seen."

Another asked, "How are you going to top that party?"

One friend said, "I think it's great to be on fire for the Lord, but I think you carried this to an extreme."

It was the Friday after the fire that we had scheduled the first session of our Christian Home Series. We planned for about forty guests with four trained couples to be group leaders. The cars began coming at 7 P.M. and by 7:30 when we were ready to start, ninety men and women had arrived. Many of the men who had not been interested before came to see the house God had spared. The publicity of the fire had doubled our anticipated attendance.

That week we hastily trained six new couples and asked our neighbors if we could borrow rooms in their homes for our groups. More came the following Friday, and we had ten discussion groups spread out in three houses.

The Miracles Never Cease

While the fire had been a catalyst for our Bible study, we had yet another miracle that year. Fred and I went to San Francisco for a long weekend before Christmas and enjoyed the usual tourist attractions. On our return we were in the air only ten minutes when the pilot announced that we had to return to San Francisco due to a faulty hydraulic system. "Don't worry," said the pilot, "there is an alternate plan and we're using it."

We came in low over the Bay and I saw the runway, but just as we were about to touch down, the pilot gunned the engines and took off almost straight up. He explained that there had been some planes on the runway, and he had decided it was better not to land. Later we found out the truth: When he had tried to slow down, he couldn't.

I looked at my watch. It was 10 A.M. Another ten minutes went by and the pilot told us he was going to try again, but that this time we should all get into the "brace position" as we were going to experience what he politely called an emergency landing.

We all had to study those cards in the seats that you never pay any attention to because you know you're not going to crash. Fred and I quickly memorized where the life rafts were, how to get the emergency door open and how to assume the brace position. We found this to be an ungainly posture created by putting your head on your knees, and locking your arms tightly under your legs to hold you firmly in one unit. The flight attendants looked slightly frantic as they hastily checked our positions and then doubled up themselves. We were told not to lift our heads and look out the window no matter what. We didn't know if we were going to crash into the water or on land—we just knew we were going to crash.

With our heads bowed, we prayed. Everybody prayed. There's nothing that makes a believer out of an agnostic faster than an impending plane crash. Finally, we hit the ground at full speed—swerved, shook, shuddered! The pilot instantly reversed all the engines and in one big heart attack, the plane rocked to a halt and the motors stopped dead. We held our breath waiting for an explosion, but nothing happened. As we raised our heads at 10:15 and looked out the window, we could see a circle of ambulances and fire trucks that had been prepared for the worst.

What we didn't know at the time was that our dear friend, Caroline Kinne, had played a part in our rescue. On the day of our flight, at exactly 10 A.M., Caroline, who was home recovering from an illness, was listening to the radio and when the announcer said it was 10 o'clock, our names came to her mind. She didn't know why, but she felt she should pray for our safety. She shut off the radio and for the next fifteen minutes prayed until she received a peace that we were safe. The next day she called us and asked if we had been in trouble. I quickly poured out our plane crash problems and told her it was a miracle that we were alive.

"Yes, it was a miracle," she said softly, and then she shared her part of God's plan for our lives.

Reflections

Have you ever been part of a miracle? We think back to Bible miracles like turning water into wine and healing lepers and know we've never personally been part of any such thing, yet God is still in the miracle business.

As I remember surviving several earthquakes, the raging flood that wiped out the only entrance bridge that connected Campus Crusade with the outside world, the wild forest fire that split graciously and went around our house instead of burning it, and the airplane crash that didn't quite crash, I realize that God has placed a big hand of protection over our lives. He has been our refuge and our fortress. He has saved us from deadly pestilence. He has covered us with his feathers. He has been our shield and rampart.

Because we love Him, He will rescue us and protect us.

What a set of promises from a God who knows us and cares.

Have there been miracles in your life that you've put out of your mind? Have you been spared when others have been harmed? Too often we feel we've survived by chance and not given God praise for His protection. He wants us to know His name and call upon Him — not just at moments of dire need, but daily. The Lord inhabits the praises of His people and He will respond when we call. He doesn't promise we will have no problems, but He will make beauty out of ashes. He will

Make the tough times count.

22

President
of the
Women's Club

Since there was a nucleus of women who feared I would capture the club, convert the members and carry them off to some religious retreat, I spent my year as first vice-president aiming for a low profile.

One fact that continues to amaze me in the Christian life is that God never wastes any talents or training we had before becoming believing Christians. Graciously, He doesn't write one script for all Christians to follow; rather, our roles are tailor-made to fit our unique personalities.

I had spent much of my life directing various secular women's organizations and the Lord let me use my experience in San Bernardino. When I had been at Arrowhead Springs for only a few months, Vonette Bright took me to the women's club of San Bernardino, a prestigious group of 350 civic-minded ladies. At her suggestion, I joined the club. Before I even paid my dues, I was given a minor board position with the impressive title of federation extension chairman. Since I have always felt Christian women in secular organizations should do a better-than-average job, I worked hard at my small assignment. At the end of the year I won a top district award.

In Federated Women's Clubs, anyone who wins an award attracts attention, and so the nomination committee decided I was a new hopeful. Vonette had been the membership chairman and third vice-president and I was nominated to replace her. I debated whether I should accept such a big position so quickly but felt confident that since I was asked, I should accept.

Shortly after the slate was announced I received two letters from ladies in the club. Both letters expressed shock that I, as a newcomer, had accepted the nomination for third vice-president. The letters accused me of trying to take over the club and one sentence read, "Even Jesus Christ had to die before He obtained the kingdom." The letters were bitter and vindictive and told me if I knew what was good for me, I would immediately withdraw my nomination.

In all my years of leadership, these were the first nasty letters I had ever received. I was aghast that anyone would write such words to me. The eight ladies who composed the two letters signed them with their first names and last initials. My natural curiosity was about to send me to the club yearbook to find out who these women were, but as I started toward the book, the Lord stopped me. It was as if He said, *I'm going to use you in this club, and you'll be more effective if you don't know who these ladies are.* I threw the letters away and asked God that if indeed He was directing me to continue with the club, He would cause me to completely forget the letters. I also prayed that if the letters were an indication I was to resign, I would be continuously upset. From the moment I threw the letters away, I never gave them another thought, and I left my name in nomination.

When election day came, I fully expected someone to nominate an opposing candidate from the floor. I waited anxiously as my name was read and the president asked if there were any additional nominations. After the traditional thirty-second pause, the president said, "Hearing no additional nominations, I declare the nomination for third vice-president be closed."

I knew the Lord had His hand on me. Within a week, the second vice-president became ill and resigned, and the first vice-president's husband was transferred and she had to leave town. Before I ever took office as third vice-president, I became the first vice-president!

Since there was a nucleus of women who feared I would capture the club, convert the members and carry them off to some religious retreat, I spent my year as first vice-president aiming for a low profile. I did nothing that was not asked of me, made no aggressive steps and tried to relieve my detractors of any serious worries. Since the by-laws stated that the first vice-president automatically is nominated for the next year's presidency, I was installed as president the following May. The signs of insurrection had disappeared.

Introducing the Club to Bible Study

One of the first areas the Lord laid upon my heart was to revitalize the ailing Religion Section. Each club is expected to have various section meetings that cover such topics as music, arts, crafts, drama, bridge, travel and religion, among many others. While most of our sections were functioning well, the Religion Section was close to failure.

I invited all ladies who would be interested in such a group to my home and asked what they felt we should do to strengthen the section. The only thing they agreed on was they did not want to do what they had done in the past. In a detached way, they had studied various types of religions — Buddhism, Hinduism, Judaism and Christianity. No one could think of what to do until my friend Lorna suggested we have a Bible study. They were unaccustomed to Bible studies, but accepted the idea. The next question was, Who would teach the Bible study? Lorna suggested me.

I was already conducting weekly Bible studies in my new home and didn't have time for an extra class, so I decided to shift my study group into the women's club. To make this move, I had to find a way for the club to allow non-members to attend the Bible study. Since any departure from the norm always requires a complete board approval, the section chairman had to ask permission to allow outsiders to come into the club. According to the by-laws, the only way we could do this was to turn our Bible studies into a special project and charge money from each lady who attended. We had never intended to charge admission to a Bible study, but it was the only way we could stay within the club rules. The last thing I wanted was a controversial Bible study. So we took care of the technicalities and laid plans for what was a new approach for the old Religion Section.

The first series I taught was on the Old Testament. I had never studied the Old Testament but I needed to eliminate any criticism that I was excluding Jewish club members. The first session drew thirty-five women, and by Christmas we had grown to sixty-five. The interest in Bible studies continued to increase and by the end of the year the section unanimously voted to have a Bible study project again.

As I conducted the business of the club as president, the Lord guided me to 1 Kings, where Rehoboam sought the counsel of the older men on how to be an effective leader. Samuel answered in 1 Kings 12:7: "If thou wilt be a servant unto this people this day and wilt serve them, and answer them, and speak good words to them, then they will be thy servants forever." I quietly adopted these words as my direction and prayed for a servant's attitude.

I kept my Christian teachings confined to the Thursday morning Bible studies, thus relieving the worried ladies of their concern about my capturing the club for the Lord. When elections came up that year, there were no objections and I was chosen president for a second term.

The Bible studies increased in popularity and we made enough money from our admission charge to give a scholarship to Carmen Mayell, a deserving student at a Christian college. The following year we continued our study group and had our first club prayer breakfast. In 1973 we not only won the district award for religion, but were given a special honor at the state convention for "outstanding achievement in the area of spiritual values and ethics." The state chairman said we had won because of the Bible studies held in our club building. This was a major breakthrough and paved the way for other clubs to have Bible studies with the approval of the California Federation of Women's Clubs.

I taught these studies for ten years until my traveling schedule made a weekly commitment impossible. Our prayer breakfasts provided an evangelistic outreach and, because of their success, the district started a prayer breakfast, then the state and ultimately the national convention for Federated Women's Clubs of America instituted a prayer breakfast. All this because our local group was willing to step out and bring the Lord into a secular organization in an inoffensive way that changed lives.

One woman summed it up when she returned after a year away and said, "I don't know what's happened in this club, but everyone seems nicer."

Reflections

The Lord has given me a ministry of encouragement and I have often been able to help women have an impact in their community by assuming leadership in secular organizations. The Lord Jesus went out among the worldly people and He loved them where they were. He didn't make every dinner party into an evangelistic rally but He let His light shine so that people could see the difference.

Unfortunately, the world perceives Christians today as standing against everything society wants or enjoys. Non-Christians become quickly defensive when they sense someone is out to convert them. But they do appreciate hard workers who do what they say they'll do and who have an above-average sense of responsibility. If you wish to have an influence for good in your community, here are some suggestions.

1. *Don't choose a group that is obviously anti-God.* In selecting an organization to work in, find one that has some basic moral principles. When I read the by-laws of the Federated Women's Clubs I found a section that said we were to invest in the spiritual values of our members. I quoted this by-law in proposing Bible studies in the clubhouse. It's amazing what's in the by-laws of any organization and you can be safe in assuming that the average member has never read them.

2. *Be willing to do insignificant jobs well.* Don't try to be president before doing some small chores and doing them better than anyone else has ever done them before.

3. *Become program chairman.* This office gives the best opportunity for influencing what speakers come into the group. You can't have an altar call at each meeting, but you can bring in speakers with a moral message and keep out some of the perverted possibilities waiting to pollute the minds of the public.

4. *Remember that there are leadership vacuums everywhere.* Few people want the responsibility that comes with being chairman or president. I was in one church where the pastor had encouraged his people to go to political caucuses and volunteer for leadership positions. When they reported in the next Sunday, many had become local party chairmen on the first meeting and almost all who had done as the pastor instructed had come away with some party office. I was impressed with how easy it is to become a leader when you are willing to volunteer and work conscientiously.

I know several women who have become PTA presidents and have been able to influence school programs and sometimes even curriculum from a position of leadership.

5. *Don't be discouraged by fellow Christians who reprimand you for "leaving the faith" for worldly pursuits.* If you feel called to serve in a secular organization, respond in the knowledge that the Lord will bless your efforts. In Philippians 2:14,15 it says: "Do all things without murmurings or disputings that you may be blameless and harmless, the sons of God without rebuke, in the middle of a crooked and perverse nation among whom you shine as lights in the world."

We are surely in a crooked and perverse nation, so go out and shine!

For those of you interested in understanding the biblical rationale for Christian activism in local politics, I would suggest you read *The Blue Book for Grassroots Politics* by Charles Phillips (Oliver Nelson). This is a complete and practical handbook for anyone interested in how to have an impact on our country's moral and spiritual values and laws.

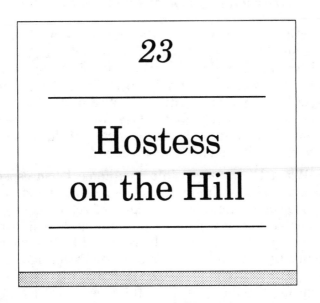

23

Hostess on the Hill

Though the move was a difficult step of faith to take, God blessed the sacrifice through expanding our ministry in ways we never would have imagined.

My children now look back on our days in the spacious house in the foothills of the San Bernardino mountains as "Mother's Hostess on the Hill Era." And in retrospect, it was.

At the time of the fire I had promised the Lord that if He would spare our home I'd dedicate it to Christian hospitality and entertaining the saints. We had constant open house. People came for dinner and stayed for weeks, sometimes years. We had a monthly covered dish supper and never knew how many would arrive. We would set up tables and chairs in our family room, turning it into a candlelit restaurant. On the second Saturday of every month about fifty people brought a casserole, salad or dessert, plus any friends, and we all met for dinner, fellowship and a program.

For eight years we maintained a well-kept hospitable home and loved every aspect of what God had given us to do. I was playing Martha, serving all who entered, plus I taught the women's club Bible study, a teen study, a couples' Friday night study and a Wednesday lunch Bible study at Norton Air Force Base. But as our speaking ministry increased, we began to wonder if this hospitality phase of our life should come to an end.

When I had moved into this home I had especially designed a study with built-in desks for Fred and me and bookshelves containing every kind of reference material imaginable. I knew when I designed the study that I wanted to write a book, but in eight busy years I hadn't composed so much as a chapter. I had created scores of original Bible messages but I had never written a book. People kept asking me, "Do you have any of this in writing?" Every time I answered no, I felt ashamed. I had all the equipment but no product; somewhat like a woman with a beautiful kitchen who can't cook.

Fred occasionally mentioned that the house was too much for me, but each time I'd dive into my chores with new energy just to show him I could handle it. At that point I was teaching a Bible study on Hebrews and when I got to chapter twelve on laying aside the weights that keep us from running the race, I prayed and asked the Lord to show me if there was anything holding me down. Immediately the house came to my mind. I rejected that thought, but it kept returning: *Your house is a heavy weight; it's slowing you down.*

I pointed out to the Lord how I had used this home to glorify Him, and how many people had heard His Word here for the first time in their lives. The message kept coming back: *Sell your house.*

Not wanting to believe these words, I put a few conditions on the sale of our home. It would have to sell quickly so we could be re-established by September for our son Fred to go to junior high school, and we would have to get close to the asking price. If it didn't sell, I would assume I should cut back on my speaking and continue to entertain and teach. Not wanting to make this an easy job for the Lord, I listed the house with the agency our daughter Lauren worked for under the conditions that they wouldn't advertise, put it in multiple listing or place a sign out front. For this house to sell, it would take a miracle.

A few days later I answered the door bell to find a lady from the real estate office. She wanted to look the house over. She was obviously a Choleric personality, as she walked briskly through the house without even opening any closet doors. When she had completed her brief tour she said, "I'll take it."

"Just like that?" I asked.

"I came through here once on a home tour you had and I vowed if this house ever came on the market, I'd buy it."

And she did. Quickly and at the right price.

Surely I had no excuse. I had asked the Lord to show me if anything was keeping me from doing His will. He had given me bad news and I had made it as difficult as possible. When the house sold in spite of me, I had to agree with the Lord and begin packing. It is never easy to leave a home that has become part of you and the thought of taking apart this dream house and packing it up was especially hard. Once again I was leaving my castle where I had planned to live happily ever after.

I walked from room to room and cried. I looked at each decorative detail that Gudrun and I had so carefully constructed. How could I leave behind the striped awnings over Freddie's beds or the Swedish arches built in front of Marita's beds with the Austrian shades that could be let down to hide her away? That house was a part of me and I loved every inch of it.

How well I remember the day when the new owner and her decorator came. He was an imperious man who barely gave me a token hello. Each room he entered appalled him. "Oh, my dear, this will never do. How could they have painted the family room brick red? We'll have to tear out these cheap little arches and pull down these tacky canopies over the beds. This is a much bigger job than I ever anticipated."

I couldn't believe he thought everything I loved was tasteless and should be removed as soon as possible. By the time he left I wondered if interior design schools had a course called Disdain 101 to teach the students how to scoff at the decorating attempts of others.

We had to relocate quickly and Lauren found us a Spanish style condominium in Redlands. In one fell swoop we got rid of our encumbrances, the weights that slowed me down, and we moved from a six-bedroom house to a 1300-square-foot condo. It was like living in a motel and almost like returning to Bungalow One.

Since I no longer had room for a study at home, I sent Marita out to find me an office where I could write. A college sophomore at that time and noted for her ability to charm others, Marita located a four-room office in an old building in the center of Redlands. The price was $200 a month, but by the time she concluded the agreement, the owner rented it to us for $80. Marita, assorted boyfriends and my son Fred painted and wallpapered the main room and we moved in furniture left over from our former home.

I never would have found the time to write if I had stayed in my castle on the hill, but within one year's time in my office I had written my first two books and increased my speaking engagements. Though the move was a difficult step of faith to take, God blessed the sacrifice through expanding our ministry in ways we never would have imagined.

Reflections

As I look back on that traumatic move, I realize how

easy it is to go up in life and how difficult it is to come down. Yet I know even more surely today that the move was right. I had prayed for guidance, using God's Word as a foundation, and He gave me clear direction. I have learned that when I pray and get an answer I don't like, it is usually the Lord speaking. I don't have to pray for direction to find a shopping mall. I can find them on my own in nearly every city.

Often people ask, "How do you know God's will for your life?"

Before you can hear God's instruction you have to be studying His Word. Be open to certain verses or passages as they draw your attention. Second, you have to be seeking His direction in prayer and then listening for His answer. When you do spend time daily in study and prayer, you will receive the Lord's counsel. Conversely, if you never have time for study and only shoot up prayers on the run, you may not ever hear His counsel or know His will.

Not every answer is what we want to hear, but as we fellowship closely with the Lord we become so in tune that we turn automatically in His direction.

Leaving my dream home was not an easy or exciting thing to do, but in retrospect it was the right thing to do. As the Lord has blessed us we have been able to

Make the tough times count!

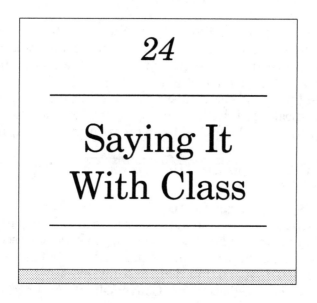

24

Saying It With Class

We all have a story to tell, but many of us don't realize that our difficulties and dilemmas, once we've had a degree of healing, can be used to encourage others.

In the fall of 1980 the Lord used a verse to call me to a new ministry. I had already been challenged by an article predicting that the '80s was to be the decade of the active woman and that women were going to be looking for all kinds of training. I knew that Christian women were going to be part of the active decade and I wondered who would be training them and what they would be learning. At this point I was studying in the Amplified Bible and found 2 Timothy 2:2:

> And the instructions which you have heard from me along with many witnesses, transmit and entrust as a deposit to reliable and faithful men who will be competent and qualified to teach others also.

As I studied, I realized how perfectly this verse fit my

story and how it challenged me to move in a new direction. I looked at my life as an everlasting training program. I had been receiving instructions forever. I remembered my father teaching me verses and poems, my mother trying to make me into a violinist like her, and my Aunt Sadie giving me piano lessons. Although I didn't have much innate musical talent, I did learn to read music and have enough of an appreciation for the melody, rhythm and style that I was later able to direct musical comedies.

I thought of my teachers and Sunday school instructors who had filled me with information and Bible stories. My high school years of serious study in order to get a scholarship to college. The extra-curricular activities in drama, poetry reading, debates, yearbook, French club and public speaking. My three college majors of English, speech and education, six years of high school teaching, one course of instructing Gracious Living, two terms of teaching psychology to adults and one year of teaching public speaking on the college level.

Added to that were my endless years of being president of everything and my understanding of Roberts Rules of Order. Plus the intense Bible study I had done and the many Christian speakers I had heard. That added up to *instructions* I had heard from God, parents, teachers, speakers, plus all my life experiences and *many other witnesses.*

What did the verse say I was to do with my own special package of learning? *Transmit* — send across. I was to teach it to others. *Entrust* as in a deposit. I was to help others become Christian leaders and speakers and writers, considering my instructions as a *deposit* in the lives of others with the possible hope that someday I might see some interest on my deposit.

Who was I to teach? *Faithful* and *reliable* people who I knew loved the Lord Jesus and could be counted on to use and not waste the information.

What would happen to these people? If I taught them

all I knew, they would become *competent* and *qualified* to *train others also*. What a way to multiply my life and make the tough times count.

Once I accepted the call, I invited forty women to come to California to be trained. Thirty-five accepted and I began to write the first CLASS, Christian Leaders and Speakers Seminars. I had assumed everyone who attended my seminars would be above average in every way and relatively trouble-free. I was going to take people with no problems and send them out to take care of those who had them. But what I learned in that last week of January 1981 was that all of us have been through traumatic times. We all have a story to tell, but many of us don't realize that our difficulties and dilemmas, once we've had a degree of healing, can be used to encourage others.

In our select group of thirty-five Christian women leaders, we had seven incest or child abuse victims, several divorces and an assortment of other major problems including drug and alcohol abuse. How exciting it was to see each woman realize she didn't need to be ashamed of her past but she could use her victimization and victories as inspiration for others in similar circumstances. She could make her tough times count!

As our CLASS ministry grew, we began using a survey called "Troubles in River City" (we got the name from the song of that title in *The Music Man*). We listed every problem we could think of and had the participants check off all of those that had happened to them or to immediate family members. In the last ten years we have added new traumas that we hadn't thought of in 1980 and we have watched the progression of problems increase. Along the way we learned that our purpose in teaching CLASS was not just to train others to speak but to help them find healing in their own lives first.

Carol came to CLASS as an experienced Bible study teacher who wanted to brush up on her technique. During the section on the four personalities she began to think,

Who am I really? She knew all the things she did, but she did not know who she was. She took her Personality Profile and was somewhat even in every personality type. I explained to her, "Either this means you are so Phlegmatic you have difficulty deciding on the words and their meaning, or you are so perfectly balanced you are about to ascend, or you've spent your life trying so hard to please everyone—be all things to all people—that you have no idea who you really are."

"It's the last one," she said quickly.

As we talked, I found she had grown up in an alcoholic home where she had learned to cover up bad situations and deny that there were any problems. In doing this she had covered up her true personality. As a Christian she was devout, legalistic and almost too sweet to be real. She had created "good little spiritual Carol."

She went home eager to find out who she really was and be done with any hypocrisy. As she read through *Your Personality Tree* she was convicted by the chapter on masking. She had been hiding behind a false face of wishful thinking. As she began to write her prayers daily and ask the Lord to show her truth—that the truth might set her free—she uncovered some sexual abuse by her alcoholic father. She set on a course of recovery from her revelation of reality and she now teaches on overcoming childhood traumas and leads support groups to help others who have had similar problems.

Carol came to pick up some new ideas for teaching her Bible studies, learned she needed some help in her own life and progressed into a ministry of far greater depth and heart than she had ever thought possible.

We have seen thousands of Carols and hundreds of men come through our CLASS in the past ten years who have been open to God's leading first in their own lives and then in meeting the needs of others.

Reflections

As I look back over the ten years of CLASS, I rejoice in what the Lord has done with so many of our alums. From my modest thought of training thirty-five women in 1981, CLASS has grown each year and has graduated over 7000. From the simple start in the basement of a bank in Redlands, California, CLASS has expanded to the Hilton International Hotel in Brisbane, Australia, and to Auckland, New Zealand, where Dame Catherine Tizard, mayor of Auckland and Governor General of New Zealand, attended. She had only meant to give an opening greeting but was so fascinated she stayed to the end. When I asked her to give a closing comment, she said, "I came to scoff and stayed to worship."

In ten years we have trained movie stars and mothers, teenagers and senior citizens, Bible teachers and businessmen, pastors and politicians to communicate more effectively whether speaking to one or one thousand. Our original thrust was to show people with something to say how to put their message into a form simple enough to reach the minds and hearts of the listeners and clear enough to be used of God to change people's lives.

We still follow this principle, but we have added the necessity of "becoming real" before ministering to others. As we saw the number of Christian leaders who were avoiding or denying their own problems, we moved slowly but surely into helping each CLASS member review their past, take off any mask they had put on for any reason and become the real person God intended them to be. In doing this, solid ministries have been created that depend on a genuine relationship with the Lord for their foundation. Whenever there has been a vague feeling of personal confusion or blockage between the individual and God, we have worked to clear away the clouds.

In order to bring Christian leaders in touch with reality and into a solid relationship with the Lord, we use the concept of the four personalities as a measuring stick.

When people come out confused or with opposite personalities, we lead them into a prayerful study of our book, *Freeing Your Mind From Memories That Bind* and a disciplined daily writing of their prayers, asking the Lord to take off their masks and make them real. Some are hesitant, but the majority eagerly respond and report later that they feel truly free for the first time in their adult lives.

The Lord has done a stripping job in my life and in Fred's over these ten years; He has brought us to a humbling point of relying on Him and not ourselves. We have put away any pretenses we might have had and He has given us a gentleness and gracious spirit that can only exist when the peace that passes all understanding is in control.

Fred and I work with many gifted people at CLASS. Our director of training is Patsy Clairmont of Brighton, Michigan, who has been with us from the original CLASS. When Patsy first came, she had no idea what God was going to do with her life. She had been giving book reviews at women's retreats and was known as "God's Little Bookie." Petite, precious and powerfully packaged, Patsy has gone from agrophobia and insecurity to becoming one of the outstanding female communicators in America today. Her unique sense of humor, transparent personality and depth of scriptural knowledge combine to make her a human dynamo.

God has transformed Patsy from a frightened country girl to a gifted presenter of His Word. He has healed her from many pains of her past and is using her to help others. When Patsy spoke on Focus on the Family, her message, "God Uses Cracked Pots—and I Am the Visual Aid," received so many requests that it placed on the list of all-time favorites. Since then, Dr. Dobson has offered her a contract for a book of the same name. If no other life but Patsy's has been transformed, CLASS would be considered successful.

Our director of management and manuscripts, Marilyn Heavilin, first came to CLASS a year and a half after her teenage son Nathan had been killed by a drunk driver. Marilyn was still grieving the loss of Nathan and only came to CLASS because I wanted her to tape a message on how to grieve and work through your pain. As she began to speak on this subject, I encouraged her to write her story. As we worked together on the foundation of *Roses in December*, we found we had many similarities in our lives. Her Matthew was born six months before my Freddie (February 9, 1960); her Mellyn within a few days of Larry (August 14, 1961). And within the next two years two of her babies died. Marilyn had multiple surgeries at almost the same time I was in the hospital. While Fred was put to bed with rheumatic fever, her husband Glen was suffering with debilitating migraine headaches.

As couples we were in deep depression and in need of supernatural healing. That's when the Lord picked us up from Connecticut and the Heavilins from Indiana and put us both down in the desert of San Bernardino at Campus Crusade for Christ headquarters. When we found each other with our almost identical lives of trauma and tragedy, we knew God had brought us together for a reason. We share a bond of love and mutual support that can only be formed by those who can say to each other, "I know what it was like. I've been there."

The Lord brought us together and allowed me to encourage Marilyn to write, speak and train others to make the tough times count.

In 1981 our daughter Marita was the child of our CLASS, but as she matured, she created new aspects and avenues of Christian leadership. She is the founder and co-chairman with Marilyn of the Southern California Women's Retreat, and now serves as our director of Christian Leaders, Authors and Speakers Services. Marita is a speaker herself, and she trains speakers through CLASS. She books speaking engagements in churches and conferences all over the country for those who have been through CLASS and she has formed a media publicity service available to major publishers to get their authors on radio and TV talk shows to promote their books. With Marilyn, Marita receives manuscripts, evaluates them and places them in the hands of publishers who might not otherwise read them.

Our daughter Lauren helped me put on the first CLASS and she has served with us frequently throughout the last ten years. She has her own ministry as a grief consultant to those women who are hurting from the loss of a child, from a miscarriage or from the birth of a retarded or handicapped baby.

Lauren's first priority is to her three sons and her husband Randy, but the Lord has used her informally to give words of encouragement to those in need. Her book, *What You Can Say When You Don't Know What to Say,* has been used by individuals, pastors and counselors to show well-meaning people what to say to those in need.

Lauren's son Randy is our first grandson and when he was little I took him to hear me speak. One day he said to me, "When I grow up, I'm going to be a speaker." I was thrilled and encouraged him. When he was about five he mentioned to me, "Someday I'm going to be a fireman." I pretended to be disappointed and replied, "I thought you were going to be a speaker." Quickly he recouped, "I'm going to speak on fires!"

Our second grandson Jonathan is a Sanguine and he loves to talk. When he was five I taught him about the personalities and then gave him the video tapes of *Your Personality Tree.* By the time he was six, he was a junior expert on the subject. I took him with me on a local speaking engagement and on the way I asked him, "Do you know why I'm bringing you along today?"

Immediately he answered, "You're going to talk about me and you want the people to see the real thing."

I introduced him as the surprise guest speaker and handed him the microphone. He talked brightly for fifteen minutes on a child's view of the personalities, ending with:

"It is not my job to make Randy Sanguine like me; nor is it his job to make me Melancholy like him. We have to learn to accept each other as we are."

The ladies were amazed at his maturity and knowledge and they clapped loudly. When the applause died down, little Jonathan, still holding the mike, said, "I do have time to stay and sign autographs."

We seem to have here a chip off the old grandmother.

Little Bryan is still too young to put on the platform, but he is very verbal and will surely add his words of wisdom in a family of communicators.

The Lord has blessed CLASS and those who have so faithfully served over the last ten years. He has given us the people and abilities to take those who come with a story to tell and show them how to communicate the truth as speakers and authors.

As I have been faithful in giving "the instructions" I have received from the Lord and many others to "faithful and reliable people," I've been blessed and they have become "competent and qualified to train others also."

I learned the hard way—without a mentor—and I've determined to share all I know with those who want to learn that they might be saved some time, some errors and some effort. In the words of the French writer Etienne De Grellet (1773-1855):

I shall pass through this world but once. If, therefore, there be any kindness I can show, or any good thing I can do, let me do it now; let me not defer or neglect it, for I shall not pass this way again.

I want to help you

Make the tough times count!

25

Freeing Your Mind

We were all so naive at the beginning, confident that there were no people with childhood sexual or emotional abuse in our church or even in our circle of personal friends.

In 1988, spurred on by the needs of people in Christian leadership to become aware of the reality of abuse in "good church families," the needs of the leaders themselves to work through the pain in their own lives and the needs of the hurting, neglected and dysfunctional families whose symptoms were being ignored, Fred and I determined to write something we could put in the hands of the hurting to help them heal. I envisioned a pamphlet with a few steps to wholeness, but as we set out to give answers to the problems we had been encountering in the churches and in CLASS, the "pamphlet" grew into a 300-page book that sold more copies in its first three months than my others had sold in their first year.

The response to *Freeing Your Mind From Memories That Bind* was so overwhelming that we were deluged with calls and letters pouring out pitiful problems and begging for help. One letter had the word HELP! printed all around the piece of paper like a border.

In his melancholy way, Fred wanted to collect data to analyze the extent of childhood sexual abuse and its effects on the adult life. He created a "Survey of Emotional Responses" to gather statistics on how many people showed symptoms of having been sexually abused in childhood but weren't consciously aware of any specific incidents. In surveying more than 2000 people in various Christian conferences, we found that 25 percent of the women had not been abused, 25 percent had been abused and were aware of it, and 50 percent had been abused (displayed the same symptoms as the abused victims) and yet didn't realize it. They had blanked out their traumatic past.

In men we found 40 percent were not harmed, 10 percent were and knew it and 50 percent were and didn't know it. The information on these surveys and other responses to *Freeing Your Mind* plus an amplification of the steps to restoration are now in Fred's book *The Promise of Restoration.*

Reflections

As we look back over this ten-year period, we are amazed at what has happened to us and to the people who have come to CLASS. We were all so naive at the beginning, confident that there were no people with childhood sexual or emotional abuse in our church or even in our circle of personal friends. And yet as time has passed and cases have piled up on top of each other, we have had to face some hard truths. We desire to help the Christian community come to some degree of awareness on this issue. No longer can we say to hurting people: "Just pray about it and it will go away"; "Forgive him and you'll be happy"; "You're just not walking in victory . . . or in the Spirit . . . or as a Christian should."

Fred and I never set out to seek a ministry with desperate people. I only wanted to train leaders to go out and train other leaders. But I decided we all need to find the source of our problems and gain some degree of healing before we can minister to others.

Perhaps you have had some abuse in your childhood: emotionally, physically, mentally or sexually. Perhaps you've denied it, covered it over or thought that's what happened to everyone.

Perhaps you have suffered migraine headaches, stomach problems, undiagnosed ailments or chronic depression and just thought you had to live with it.

Perhaps you've worked hard and somehow not quite made it, failed just before you reached success, self-destructed when you should have achieved the goal.

Any of these unexplained failures or emotional and physical symptoms could stem from some problems so far back that you have never connected your childhood traumas with your adult dilemmas. Begin today to prayerfully ask the Lord if there's some connection you've missed, some childhood abuse you've blocked out. Get a copy of *Freeing Your Mind From Memories That Bind* and carefully go over the sections of "identification," "explanation" and "restoration." As you pull the loose ends of your life together, the Lord will use you to help others.

As Fred and I have been faithful to God's call, He has equipped us to handle the hurting without counting the cost in time or dollars. As we have taught others to speak and write from their own heart issues, we have been blessed to see many published books written by potential authors we encouraged. As we have been open and transparent about our own lives, we have been able to show thousands of others—many just like you—how to

Make the tough times count!

26

Confronting in Love

Because Fred had always been a loving husband, polite, gracious and generous, I had denied or ignored any recognition of deep-seated problems in his life.

All of us like stories that have happy endings. Women love to see Cinderella marry Prince Charming, ride off into the sunset, buy a big castle with a moat and raise adorable little children and fluffy little dogs. Men dream of business and financial success and some hope to be athletic heroes.

Fred and I were typical. We really thought we could get married and live happily ever after, but right from the start we found we were nothing alike and didn't see eye to eye on anything. We didn't think our church backgrounds would make much difference, but we couldn't agree on a mutual denomination. We found out our personalities didn't match; I wanted fun and he wanted things perfect. We thought we'd have adorable children who'd grow up to be brilliant and successful, but we lost our two longed-for sons. I thought Fred would make lots of money and we'd live in lavish houses. Sometimes he did and sometimes we did. But sometimes we didn't. Our whole life story could be charted out in the ups and downs of houses.

When we committed our lives to the Lord Jesus we thought, *This is the answer. Now we'll be happy.* The adoption of Freddie certainly should have cheered us up. But I had operations, depression, disappointments. We moved to the desert of California to go into full-time Christian service. Surely God would bless such dedication, but after losing money on our Connecticut home and putting money into Bungalow One, we were forced to leave it all and move on.

We built a big house and entertained the saints. I pictured living in that home forever, that home the Lord protected from the fire, but with financial problems and a call from the Lord we sold the dream and moved to a tiny condominium. We started CLASS. We moved to a normal house. I wrote seventeen books, and I spoke all over the country. Did we finally get to Happy Ever After time? Were the tough times over? I thought so.

Caring Enough to Confront

Throughout our married life I had little to do with Fred's businesses. I had married him expecting financial security and yet through all our years we had never really reached it. We'd had many good years, but then something would happen and Fred's plans often failed. He always had logical excuses and I had no choice but to believe him. He was always optimistic and couldn't see why a loss of money bothered me. "It's only money," he'd say. He never understood that because I had grown up poor in a store I had a desperate desire to be financially secure. I didn't need to be rich; I just needed to know the bills were paid.

As my speaking and writing ministry grew, I had even less to do with Fred's business. He always led me to believe things were going well until I came home from one weekend retreat to find we'd had some major financial losses and some legal entanglements. There was no dishonesty or malicious intent, but the situation was upsetting and humiliating.

Marita and I discussed what we should do about Fred's apparent inability to succeed for any length of time. We were also concerned about the anger he seemed to have pent up inside him. I had never really thought of him as angry before because he never yelled or hit me. Yet as Marita and I talked over the situation, I realized that the reason he didn't display his anger was because I had learned to avoid triggering it. As long as I was supportive and submissive, he didn't get mad. If I questioned his decisions or directions, he'd give me what I called "The Look," a flash from his eyes that said, "I dare you." I never dared.

Because Fred had always been a loving husband, polite, gracious and generous, I had denied or ignored any recognition of deep-seated problems in his life. But this financial and legal turmoil brought up feelings I didn't know I had.

I tried to tell Fred that I felt he had some hurts in his past he hadn't dealt with, but he flatly denied it. When I suggested I felt he had an odd relationship with his mother, he angrily defended her and said sternly to me, "Don't you ever say a bad thing about my mother."

I continued trying different approaches to make him realize the source of what I felt was a long-range problem, not just the financial crisis of the moment. He could not see that his repeated business difficulties were anything more than occasional bad luck.

When I felt I was getting nowhere, Marita and I decided we needed a time of confrontation. With our friend and counselor Lana Bateman as the outside, objective party, we asked to speak with Fred about a serious matter. When we told him we saw a lot of anger inside him, he denied it and got angry. As we enumerated examples, he began to listen and suddenly his reaction softened and he agreed to see a male counselor we had already consulted. In the interim we were functioning as usual.

One day as we were waiting to appear on the PTL Club with Gary McSpadden, we turned on the television monitor to see Becky Tirabassi. Becky has a testimony of teen-age alcoholism. She pledged to the Lord that if He would save her, she'd spend at least one hour a day in written prayer. As Fred watched her story, the Lord convicted him that he should write his prayers and he began the next day.

During the three months before he went for his two weeks of intensive therapy, Fred wrote out his prayers each day. By the time he got to the counseling he was ready for God to do a great work.

In counseling, Fred learned that he was a victim of rejection by both his mother and father. They were always working and never came to any of his sporting events or performances. Instead of encouraging young Fred, his mother had, in fact, told him he'd never succeed at anything. Little did we understand at the time that Fred's inability to stay on top for long was a fulfillment of that prophecy of doom.

He also learned that his mother had a lot of anger in her that spilled out on Fred as a child. He was always made to say he was sorry even when the situation was not his fault. He'd stuffed his anger inside him because he couldn't vent it on her. As we look back now, he had unconsciously done the same with me. Whatever the problem, I had to apologize. After a while I had learned to do it without feeling, as a cheap price for peace.

When Fred told the therapist that after his father's death his mother had moved him into her bedroom and made him her new husband in every way but sexually, the counselor explained this was an emotional form of sexual abuse.

Fred did not come home healed; instead, he was confused, introspective and remote. He had done what we'd asked him to do and he felt worse. He continued his written prayer, began to read everything he could on rejection and abuse, and spent hours in Bible study seeking God's answers for his life. Gradually we saw changes: "The Look" was gone and there was a new peace in his demeanor. As Marita and I saw the difference, we encouraged him. The Lord began to bring people to him who had hidden their pains of the past and couldn't figure out why they were angry. As Fred helped others, he developed steps that God used to heal him and those he counseled.

So much happened so quickly. As Fred became vulnerable and willing to share and as the Lord used him to help others, he felt strongly led to write *Freeing Your Mind From Memories That Bind*. He had never written before and really had never planned to, but as he says now, that was because he had nothing to say. Now he does.

The Lord has given him a special gift for uncovering the root of people's problems and filling in the gaps in their memories. We have learned that until someone finds out the *cause* of their problems (the source of the pain), the symptoms don't go away. The Lord only heals what we bring to Him.

As Fred has been the instrument in encouraging others to write their prayers daily, he has continued this discipline himself and I can attest to it. Through his "seeking first the kingdom of God" each day he has also uncovered that fact that he was a victim of sexual abuse sometime before the age of two-and-a-half. He tells about this in his book *The Promise of Restoration*.

The Lord showed Fred that he should get out of business ventures and trust that we could support ourselves in speaking, writing and ministering to others. With the Lord's blessing this has become possible. Now as we travel full-time together, being home only a few days a month, we have learned to love each other in a new dimension and feel as if we are on a perpetual honeymoon. We've faced our problems squarely. We've sought the Lord's wisdom and He has helped us to make the tough times count.

Reflections

What has all this meant to our marriage? It means that as Fred has dealt with his own hidden hurts and has come to a closer relationship with the Lord, he has become a real person.

Fred never intended to be a phony. None of us do, but the repressed anger and rejections in Fred's past had caused him to live an artificial life. He didn't realize this nor did I, but in retrospect I see how difficult it was to love a person who wasn't genuine. There was always that missing piece to the puzzle. We had learned to function well together. We even admired each other's talents, but we didn't know what love really was. Since we got along so much better than everyone else we knew, we thought we had a good marriage but we were missing the key ingredient. We could communicate intellectually, socially and spiritually, but not emotionally.

Does any of this sound like you? Do you have a marriage or relationship that seems to be missing something? Maybe it's time to prayerfully confront your mate and think about the possibility that there may be some childhood problems that are still influencing your behavior today. If you wish to look together at possible damaging emotions from the past, use the questions in *Freeing Your Mind From Memories That Bind*. We've had people ask each other these background questions and discover things about each other they never knew before.

Marilyn and Glen Heavilin, both on our CLASS staff, used the *Freeing Your Mind* questions as a conversational tool on a long trip. As Glen drove, he asked Marilyn questions about her childhood. "Tell me about the house you lived in as a young child." "How do you feel about that house?" "Did you ever have babysitters?"

As Marilyn answered yes to that question, a scene formed in her mind that was so vivid she was able to describe the carpet on the floor, the color of the couch, the clothes she had on and the clothes the babysitter — a teenage boy — was wearing. This event happened more than forty-eight years ago, but Marilyn was able to recall a very uncomfortable situation with this young boy which she now realizes created fears that she has been dealing with since that time. She also remembered the bathrobe she was wearing and that her parents left her because she was ill.

Shortly after recalling this memory, Marilyn was able to verify with her mother the reality of what she remembered. Because she had whooping cough, Marilyn had been left with this boy for a short while so her parents could attend a wedding.

Marilyn says, "Although I have been with others when they retrieved memories from their childhood, I must admit I wondered sometimes if these events really happened. It seemed almost too easy. But God allowed me to see through my own experience that if we are really seeking the truth in order to be more usable vessels, He is willing to reveal the truth to us with very little fanfare or effort on our part. All we need is a willing spirit. When the time is right, the truth will be revealed to us. I needed to be released from these fears that followed me from childhood, and when I was willing to confront the issue in prayer, God allowed me to be released from my past."

Marilyn is typical of many who have some hidden hurts in their lives that they have not even known about and, therefore, have not dealt with or brought to the Lord for healing. You may need to examine your own life or encourage your spouse to seek counsel. If there is resistance or if you have a situation where there needs to be some personal confrontation, I'd suggest a few guidelines.

1. *Determine if there is a need to confront.* Is the behavior of the individual in question threatening the emotional health of at least one other family member? Is there any physical abuse going on? Is there an addiction — drugs, alcohol, gambling, pornography — that shows no

signs of stopping? Are there continued business failures or other patterns that are damaging to the family? Is there a fear of blow-ups, temper tantrums, fits of rage?

If any of these types of problems exist now and are getting worse and not better, there is a need for confrontation. I have talked with women who have been beaten and abused by their husbands who felt it was their cross to bear. They felt if they were really submissive enough and Christian enough, he would stop tomorrow. In my experience, women who tolerate abuse in a marriage over a long period of time do so because they were abused as children. They have learned to "take it." Be sure to check your own emotional stability before attempting to confront someone else.

2. *Seek the Lord's direction.* Do not hastily jump into a confrontation or you may end up defeated. Daily write to the Lord in prayer, asking His guidance in the situation. Make sure you are spiritually ready and divinely inspired.

3. *Read at least one book on confrontation* to better prepare you for what may happen.

4. *Find an independent, outside person* who is willing to stand with you as a mediator, not an attacker. Explain the situation as objectively as possible and have this individual ready to do the confronting if necessary.

5. *Enlist family support.* It's almost impossible to implement family change if the group is not with you. If they all feel you are off balance, you will need some family counseling first to decide where the problems are rooted and what the others feel should be done.

6. *Develop a plan for possible solutions.* Before we expressed to Fred that we felt he would benefit from counseling, we had talked with a therapist about the situation and knew when he had a block of time available. Don't go into any confrontation until you have looked into possible solutions and have the phone numbers of professional help in hand.

7. *Be willing to hang tough.* No confrontation is easy and the person may turn on you and try to browbeat or reason you into changing your mind. He or she has probably already done that many times in spontaneous confrontations you've had in the past. You must be prepared and determined that life cannot go on like it is any longer.

8. *Be prepared for the worst.* We don't want to approach this meeting with a negative attitude, but we must be alert to the possibility that the person we confront will pack up and leave.

9. *Set an appropriate time.* No time is perfect for a confrontation, but make sure you choose a time when the individual will be under the least amount of stress and when he or she is not under a time pressure to leave.

10. *Approach with love.* Don't make the confrontation an attack. It is shocking enough for the person to find himself in a position where everyone seems to have suddenly turned against him. Continue to say, "We love you. We want the best for you, but we need some changes made." Be willing to modify your own behavior and compromise in minor areas as long as the confronted person is willing to take major steps.

These suggestions are from what I learned personally. They are not a complete manual on confrontation, but they will at least give you some guidelines if confrontation is necessary.

Our time of facing reality was not easy, but it was necessary and the changes have been remarkable. God has blessed our ministry and given us a new depth and understanding. He has

Made the tough times count!

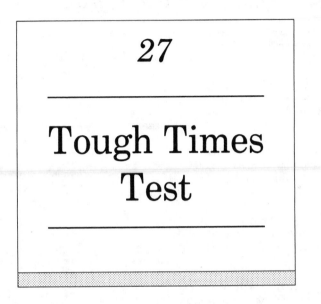

27

Tough Times Test

Check off the answer which is closest to your feelings.

	Column A	Column B	Column C
1. When you think of that ideal childhood in a garden of verses, a meadow of daisies or a fountain of blessings, do you feel you were surrounded by flowers?	Never	Sometimes	Always
2. As you look back, were your childhood days dull, drab and without beauty?	Always	Often	Never
3. Did you wish for a better home or car? Did you wish you could live on the other side of the tracks?	Definitely	Sometimes	Never

4. Do you remember

Christmases as disappoint-
ing or quarrelsome?

Many	A few	None

5. When you look back, was
substance abuse a part
of your childhood?

Constantly	Often	Never

6. When you think of the
clothes you wore as a child,
what is your first reaction?

Hated them	Okay	Loved them

7. Was there any shame or
ridicule attached to your clothes,
shoes or hair as a child?

Always	Sometimes	Never

8. Was there anything stuck
on you (nickname, reputation,
family problems) that you
couldn't seem to shake off?
What was it? _____
Did this bother you?

All through childhood	Sometimes	For a brief time

9. Did you set specific goals
for yourself?

Never	Once	Definitely

10. Did either parent teach
you positive principles that
have helped you in life?

Not really	Off and on	Often

11. Where did you learn
the facts of life?

Friends	Books	Parents

12. Did you ever feel that
getting out of your hometown
was your only hope for success?

Yes	Didn't matter	No

13. Would you feel better about
yourself if you had more

education?

	Definitely	Perhaps	No

14. Were there any deaths in the family when you were young?

	More than one	One	None

15. From teen years to now, how many deaths of family members or close friends have you experienced?

	Several	One	None

16. Do you feel you were allowed to grieve? Were you encouraged to share your feelings about these deaths?

	Not at all	Once	Yes

17. Were you encouraged to study and get an education?

	Not at all	One parent	Constantly

18. Did financial or emotional problems exist in your family?

	Constantly	Occasionally	Never

19. Was there divorce in your family (parents, sisters, brothers, yourself)?

	More than one	One	None

20. Did you have a parent who leaned on you for support and/or drained you emotionally?

	Both	One	Neither

21. Were you ever in a position where you were embarrassed about your body (doctor's office, physicals, group showers)?

	Several times	Once	Never

22. Did getting married raise

your feeling of worth and
give you more confidence?

Not at all	At first	Yes

23. Was your honeymoon
a positive experience?

No	Average	Great

24. Do you feel your mate set
out to make you over?

Definitely	A little	No

25. Do you both communicate on
an emotional, heart-felt level?

Seldom	Off and on	Yes

26. Have you been tempted
to be unfaithful?

Often	Once	Never

27. Have you ever longed for
someone who really would
understand you?

Often	Sometimes	I have one

28. Have you (or your mate)
had any problem pregnancies
or miscarriages?

More than one	One	None

29. Have you (or your mate)
given birth to a baby with
birth defects or retardation?

More than one	One	None

30. Do you feel you've worked
through the grief of these
traumatic births?

Very little	Somewhat	Completely

31. Have you had
major surgery?

More than once	Once	Never

32. Have you experienced
any misdiagnosis or neglect?

Each time	Once	Never

33. Have you ever had feelings
of rejection or loneliness?

For years	In the past	Never

34. Were you sexually abused
or touched inappropriately
as a child?

Many times	Once	Never

35. Have you given complete
control of your life to
the Lord?

No	Sometimes	Yes

36. Have you been so hungry
for the Lord that you've stayed
up half the night to talk with
Him?

Never	Occasionally	Often

37. Have you thought the Lord
couldn't use you because you
were divorced, untrained or
for any other reason?

Definitely	Occasionally	No

38. Have you ever had to move
from a home you loved to one
less desirable?

Many times	Once	Never

39. Have you and your mate
ever disagreed on what the
Lord was calling you to do?

Frequently	Occasionally	Never

40. Have you experienced a
major catastrophe, such as
fire, flood or earthquake?

More than once	Once	Never

41. How would you classify
your leadership roles?

Troubled	Accepted	Praised

42. How would you classify
your witnessing attempts?

Offensive	Not tried	Successful

43. Do you use your house
for Christian hospitality?

| _____ | _____ | _____ |
| Never | Sometimes | Often |

44. Have you used your
tough times to help others?

| _____ | _____ | _____ |
| Never | Sometimes | Often |

45. How would you
classify your memory?

| _____ | _____ | _____ |
| Lots of gaps | Wanders | Clear |

46. How would you describe
your brothers and sisters?

| _____ | _____ | _____ |
| Emotionally unstable | A little mixed up | Emotionally stable |

47. Do you ever feel insecure
about who you really are?

| _____ | _____ | _____ |
| Often | Sometimes | Never |

48. Have you thought of
your life as difficult?

| _____ | _____ | _____ |
| Yes | Occasionally | Never |

49. Have you failed when you
could have succeeded?

| _____ | _____ | _____ |
| Often | Once | Never |

50. Have you realized in the
past that God would make
the tough times count?

| _____ | _____ | _____ |
| No | A little | Yes |

Now add up each column and give yourself 3 points for each answer in Column A, 2 points for Column B and 1 point for Column C.

	Number	Points	Total
Column A	_____	x 3	= _____
Column B	_____	x 2	= _____
Column C	_____	x 1	= _____

Grand Total _____

Now that you have taken the Tough Times Test, what are you going to do with the results to make them count?

If you scored 50 or below, your life has been relatively trouble free. You are emotionally balanced and have little difficulty in human relationships. You may not understand someone whose life has been one calamity after another, but you have the ability to develop compassion and concern for those in perpetual problems if you so desire. Help others find the steps to hope and healing. God can use you in a mighty way as you make yourself available to minister to those in need.

If your score is between 51 and 90, you have had your share of problems, but you've not been defeated by them. You have made the best of bad situations and you have learned from your own mistakes. If you wish to go beyond the average and make the tough times count, read the steps to making the tough times count (below) and follow those that apply to you.

If your score is above 90, you can surely say you have experienced tough times. But that doesn't mean you are a failure or a hopeless human being. My score was 102, and most people would feel I have lived a positive and productive life. Your score only means that you are now at a point where God can begin to work in you in a new and powerful way.

The apostle Paul prayed fervently to have God remove his "thorn in his flesh." In writing to the Corinthians, he summed up his situation by saying his problems kept him from glorying in himself and from exalting himself above measure: "So for the sake of Christ, I am well pleased and take pleasure in infirmities, insults, hardships, persecutions, perplexities and distresses; for when I am weak (in human strength), then am I [truly] strong—able, powerful in divine strength" (2 Corinthians 12:10, Amplified).

There are few people in the world who have not suffered, but often as Christians we are made to feel that if we were really spiritual we'd be healthy, wealthy and wise. Author Oswald Chambers writes that when we finally get to the end of ourselves God will begin to use us in a new way:

> As long as you think there is something in you, He cannot choose you because you have ends of your own to serve; but if you have let Him bring you to the end of your self-sufficiency then He can choose you to go with Him. . . . The comradeship of God is made up out of men who know their poverty. He can do nothing with the man who thinks he is of use to God.[1]

Fred and I can attest to that.

Steps to Making the Tough Times Count

1. Know your poverty.

Because you have read this book and taken the Tough Times Test, you now know that you and I are poverty cases. I grew up poor in the Depression and thought that once I got some money and position I'd never be poor again. But over and over I've been brought to a point of poverty of the spirit, a place where I wanted to give up, a time when I thought my efforts were of no avail. Jesus says in His beatitudes, "Blessed are the poor in spirit; for theirs is the kingdom of Heaven" (Matthew 5:3, KJV). When we get to the point of poverty, the Lord can move in a mighty way.

2. Set aside a time of seeking.

Don't sit in poverty and wait for the Lord to drop spiritual riches in your lap, but set aside some time to evaluate your life. You've gone through this book and know what has happened in my life. I had to analyze myself and seek wisdom from the Lord and help from respected friends. I spent a full day in counsel and prayer with Lana Bateman going back over my life and dealing with each area of hurt or bitterness. Fred gave up two weeks to receive guidance from a counselor and uncover the roots of his rejections. Together we spend hours each week in Bible study and prayer and help others to uncover the source of their problems so they may move on to the solutions.

3. Understand your personality.

When we first started working with the four basic personalities in 1967, we did it as a parlor game. But I was amazed to see people's lives changed as they suddenly understood the source of their relationship problems. Using the Personality Profile as a tool has helped so many thousands of people to understand their strengths and weaknesses: The Sanguine who wants to have fun but is undisciplined; the Choleric who takes control but is often bossy; the Melancholy who aims for perfection but gets depressed when things go wrong; and the Phlegmatic who is peaceful, well-liked and inoffensive but would rather rest than work.

As we used the Personalities as the core of our messages, we began to find people who "didn't come out right." They had conflicting scores on their Personality Profile. By working with them we found that somewhere along the line they had been forced to put on a mask for survival. Many had been abused or lived in dysfunctional homes; almost all had deep feelings of rejection. The study of the personalities went far beyond what we had originally tried as a simple game.

If you have not worked with the personalities or have looked at them superficially, I would suggest you start with *Personality Plus* and *Your Personality Tree* and make this study a family project. *Your Personality Tree* is set up with discussion questions and plans for a family tree scrapbook.

4. Read anything pertaining to your problem area.

Today there are good Christian books on just about every possible area of need. As you read, highlight anything that speaks to you specifically and then go back and reread it. Buy magazines that have articles which relate to your problems.

5. Pray specifically.

In James 1:5 we read that if any lack wisdom, we can ask God for it. Proverbs tells us that wisdom is more precious than gold. And yet few people pray specifically for wisdom in their own area of need. In his counseling situations, Fred has found that when an abuse victim asks God to show him where the abuse first started, a scene usually comes before him as he prays. Many have gone to counseling for years and prayed in general, but they have never asked for the wisdom to find the specific source of their pain. The Holy Spirit brings recall of what we need to know in order to be healed. Whatever your need may be, we strongly recommend a daily discipline of written prayer, pouring out your concerns to the Lord.

6. Free your mind.

If you feel that because of your repeated problems you need some extra help, you may be right. Turn to the Survey of Emotions and Experience on page 279 and check off any that now apply or ever have applied to you. If you check more than 10, you probably need to get *Freeing Your Mind From Memories That Bind* and work through the entire book carefully.

We have received tremendous response from people who had never understood why they had continual tough times until they read *Freeing Your Mind* and prayed specifically for wisdom. Suddenly their past problems have come into focus and they could see their pattern of victimization and/or rejection.

7. Look for the lesson.

Whatever your problems may be and whatever circumstances you've lived through, look for the lesson. What have you learned about yourself? Has there been a consistency about the problems you've faced? What moral is there to your story? Have you acted upon what you've learned? Do you need to confront some issue or some person? Have you just hoped it would all go away someday?

Our heartaches are only of some value if we've looked them over and learned from them. James says, "Is your life full of difficulties and temptations? Then be happy, for when the way is rough, your patience has a chance to grow. So let it grow, and don't try to squirm out of your problems. For when your patience is finally in full bloom, then you will be ready for anything, strong in character, full and complete" (James 1:2-4, TLB).

Don't just wish the problems away; look for the lesson, learn it and apply it.

8. *Help others in similar situations.*

One of the best ways to lessen our own pain and make the tough times count is to help others who are in a similar situation. You don't have to be a registered psychologist to say, "I know how you hurt. I've been there."

You might be thinking, "How will I find people to help?" You don't have to look; just let God know you're ready. If He agrees with you, He will send those who can use your special touch. I find them in ladies' rooms, at airports and in supermarket lines. They see the compassion and concern in your eyes and they pour out their life story. When you are ready, God will do the selecting.

The greatest thrill I have is to see those who come to CLASS doubting that God could ever use them, suddenly see the light and begin to make the tough times count.

I lived through poverty and charity dresses. I learned the hard way that after every wedding comes a marriage. I suffered with double deaths and depression. I lived through floods, fires, earthquakes and a plane crash. I went through surgeries and searchings.

But with the guidance of the Lord Jesus, I've been able to know and accept my poverty, set aside time for introspection, seeking and study, understand my personality strengths and weaknesses, read extensively on many subjects of interest, pray specifically for Fred's willingness to seek counsel, watch him free his mind from memories that bind, find the lessons in adverse circumstances and help others in similar situations.

I can't say that I'd like to ever experience those tough times again, but I do know I'm a stronger person today because I've worked through them and the Lord has made beauty out of ashes.

One day when my son Fred was ten years old, he said, "Mother, I'm sorry for the problems you've had with your two boys, but I was just thinking. If it hadn't been for them, I wouldn't be your son. I would have been born anyway, and someone else would have adopted me, but it wouldn't have been you, and I might not even be a Christian today."

While I would never want to repeat the trials or troubles in my life, Fred's words reminded me that "All things work together for good to them that love God, to them who are called according to His purpose" (Romans 8:28, KJV).

The verse doesn't say everything that happens *is* good but that someday, down the line, God will redeem the tragedies and use the lessons for good. But not to everyone; only to those who love God and are called according to His purpose. I am so grateful today that our family loves the Lord and He has called us to help others

Make the tough times count!

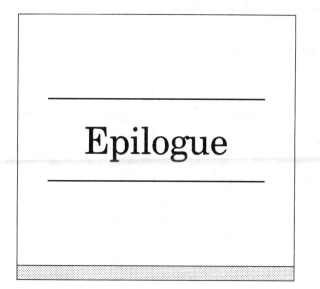

Epilogue

All Cinderella stories end with the transformed heroine and her Prince Charming riding off toward their castle to live happily ever after. While I programmed myself for this fairy-tale existence, knowing that *if only* I could achieve my goals I would be happy, the traumas of my life brought me from romance to reality.

While the Declaration of Independence guarantees the pursuit of happiness, neither government action nor personal determination assures we will find it. If anyone ever tried to pull life all together, I did. If anyone ever had the strength and drive for success, I did. Yet, I learned that as long as we seek perfect circumstances, we'll *never* be happy.

I started out as a poor little girl in need of a transformation. I looked for a nonexistent fairy godmother and when I couldn't find her, remade myself. I married a Prince Charming and decorated a whole series of castles, yet when my walls were attacked, I crumbled. I had to admit defeat and reach out to Jesus, who provided the transforming power I had looked for all my life.

While my circumstances have never reached perfection, the Lord has given me the ability to rise above my problems. He has taught me through one verse, 1 Corinthians 10:13, that I am not the first person to have problems, nor the last, but He will help me bear my burdens: "There hath no temptation taken you but such as is common to man: but God is faithful, who will not suffer you to be tempted above that ye are able; but will with the temptation also make a way of escape, that ye may be able to bear it."

While I do not enjoy tragedies, God gives me the ability to bear them, to have joy in adversity and, most of all, to make the tough times count.

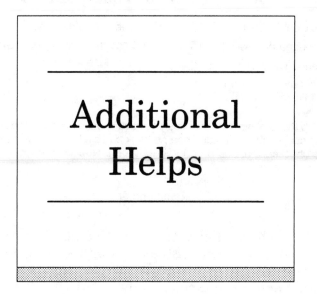

Additional
Helps

Survey of Emotions and Experience

The following survey may help you to determine the root causes of your tough times. Please check each box that applies or has ever applied to you. Leave blank any that do not apply or you are not sure of.

Alcoholic parent	☐	Lack of trust	☐
• Childhood "bad houses or rooms"	☐	Low self-worth	☐
Childhood depression	☐	Marital sexual disinterest	☐
• Early childhood anger	☐	• Memory gaps in childhood	☐
• Early childhood masturbation	☐	• Obsessive fear of rape	☐
Emotionally abused as a child	☐	• Panic attacks	☐
Fear of being alone	☐	PMS	☐
• Feel unworthy of God's love	☐	Recurring bad dreams	☐
• Feeling "dirty"	☐	Rejection feelings	☐
Guilt feelings	☐	• Same-sex attraction	☐
• Hate men	☐	• Self-hatred	☐
		Sexually abused or molested as a child	☐

279

Suicidal feelings ☐   Uncontrollable anger ☐

Teenage promiscuity ☐   • Uncontrollable crying ☐

Tendency to overreact ☐   Undiagnosed pains
                             and aches ☐
• Uncomfortable with
  nudity in marriage ☐

Add up the total number of boxes you have checked and put the number in the space labeled **Total**. Then go back and circle every symptom you have checked that has one dot in front of it. Now write in your total of one-dot symptoms.

Total _____   **Total with one dot** _____

If you have checked ten or more of these items and at least one (if not more) of the items with a single dot, you may be discovering some deeply buried tough times in your life that need to be exposed to the light of freedom in the Lord.

You may be surprised to know that everything on this list is a *possible symptom* of childhood sexual interference. The presence of one-dot items almost always indicates childhood sexual abuse in some way. This may very likely be the root of all the issues you are experiencing in your life today.

If you have ten or more checks, we strongly recommend you work through *Freeing Your Mind From Memories That Bind* and its companion book *The Promise of Restoration*. Both are published by Here's Life Publishers and are available at your local Christian bookstore, or you can order them on the next page.

Note

If the Recommended Resources Order Form (page 281) has already been used, you may order materials or obtain another copy of the order form by writing to

CLASS
1645 So. Rancho Santa Fe, #102
San Marcos, CA 92069

Recommended Resource Order Form

	Number Ordered	Total

Personality Plus. Florence's first book on the personalities will give you an excellent understanding of the four basic personalities and the ability to get along with people who are nothing like you. $8.00

Your Personality Tree. This sequel to *Personality Plus* starts by reviewing the basics but quickly moves to the deeper areas of the personalities including an insightful chapter on masking. $9.00

How to Get Along With Difficult People. Using the church as a setting and fictional characters such as Sally Spiritual and Gilda Guilt, Florence shows you how to deal with the difficult people in your life. $6.00

Freeing Your Mind From Memories That Bind. Fred and Florence join together to give in-depth help and healing. Included are fifty pages of self-analysis that will help you identify the exact source of your emotional pain. $9.00

The Promise of Restoration. Fred's penetrating new book shows men and women who are struggling with emotional issues how to identify and dig out the root causes. Gives clear steps to restoration. $9.00

Hope for Hurting Women. This helpful book will show you how fifteen women took the tough times of their lives (alcohol, drugs, agoraphobia, physical and emotional pain, adultery) and made them count. $9.00

Blow Away the Black Clouds. Who gets depressed? What are the symptoms? How can you deal with it personally and spiritually? How can you help others? Florence gives a light touch to a heavy subject. $7.00

Silver Boxes. Florence relates touching personal stories that show the value of encouraging words. Lifting others up will help you make your tough times count. $13.00 (hardback)

It Takes So Little to Be Above Average. Through this book you can move beyond average and gain confidence in leading groups, thinking creatively and praying with heart. $7.00

After Every Wedding Comes a Marriage. Steps for a successful marriage which Fred and Florence have taught through years of marriage seminars will help you to get beyond some of your tough times. $7.00

Roses in December by Marilyn Heavilin. After experiencing the death of three of her sons, Marilyn is well qualified to help those who are grieving and lead them to healing. $8.00   _____ _____

When Your Dreams Die by Marilyn Heavilin. Grief is the process of facing the death of a dream. Marilyn will give you guidance on letting go of the old dreams and launching out to new dreams. $8.00   _____ _____

What You Can Say When You Don't Know What to Say by Lauren Littauer Briggs. In this book, Lauren shows you how to say the right things when others are in the midst of their tough times. $7.00   _____ _____

My Utmost for His Highest by Oswald Chambers. A special CLASS edition of a favorite daily devotional, written especially for those who hope to become leaders. $6.00   _____ _____

Tapes

Reaching Out. In these tapes from their Reaching Out seminars, Marita Littauer and Marilyn Heavilin will teach you how to utilize your personal experience and develop your own ministry through speaking and writing. Two cassettes/$12.00   _____ _____

CLASS Tapes. The three-day seminar is available on cassettes and will show you how to share your story with others and make the tough times count. Thirteen cassettes with workbook/$100   _____ _____

Your Personality Tree Video. Two video tapes give eight half-hour messages useful for personal or group study. Florence shares her testimony, lessons on personalities and concludes with *Silver Boxes*. Two video tapes/$50   _____ _____

Subtotal	_____
Shipping and Handling (Please add $1 per item.)	_____
California residents please add 6.75% sales tax	_____
Total Amount Enclosed (Check or Money Order)	_____

Charge: Mastercard/Visa #_____

Name on Card_____ Expiration Date_____

Make Checks Payable and Mail to: CLASS BOOK SERVICE
1645 So. Rancho Santa Fe, #102
San Marcos, CA 92069
800-433-6633

Family Photos

Florence Marcia Chapman, c. 1929

Three Rooms Behind a Store, c. 1937

Clockwise from left: Walter Chapman, Florence, Jim, Ron

Florence and Broderick Crawford
November 5, 1951

"Since there were no resident movie stars in Haverhill to pair up with Broderick, the committee chose the only dramatic celebrity – me!"

The Littauer Family Home, c. 1952

"I was overwhelmed and close to speechless when I arrived at a spacious English Tudor mansion."

**Marita Littauer, Fred, Florence, Katie Chapman
April 11, 1953**

"What more could a girl ask for? I was marrying Prince Charming. I was to be in *Life*. And I hoped to live happily ever after."

ON LAST DAY in school Miss Chapman presents new teacher, Edwin Johnson, to one of her classes.

Pupils Help A Teacher Get Married

ADMIRING TEEN-AGERS TAKE OVER CEREMONY

When Florence Chapman, a high school teacher in Haverhill, Mass., announced her engagement last winter, her pupils promptly besieged her with offers to help out at her wedding. Miss Chapman, who teaches public speaking and dramatics, accepted their offers and began assigning their duties like homework. For the pupils, who designed the wedding costumes, decorated the reception hall and helped prepare and serve the food at the reception itself, their teacher's wedding had everything that a class play would have and romance too. Most of them had never been so close to an actual wedding before. But after it was all over and the bride and bridegroom had departed—in a car driven by a pupil —one of the girls confessed, "It was lots of fun but I'd rather get married more privately."

CLASS PRESENT is complete china place setting in her pattern. "Look at her shaking!" said someone.

SURPRISE SHOWER in school auditorium ends with real shower of confetti released by boys above.

188

A Page from LIFE Magazine
May 18, 1953

A MERRY CHRISTMAS

Hope yours is a howling New Year, too –
THE LITTAUERS

Marita, Fred III, Lauren—December 1960

"For some strange reason I decided to use the picture of three crying children for our annual newsletter. How could I have done that?"

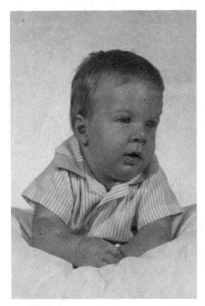

Frederick Jerome Littauer, III
6 months old

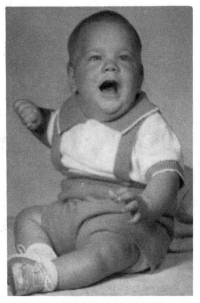

Laurence Chapman Littauer
6 months old

Our New Family, 1964
Freddie, Marita, Lauren

A GREAT TIME AT "GOOD TIME CHARLIE'S"

It being a hot night last Friday, the Chronicle decided to go to a party at "Good Time Charlie's", the new, Roaring Twenties-type night club opened up by Mr. and Mrs. Fred Littauer on Route 5 in North Haven.

And what a night it was, as these pictures show.

A handpicked combo plays hot jazz.

Charles Messier laughs it up with Mrs. Clinton B. Scoble.

...t but happy! L-r are William ...s. Edward Davis, Mrs. Don ...ward Davis, Louis Guyott,

Don Campion Mrs. Guyott and Mrs. Gamble.

In center photo, just for fun Mrs. Schiavone dons her Parisian sequin dress of the 20' era for the evening at Good Time Charlie's. She's pictured with Mr. Schiavone.

At lower right, Mrs. Frederick Littauer chats with Michael Schiavone, Charles Scholhamer and Joseph Schiavone.

A Page from the CHRONICLE
July 15, 1965

That House That Didn't Burn
November 13, 1970

"The flames advanced in a straight path as far as we could see, left and right, heading down the mountainside to the canyon below us."

Florence Today

Fred and Florence Littauer

Help for People
Who Are Hurting

Quantity   Total

_____   **GOD IS NOT FAIR: Coming to Terms With** $_____
Life's Raw Deals *by Joel A. Freeman.* Sensitive,
positive help for all who may feel or say, "God Is
Not Fair." A popular, humorous style that intro-
duces readers to the sovereignty of God.
ISBN 0-89840-189-5/$6.95

_____   **FINDING THE HEART TO GO ON** by Lynn $_____
Anderson. A beautifully written book about the life
of David that will help you find the heart to go on in
the face of hopelessness. ISBN 0-89840-309-X/$8.95

_____   **PUTTING YOUR PAST BEHIND YOU** by Erwin $_____
W. Lutzer. There is hope—you can put your past behind you. The author provides steps you can take to
turn traumas into triumphs.
ISBN 0-89840-290-5/$7.95

**Your Christian bookseller should have these products in stock.
Please check with him before using this "Shop-by-Mail" form.**

Indicate product(s) desired above. Fill out below.
Send to:

HERE'S LIFE PUBLISHERS, INC.	**ORDER TOTAL** $_____
P. O. Box 1576	SHIPPING and
San Bernardino, CA 92402-1576	HANDLING $_____
	($1.50 for one book, $0.50 for each additional. Do not exceed $4.00.)
NAME_____	
ADDRESS_____	APPLICABLE SALES TAX $_____
STATE_____ZIP_____	(CA, 6.75%)
	TOTAL DUE $_____

☐ Payment (check or money order only) | PAYABLE IN U.S. FUNDS.
   included
☐ Visa   ☐ Mastercard #_____

Expiration Date_____Signature_____

**FOR FASTER SERVICE
CALL TOLL FREE:
1-800-950-4457**

PLEASE ALLOW 2 TO 4 WEEKS FOR DELIVERY.
PRICES SUBJECT TO CHANGE WITHOUT NOTICE.